# NEWSCHASER
The Rhetoric of Trump in Essays and Commentaries

# NEWSCHASER
The Rhetoric of Trump in Essays and Commentaries

THE EDITOR:
## Daryl Taiwo Harris, Ph.D

FOREWORD: **Michael D'Antonio**- Author | Political Pundit

**W•** Universal Write Publications LLC

No part of this publication may be reproduced in whole or in part, or stored in a retrieval system, or transmitted in any form or by any means, electronic, mechanical, photocopying, recording or otherwise, without written permission from the publisher, except in the case of newspapers, magazines and websites using quotations embodied in critical essays and reviews.

***NEWSCHASER: The Rhetoric of Trump in Essays and Commentaries***

Copyright © 2017 Universal Write Publications LLC
All rights reserved.

For information:
For information email AdvisoryBoard@universalwrite.com
Website at www.UniversalWrite.com
Publisher: Universal Write Publications LLC

Mailing/Submissions
Universal Write Publications LLC
421 8th Avenue, Suite 86
New York, NY 10001

ISBN-10: 0-9825327-3-3
ISBN-13: 978-0-9825327-3-7

# Table of Contents

**FOREWORD** — xi
Michael D'Antonio

**PREFACE** — xvii
Ama Mazama

**INTRODUCTION** — xxi
Daryl Taiwo Harris–*The Lamentations of Twitter Duped and Twitter Dumped On*

**HISTORICAL PERSPECTIVE AND SIGNIFICANCE** *Op-Ed* — xxxi
Molefi Kete Asante–*Why I Voted in the Presidential Election of 2016*

**CHAPTER ONE – The Fallacy of Trumpism** — 1
Molefi Kete Asante -*Donald Trump and the End of American Political Rhetoric: A Contrast with Ethical Tropes in Ancient Africa*

**CHAPTER TWO – Rhetoric and the Whispers of Race** — 15
Clarence Lusane–*We Can Hear You: Dog Whistles, Blaring Trumpets and Race Language in the Obama-Trump Era*

**CHAPTER THREE – Misogyny on the Campaign Path** — 37
Marquita Pellerin-Gammage -*Political Terrorism Against Women: Analyzing Trump's Campaign Tactics Designed to Scare the American Public into Supporting White Male Leadership*

**CHAPTER FOUR** – Feeding the Trump Base    53
    Kola Abimbola -*Police Culture: Theory and Proof in Pre-Trial Criminal Evidence*

**CHAPTER FIVE**- The Art of the Rhetoric of White Nationalism    81
    KenZoe Brian J. Selassie–*Yurugu Rhetoric: Psychopathy and Savagery*

**CHAPTER SIX** – Us Against Them    95
    Jude Chinweuba Asike–*Conceptions of Cultural World Order and Ethnic Nationalism: Analysis of Trump's Naïve Realism*

**CHAPTER SEVEN** – Islamophobia and Anti-Immigration    103
    Luqman Abdullah–*Capitalizing on Fear: Donald Trump's Immigration Policy in a Nutshell*

**CHAPTER EIGHT** – Radical Conservatism    117
    Justin Gammage -*Making America Great Again: The Return of Conservative Political Thinking and Rhetoric that Marginalizes Black Social Movements*

**CHAPTER NINE**- Anti-Intellectualism and For Profit Education    133
    Brian L. Wright–Jemimah L. Young; Donna Y. Ford–*Will Every Child Count? Exploring What Early Childhood and Gifted Children of Color Risk Losing Under a Trump Administration*

**CHAPTER TEN** – Anti-Immigration and Isolationism    149
    Aitza Haddad–*Trump, Latin America, and the Future of International Law*

**CHAPTER ELEVEN – Privatizing Education**  163
Ann-Marie Waterman,–*President Donald Trump's Rhetoric on Education*

**CHAPTER TWELVE –White Nationalism**  177
Sara Swetzoff–*The Trump in All of Us: Settler Colonialism and the White Nation*

**CHAPTER THIRTEEN-*Racism and Discrimination***  185
Ashley L. Lewis–*Black Activism as the Face of Terrorism? Donald Trump Pins Black Lives Matter a Terrorist Organization*

**CHAPTER FOURTEEN- *Politics and Race***  197
Denise Rosier *AKA* Ayo Sekai- *Linguistic Imperialism: Trump and Making America Great Again*

**CHAPTER FIFTEEN-*Racism and Rhetoric***  211
Jaimee Swift–*Trump Eugenics, and the Black Inferiority Complex*

**CHAPTER SIXTEEN- *Islamophobia***  221
Stephenie Howard–*Trump's Anti-Muslim Rhetoric and the Implications for Clinical Social Work Practice*

**CHAPTER SEVENTEEN- *Racism and Rhetoric***  231
Paula Lezama: *An Unfair Burden: Donald Trump's Rhetoric and Latino Families*

**CHAPTER EIGHTEEN- *Racism and Rhetoric***  243
Aaron Smith–*2 Faces of Evil: Donald Trump as the Poster-Child for Political Eurobliviousness!*

**CHAPTER NINETEEN- *Misogyny***  251
Anjerrika Bean -*Donald Trump: Racism, Rhetoric, and Women*

# Foreword

## *President as Cult Leader*

No one should doubt that as much of the world struggled to understand the bizarre candidacy and then presidency of Donald Trump that this attention, the mere fact that so many people were focused upon him, was the reward Trump has sought throughout his life. As the ultimate man of his time, an era when a person's appearance in the media could make one rich, powerful, and ultimately *real* in the eyes of others, Trump has achieved his true goal. His name and likeness are known to the world. And it is up to us to grapple with the reality of his occupation of the world's most powerful office.

Everything about Trump's ascendance defied what most people associate with the regular course of events. From the moment he arrived on the public stage, in the 1970s, he was regarded as a paragon of ill will, a preening buffoon who insulted others, boasted relentlessly, and lied with abandon. (This included adopting fake personas to claim that the some of the world's most beautiful women were enamored of him.)

Although he said he was a real estate development, Trump's main construction was his own image, which was a confection made of gold-colored metal, advertising, and cosmetics. Citizens of his hometown, New

York City, routinely dismissed him to pollsters, with roughly 65 percent offering consistently negative views on the man at every stage of his life. However Trump understood that in world of infinite options, support from 35 percent of the people would be more than enough to assure him of customers for his business and, later, an audience for his TV show.

Throughout his life before the 2016 presidential campaign Trump made racist and misogynistic statements and gleefully bullied both public figures and consumers who were duped by businesses like the so-called Trump University. These transgressions were revealed in the press but for the most part the facts eluded the great masses of people who would eventually vote for Trump to be president. By the time of the election, Trump was an attitude as much as a candidate. His stump speeches were performances devoted to the expression of ego, certainty, and defiance and they thrilled his followers who found a kind of emotional release in hearing someone express disdain for those whom they disdained and promised to save them from an apocalypse that loomed on the horizon.

The idea that something is terribly wrong in America and that various forms of evil including terrorism, global economic competition, and incompetence in Washington threatened the nation, occupied the center of the portrait of the nation Trump painted for his followers. The appeal was a deeply psychological one. It touched on the universal human sense that we, each of us, contain all that is good and evil in humanity and our fear that the evil may be ascendant. This feeling underpins the messages of apocalypse that have been preached for as long as human beings have organized themselves into communities and became a strain in American political rhetoric in the 19$^{th}$ century. Trump absolved his supporters of responsibility for this evil by projecting it onto others, from President Obama to the world's Muslims, and assuring them that they are the "good people."

In opposition to the vision evil, what Trump called the "carnage" facing us in the future, he offered himself as the savior. The system was 'rigged" he said. The world was "laughing at us" because we were failing. "Only I" can solve America's problems, he preached repeatedly. "Only I can fix it." Not even Christ made such a promise.

More thoughtful listeners would hear Trump's words and catch the scent of treachery in his performances and find them unnerving. He spoke and moved in an authoritarian style that evoked dictators both living and dead. Opposing politicians and serious journalists repeatedly unmasked Trumps' deceptions and warned of the danger that he posed. The clarions were sufficient to move the majority of Americans to reject his candidacy in favor of his flawed opponent, Hillary Clinton. But while Clinton prevailed by three million votes, the quirks of the Electoral College installed Trump in the White House. Ever since, he has continued to act and speak with little regard for the truth or the needs of a nation divided by partisan rancor and riven by fear, most importantly, fear of *him*.

At home, many American have watched in alarm was extremists have carried out hate-based, anti-immigrant killings in Kansas and Oregon. Abroad, allies and enemies alike have been appalled by Trump's rhetoric and behavior. Trump has treated nations who shared America's interests as members of North Atlantic Treaty Organizations as props for his xenophobic grandstanding and nothing said by any world leader could stop him from joining Nicaragua and Syria to reject the Paris climate change accord, which the rest of the world has embraced.

Just five months into his presidency Trump has created so many controversies that it's impossible to keep up. His embrace of Vladimir Putin was eclipsed by his sharing of secrets with Russia's ambassador who was overshadowed by his firing of FBI director James Comey. He has done so many bizarre things that disruption is slowly becoming accepted as the norm, and those who call Trump to be "presidential" would have grown hoarse and exhausted.

The exhaustion felt by those who are terrified by Trump is part of his method. He has always sought to wear down his opponents and normalize his own depraved behavior by continually pushing toward ever-worse extremes. Borrowing from Malcolm X, he will pursue power and the satisfaction of his ego by any means necessary.

The difference between Malcolm and Donald is, of course, that Malcolm sought to advance a people and Trump seeks personal gratification. His manipulation of the nation's psyche and his disruptive and destructive political choices are not part of a well-considered plan, nor do they reflect an ideology. Trump does not have a political philosophy and he has no strategy beyond the indulgence of his own impulses. He has purpose other than self-aggrandizement, which means that he wants attention in any form offered. In this way he is more cult leader than politician and his supporters are not citizens but devotees.

In the enlightening essay in this book you will come to understand Trump as a person and, more importantly as a phenomenon. Racism, misogyny, extremism and other elements are all part of the dynamic that occurs inside of Trump and they are present in his relationship with the world. This truth, revealed here by scholars writing in a variety of disciplines. However in total, this volume is a powerful call to those who may be exhausted by the challenge this man presents and despair of effectively calling him to account. They call us to stand against Trump's efforts to distort reality and exploit the worst in human nature. As a biographer of the man, I can attest that the only thing that has ever stopped him has been resistance that is as determined and relentless as he. Let this book help us understand why and how that resistance must be developed and sustained.

Michael D'Antonio
Author, Screenwriter, Political Pundit
Long Island, New York

## Bio

A Pulitzer-Prize winning writer of books, articles, and original stories for film, Michael D'Antonio has published more than a dozen books, including Never Enough, a 2015 biography of presidential candidate and billionaire businessman Donald Trump. Described variously as "luminous," "captivating," "momentous" and "meticulous" Michael's work is renowned for its clarity, balance, and thoroughness.

His works have been noted as "best books of the year" or "editors' picks" by The New York Times, The Christian Science Monitor, BusinessWeek, The Chicago Tribune and Publisher's Weekly. He has appeared on Sixty Minutes, Today, Good Morning, The Morning Show, America, Larry King Live, Morning Edition, All Things Considered, Diane Rehm, Coast-to-Coast, and many other programs.

Before becoming a full-time author, Michael worked as a journalist in New York, Washington, and Maine. He has written for Esquire, The New York Times Magazine, The Times of London Magazine, Discover, Sports Illustrated, The Los Angeles Times Magazine and many others. He has received numerous awards including the 1984 Pulitzer Prize, shared with a team at Newsday that explored the medical, legal, and ethical issues surrounding the Baby Jane Doe case.

In 2016, Michael became a regular contributor for CNN, both on-air and on their website. His pieces can be read here: http://www.cnn.com/profiles/michael-dantonio

D'Antonio has been the recipient of the Alicia Patterson Fellowship, the First Amendment Award, and the Humanities Award for his Showtime film, Crown Heights. Born and raised in New Hampshire, Michael now lives on Long Island with his wife, Toni Raiten-D'Antonio who is a psychotherapist, professor, and author of three acclaimed books.

Bio Credit *www.michaeldantonio.net*

# Preface

Perhaps at no time in the history of American politics has a political personality given scholars such a trove of figures, tropes, and rhetorical devices as Donald Trump did during his campaign for the presidency in 2016. Without exaggeration, one can say that Trump drove the television and radio pundits and commentators speechless with his hyperbole, accusative rhetoric, name-calling, and big lies. Although politics has the capacity to bring out the most worrisome type of double-speak and ill-informed discourse, never had the American electorate met with such political and personal narcissism as displayed by Donald Trump.

*This Rhetoric of Donald Trump* compiled by Daryl Taiwo Harris, one of the leading political science theorists in the contemporary academy, seeks to bring to light some of the most telling aspects of the Trump phenomenon. In 19 chapters, this book covers the entire spectrum of the Trump rhetorical campaign, pointing out the various ways the candidate rose to the top of a very large field of professional and experienced group of politicians. He defied the routines and the accepted principles of discourse behavior to claim the mantle of being a transformative figure in the political arena.

One can cite many instances where Trump blew off the customs and rules that had governed political discourse in American politics for decades. It was almost as if he had taken a page out of the rhetorical textbook of National Socialism during the 1930s. He inundated the population with false information, told in a confident and unashamedly bold manner, and many people fell for the rhetoric. They became assured by Trump's boldness that they were also bold. They dumped onto Trump all of their insecurities and he folded them up into his own language of attack, assaults, and activism.

Authors take on: Ethnic Nationalism, Naïve Realism, immigration policy, World Order, Marginalized Black Social Movement, Eugenics, political terrorism against women, Black inferiority complex, Latino families, Islamophobia, police culture, education, and linguistic imperialism. All of these issues appear in the total corpus of the Trump Presidential rhetoric.

The intelligence of these studies and reports represent among the first real thinking of African American scholars on the Trump phenomenon. Experts in communication, Africology, sociology, and political science make this book all the more remarkable for it comprehensiveness and depth. I urge the reader to pay close attention to this book during the Trump Administration to see the prescience of the writers who have taken on the material and symbolic meaning of Trump's call for change. Nothing should obscure the fact that African people must continue to work for their own victories despite the fact that we are in a hegemonic situation. I applaud Daryl Taiwo Harris for the boldness of his vision and the brilliance of his conceptualization on these issues.

Ama Mazama, Ph.D.
Professor and Graduate Director, Africology
Temple University

# Bio

Ama Mazama (aka Marie-Josée Cérol) is Associate Professor and Director of the Graduate Programs of the Department of Africa American Studies at Temple University. She received her PhD with highest distinction from La Sorbonne Nouvelle, Paris III. After graduating from La Sorbonne with Highest Distinction in Linguistics for her doctorarte, Professor Ama Mazama taught at the University of Texas, Pennsylvania State University, before arriving at Temple University in 1993. She established a reputation as the principal exponent of the African origin of the Guadeloupian language. In two books, Langue et Identité en Guadeloupe: Une Perspective Afrocentrique and Une Introduction au Créole Guadeloupéen.

She is the Managing Editor of the Journal of Black Studies. Her publications appear in journals in three continents. Well known as an educational consultant for the infusion of African content in American schools Mazama has written several books for teachers in addition to her major scholarly works in Afrocentric philosophy and theory. Two co-edited encyclopedias, the Encyclopedia of Black Studies and the Encyclopedia of African Religion, earned praise for their pioneering work from the National Council of Black Studies. Her scholarly works critique domination and hegemonic philosophies, reveal the cultural, linguistic, and religious bases of Caribbean culture, especially Vodu, and examine cultural and critical methods of establishing an ethic of justice and equity.

Bio Credit *www.youtube.com*

# Introduction from the Editor

## *The Lamentations of Twitter Duped and Twitter Dumped on*

### Daryl Taiwo Harris

Over the course of the 2016 election cycle, the American public was treated to the truly startling spectacle of Donald Trump assuming presidential power. The specter of Trump wielding the awesome power of the presidency is compounded by the fact that, alongside his meteoric political ascent, conservative Republicans effectively secured control of all three branches of the national government; and, complementing their grip over the federal government, Republicans hold virtual dominance in all southern state legislatures, as well as in three-fifths of all state legislatures. Trump began his ascent in the American imagination first as narcissistic excess in Atlantic City's casino world, then as comic relief on reality television's *The Apprentice* program where he regularly derided other people as "losers."

The idea that Trump might morph into a political force gained momentum in 2011 when he began to malign Barack Obama as the dark imposter who usurped presidential power and authority from its rightful, white inheritance. Trump's haranguing of Obama even caused Obama to publicly present his birth certificate attesting his citizenship. But Trump's smear campaign continued—he could hardly do otherwise because of its general acceptance and popularity among the Republican electorate. Throughout Obama's presidency, for instance, fully 72 percent of Republican voters held suspicions of his American citizenship, and half believed that he was secretly a Muslim. So accepting was the Republican electorate of vilifying Obama that in August 2016, just months before the election and the end of Obama's presidency, it applauded Trump's pernicious claim that Obama founded the terrorist group ISIL (Nelson, 2016). Trump excels at being indelicate, all the while appealing to the most ignoble proclivities in American society: racism, sexism, nativism, and religious chauvinism, among others—his incivility, of course, is part and parcel of his character, and hearkens back to at least when he assumed substantial authority in his family's real estate business.

As a political novice who arose out of relative political obscurity, Trump dumbfounded the American political establishment. First, he vanquished the crowded field of Republican candidates seeking the party's nomination for president. He then eked out an electoral college vote victory over Democrat Hillary Clinton in the general election, although she won nearly 3 million more popular votes. It appears that Trump prevailed in the 2016 general election because several white demographic categories coalesced behind him. Most notable in this regard was the strong support he received from non-college educated whites, some of whom are pejoratively referred to as "bubba" voters (that is, disenchanted white Democrats who cross over the partisan barrier to vote Republican). As it were, non-college whites backed Trump hugely, giving him 67 percent of their vote, compared to Clinton's 28 percent. Trump even outperformed Clinton among college-educated whites, although by the much narrower margin of 49 percent to 45 percent. Of those bubba voters, their lineage arguably dates to at least the 1980s when they crossed over to support Ronald Reagan. Bubba voters, of course, reside all over the country, but their stronghold is mainly in the formerly industrial powerhouse states of Ohio, Pennsylvania, Indiana, and Michigan. With industry's decline over the past half century, however, their economic fortunes likewise have declined (Wilson, 1997). No longer solidly middle-class, and having no viable means to reclaim it, they are especially prone to being simultaneously duped and appeased by politicians who attribute their misfortunes to such culprits as ideology (liberalism, for instance), immigrants (especially Black and Brown ones), big government, and social welfare programs. Ironically, even as non-college whites (especially bubba) are seemingly misled on the source of their woes, they nonetheless are susceptible to being dumped on as well. Trump and Republicans' repeal and replace designs on the Affordable Care Act of 2010 highlight this problem.

Trump successfully ascended the political ladder, but seems incapable of moderating his Twitter rants one iota. Indeed, as president he continues to use the social media platform almost daily to berate and belittle those he counts as opponents, enemies, and "losers." In this way, he provides a trove of rhetorical data for analysis, commentary, and critique. Trump's mouth, simply put, is the gift that keeps giving, as he is overly talkative but in the worst way. He presents neither secrets nor complexities. And yet his impulsive, rhetorical volleys on social media and elsewhere would be vacuous were it not for the fact that he wields and exercises presidential power. Up till now Trump has only demonstrated an adeptness at issuing executive orders—he has yet to show adroitness in pushing a viable legislative agenda—but he has already confirmed that he is perfectly capable of causing duress and great harm to Black and Brown peoples, immigrants, Muslims, the environment, women, and little people in general.

The authors of these essays and commentaries recognize the artifices and discordances Trump augurs for American governance, and thus have set their analytical visions on the effects they portend for the country. Still, it might be useful here to survey some of the most consequential policy issues that are in the Trump administration's crosshairs.

## Duping and Dumping on the American People

To contend that Trump's loyal constituency is comprised of those who were and are duped in some manner is not entirely accurate—actually, his devotees can be regarded as true believers who indulge in the same nativist tendencies, and who embrace in varying degrees the policy prescriptions Trump espouses.

## On the Environment and Climate Change:

If there is an issue area in which the Trump administration is truly aiming to dupe the American people on, it would undoubtedly be the environment and climate change. Calling global warming a hoax, Trump and fellow climate change deniers, reject the science that says the earth's climatic patterns are being catastrophically altered due to the excessive use of fossil fuels. In late March 2017, just two months into his administration, Trump signed an executive order effectively rescinding Obama-era climate policies. Obama aggressively sought to position the United States as an international leader in reducing carbon pollution. Toward this end, the Environment Protection Agency (EPA) devised the Clean Power Plan which, under the Clean Air Act of 1963 (last amended in 1990), sought to reduce and freeze construction of coal burning plants, and replace them with clean energy, such as solar. Also under Obama, the United States became a signatory to the Paris Agreement in 2016, ostensibly to help mitigate greenhouse gas emissions. Trump's retreat on the Clean Power Plan—and threatened withdrawal of the United States from the Paris Agreement—while mollifying energy industry firms and workers, is certainly imprudent, and makes him an irresponsible steward of the earth.

Unfortunately, Trump's executive order did not end his reckless assault on responsible environmental policy, for he envisions an environment unmoored from so-called burdensome government regulations. Presumably, this would enable the energy corporatists to innovate and create a flood of energy industry jobs. To unleash them, Trump's FY2018 budget proposal aims to slash the EPA's funding by a whopping 31 percent, to

$5.6 billion. Not a fan of the EPA—having campaigned to eliminate it "in almost every form"—Trump's proposed cut to the agency would be the largest cut to any federal agency. His plan also calls for laying off 3,800 EPA employees, and scaling back or discontinuing many cleanup programs, such as Superfund (which cleans up toxic-chemical spill sites) and those that protect the Chesapeake Bay, the Great Lakes, and the Atlantic and Pacific coasts. Trump also wants to significantly scale back the EPA's federal enforcement office by cutting the office's budget by 40 percent. This coincides with EPA director Scott Pruitt's belief that states can better monitor the corporations in their jurisdiction on their adherence to federal environmental rules. This is the same Scott Pruitt who as Oklahoma's attorney general before being appointed EPA's director repeatedly challenged the agency's regulatory reach.

Writing in *The Atlantic*, Robinson Meyer pretty much sums up Trump's intentions for the environment: "If he had the power, Donald Trump would allow polluters to spew carbon and chemicals into the air and water, muzzle the science that identifies why that's a problem, and cut off the research and development which is finding a more renewable way of generating power" (Meyer, 2017, p. 4).

It is important to appreciate that Trumpism as an ideological movement endeavors to have far- reaching impact beyond a few issues. Trumpism certainly wants to make policy prescriptions on a host of issues. But it also cultivates fantasies of a monocultural space where diversity and multiculturalism are mere catchphrases. The appointment of Stephen Brannon (the alt-right firebrand who traffics in white supremacist nationalism) as White House chief strategist signifies that Trump neither understands nor respects diversity and multiculturalism. Moreover, diversity and multiculturalism often denote claims of social justice and equality and, as such, they also suggest that the Trump administration would be unkind on criminal justice reform.

## CRIMINAL JUSTICE REFORM:

Trump's vision of criminal justice reform is akin to rekindling the "tough on crime" mass incarceration measures of the past 40 years (Alexander, 2012). Notwithstanding that bipartisan initiatives, along with President Obama's efforts, to reform America's criminal justice system were nearing fruition, Trump and Attorney General Jeff Sessions have set a course heading in the opposite direction. Notwithstanding that over the past seven years the national incarceration rate has declined, and that the nation's crime rate remains at a 20-year low, the Trump administration still put the brakes on. Hardly a few weeks into his tenure, Sessions announced that the Justice Department would reinstate the use of private prisons for federal incarceration, effectively rescinding Obama's executive order to discontinue their use. Private prisons are needed, according to Sessions, "to meet the future needs of the federal correctional system." Sessions, of course, has wide-ranging authority over federal prosecutors and federal law enforcement, and his guidance will affect the degree to which federal law enforcement ramps up policing and criminalization in Black and Brown communities.

To be clear, social control policing and criminalizing Black and Brown people are not new. From Jamestown, VA, in 1619 to New York City in 2017, Black people have been subjected to heavy-handed policing and criminalization. Prisons, of course, were a natural and necessary extension especially of the slaveocracy regime, but also of the Jim Crow system that replaced it (Wilson, 1990; McIntyre, 1993). Times have changed, however. The staggering economic and human costs of mass incarceration are such that even some conservatives have come to their senses on continuing or rekindling the "tough on crime" mantra.

Notable about Trump's posture on criminal justice is that he relies on stoking fear of a dangerously high crime wave, and that only he, via "tough on crime" measures, can make America safe again. Their fears appropriately stoked, Americans presumably would embrace a national stop and frisk policy, a border wall with Mexico, and mass deportations.

Since taking office, Sessions has championed a return to harsher federal sentencing charging policies, issuing a call to all U.S. Attorneys to anticipate a policy shift in this direction. Session simply wants to incarcerate more people, for less serious criminal offenses. A year ago, then-Senator Sessions led a fight to defeat the bipartisan effort to pass the Sentencing Reform and Corrections Act, which would have reduced mandatory minimums for some nonviolent and drug crimes. He mocked it, labeling it the "criminal leniency bill."

The problem of police beatings and killings of Black people is ancient. Black people have always lamented this problem. Hardly anyone can recall a time when Black people did not bemoan police violence. And while police are rarely punished for beating and killing Black people, there have been instances when the Justice Department has intervened with corrective measures. This usually occurs when civil rights violations are committed by local police departments. Under Obama, for instance, the Justice Department opened more than 20 investigations of police misconduct, and arranged consent decrees in more than a dozen of them—Ferguson, MO, Cleveland, and Baltimore are among those. Consent decrees, which are overseen by a federal court, requires police departments to work with communities and improve their practices. Sessions vehemently opposes federal oversight of local police departments, feeling that police forces are already under siege. We would be remiss if we did not comment on Trump's immigration enforcement stance. Since taking office, Trump has directed the Justice Department to ratchet up its enforcement of immigration law. Sessions has sense hired new agents, and threatened to strip funding from so-called sanctuary cities.

## HEALTH CARE: TO REPEAL OF NOT:

Of all the policies that Trump pledged immediate action on, health care easily ranks at the top. Indeed, since 2010 when it was enacted the Affordable Care Act (Obamacare) galvanized conservatives like no other issue. Congressional Republicans repeatedly clamored for its repeal on the grounds that it was a budget buster; they even cast symbolic votes to repeal the law, but that was before they gained control of Congress. Recently, however, Republicans in the House of Representatives did pass a bill to dismantle Obamacare. But all is not easygoing for Republicans. The Congressional Budget Office reported that if enacted, by 2026 the Republican bill would leave 23 million more people uninsured than under Obamacare. What is worrying Senate Republicans, who would have to go along with House Republicans, is that millions of Trump's supporters, especially the bubba voters in coal country Kentucky, or in steel mill valleys in Ohio and Pennsylvania, would be counted among the tens of millions to lose health care coverage. Not only would they have been duped by Trump's assurances of universal and inexpensive health care insurance, they would also join the ranks of the dumped on (that is, those who would be negatively affected by Trumpism.

It is worth saying again that in these essays the authors highlight in considerably more detail the significant harm that Trump's policy initiatives will exact on Black and Brown people, women's health and reproductive rights, immigrants, Muslims, and the environment. Perhaps we should conclude with the contention that Trumpism is but a scornful, white supremacist sensibility that only knows might as power. It enjoys lumbering along, thinking that it merits adoration, but causes distress, heartache, and havoc along the way.

# Bio

**Daryl B. Harris** is an associate professor and former chair of political science at Howard University. He was the recipient of a 2014-2015 Fulbright Distinguished Research Award. The scholarly focus of his teaching and research is the philosophical underpinnings of Black political phenomena. His work combines methods of Africological and political analyses with the goal of advancing Afrocentric understandings of the world. In exploring the nuances, interstices, and subtleties of previous critical works, Harris has found that the opening for innovation in the way we assess racial and cultural conflicts remains wide open. Harris has taught Black Politics and political theory courses, first at the University of Connecticut and then at Howard University, his current institutional affiliation since 2003.

## REFERENCES

Alexander, Michelle. (2012). *The New Jim Crow: Mass Incarceration in the Age of Colorblindness* (New York: The New Press).

McIntyre, Charshee. (1993). *Criminalizing a Race: Free Blacks During Slavery* (Kayode Publishers).

Meyer, Robinson. "What Does Trump's Budget Mean for the Environment?" *The Atlantic* (May 24, 2017).

Nelson, Louis. "Trump Escalates Claim that Obama Founded ISIL," www.politico.com (August 11, 2016).

Wilson, Amos. (1990). *Black-on-Black Violence: The Psychodynamics of Black Self-Annihilation in Service of White Domination* (New York: Afrikan World Infosystems).

Wilson, William Julius. (1997). *When Work Disappears: The World of the New Urban Poor.* (New York: Vintage Books).

# *Historical Perspective And Significance*

## Why I Voted in the Presidential Election of 2016

### Molefi Kete Asante

I am the sixth generation of my family to live in the United States. Neither my father nor his father voted. None of their fathers to the first that we know voted in any elections. My mother did not vote, and her mother could not vote because it was illegal for African women to vote until 1920. Black people in the South where I was born fought to declare our right to vote. I was a dedicated member of the Civil Rights and Black Power Movements, becoming leader of the SNCC chapter at UCLA supporting and participating in voting rights drives and political consciousness raising. I have the same mission today. But I have always known that the so-called democracy of the United States was terribly flawed but I had the historical consciousness to see that my early heroes, Fannie Lou Hamer, Malcolm X, Martin Luther King Jr., John Lewis, and A. Philip Randolph knew that many whites in the nation feared most of all the power of African Americans voting. As I have said many times before, we must challenge, as we have challenged before, the core element in our enemies' plan to subvert our growing power in the nation. The fear that the sleeping and disinterested black voters will one day awake in force has kept many vile and obscene bigots in power and office with the intent to suppress our rights and opportunities to vote. Democracy is rule by talk, but so is demagoguery and the best way to stifle the demagogue is to vote. Those whose aim is to limit our power know that if we disempower ourselves they have won. They have often tried to prevent us from exercising our right to vote.

This was the meaning of the killing of our ancestors who went to the polls and were shot down in the streets. This was the meaning of the demand that our people quote various articles of the Constitution before they were given the ballot. This was the aim of those who placed a price on the voting polls and who demanded to see our receipts from the previous year's trek to the polls. This was the meaning of the threats and the intimidation of black people who dared to exercise the right to vote. No one should be able, on the blood of our ancestors, to counsel Africans not to vote in national elections where the only power is the bullet or the ballot. Where difference can be made; it must be made in the deepest sense of political interest. All politics is interest politics and if we believe that we do not have an interest in the state of the economy, the survival of the earth, the management of the natural resources of this nation, and the political posture toward Africa and the world, then we are worse off than our mothers and fathers were before the Voting Rights Act of 1965. I still stand in awe of the courageous and heroic men and women who challenged the racists and bigots who feared our vote.

I will never abandon the dreams of Kwame Ture, H. Rap Brown, Fannie Lou Hamer, Ella Baker, Fred Gray, Marion Barry, William Barbee, and Diane Nash whose legendary efforts, among thousands of others, established the moral high ground of our political will to change the South. Forcing the nation to pass the Voting Rights Act of l965 was one of the great successes of the Civil Rights Movement. The prohibition of racial discrimination in voting was meant to ensure that the 14th and 15th Amendments would be enforced, mainly in Southern States, but the entire nation has become a gathering place where attempts by Republicans to suppress the African American vote is quite commonplace. Why would the Republicans want to shorten the voting time, to reduce the number of polling places, to keep people from voting who do not have certain pieces of identification? They do it to keep black people from acting in our own political interest.

My vote is my most powerful act under the Constitution. I chose to support the candidate who best represents what I see as my people's interests. That does not mean that I am blind to the flaws in this candidate, but I am certain that the opposition candidate is a narcissistic bigot as I have indicated in previous writings.

Yet I know because I took the time to read the platform that the Democrats have a far more progressive set of ideas than the Republicans. Certainly the party was pushed by the socialists to underscore the rights of the masses in ways that were not nativist like the Republicans who played to a forlorn white nationalism. As W. E. B. Du Bois recalled his own history of voting in 1956, he cited the times that he, living in the North, could vote for the candidate who dealt with the "Negro Problem."

I am firmly convinced that the Republican candidate's election would bring the worst type of anti-African American racism in the national polity. While it has always been present it has waned and waxed according to our own strength and demands. The African American people have always been the most progressive cadre in the American political arena, and with the growing Latino voting bloc it is possible that a new coalition alongside the progressive white population will bring about a transformation in the politics of the society. So I voted for Hillary Clinton in the election of 2016 to express my right and my will to choose that I think will serve best the interests of African American people. In such a vote I decided against racism, white nativism, Islamophobia, climate change denying, political ignorance, misogyny, sexism, Mexican bashing, and anti-African American history and culture.

# CHAPTER ONE

## *The Fallacy of Trumpism*

### Donald Trump and the End of American Political Rhetoric: A Contrast with Ethical Tropes in Ancient Africa

#### Molefi Kete Asante

When *The Eloquent Peasant* was written in ancient Kemet it was a demonstration of the highest ethical values known to humans because it was an appeal to compassion, fairness, and justice (Asante, 2001). Donald Trump's rhetoric of dismay has completely reduced the content of public rhetoric to the most base of human appeals. It is neither the rhetoric of hope nor the authentic rhetoric of a call for peace and national unity, but rather the naked reactions of despair created by the dire possibilities looking racism squarely in the face in a country that is increasingly black and brown.

In this chapter I intend to use one of the oldest African sources of eloquence as demonstrated in Khunanup's appeal to the magistrate for restorative justice as a relief backdrop to Donald Trump's banal and vile appeal to revenge and indignity based on racial animus. To begin with one must be clear that the American society has not been well served by its media institutions, but that is probably no fault of the institutions themselves but the results of media executives and media pundits, interviewers, hosts, and reporters who have abandoned the best principles of the news gathering and reporting for whatever profit can be gained by entertainment. If we say that we have healthy institutions and for the most part the society has produced a plethora of strong and diverse media institutions, then we must ask what has been the response of those institutions to the political rhetoric of the time? The problem is therefore not the fact that this is a society devoid of the institutions that could, if they were used properly, deliver to the people the kind of analysis and information we need to make good judgments. Our problem, that is, the American problem lies in several spheres of the communication universe now that Donald Trump has been duly elected to the highest office in the land.

The first part of this chapter will outline my general position on the Trump phenomenon. The second part will expose a classical African idea of eloquence engaging the moral ideal, and then I will make a concluding comment about the place of Donald Trump in the political realm. What remains to be done by a communicationist is the detailed study of each of Trump's major speeches to ascertain the creative use of language that he employs to persuade his audiences to vote for him or to attend his rallies. One also has to raise the curtain of his entertainment value for audiences on television as a reason for the passion at his rallies. My essay will not examine this role, as I believe there is something far more sinister in the Trump phenomenon.

## First Part

There are three aspects to this American rhetorical problem with Donald Trump. The first is the inability of the journalists because of lack of knowledge, history, and courage to cut through the dense intellectual tundra of a barren rhetorical environment devoid of facts, compassion, or reason. The second is the inability of a media system reduced to capitalist profit motives to rein in the indomitable narcissistic personality of a potential tyrant who parades his populist message while donning the garments of his plutocratic style. The third aspect of this problem is the white racism that permeates the majority white population, especially men, with a sense of entitlement when it comes to leadership of the society (Tillotson, 2013). The election of Barack Obama might be said to have completely shifted the rhetoric of the American society to something like the Hitlerian hysteria after the first great European International War when the German population was in despair over the economic conditions in the country. The idea of a savior, someone who could by the dint of his personality and the force of his rhetoric transform the society, was a core of people's willingness to give up their liberties to a megalomaniac. It is this heroic idea, morphed into the rhetoric of revenge and hate that carried Trump to victory over other Republicans, and indeed, over Hillary Clinton in the electoral vote. Of course, she beat Trump by three million votes in the popular votes.

The critical test of the American society will always be will the citizens of this free state ever allow their fears to triumph over reasons and vote for their own master. I am not so sure that any society, loose from the ethical principles, that are the foundation of free and open democracy, can ever be immune to such rhetoric. Certainly the American public has proved that there is no exceptionalism in this nation when it comes to the idea of the poor, weak, and disenchanted voting into office someone who shares neither class nor popular interest with them. They think that the billionaire who dwells in Trump Tower in Manhattan will fight for the bygone industry in the small Midwestern towns!

### *Journalists and Trump: The Improbability of Truth*

In order to interview a politician it is necessary for the interviewer to know the lay of the territory as much or more than the politician. This is the first rule to prevent being conned by a great con artist. Donald Trump has demonstrated all of the characteristics of the con artist. He is a great sloganeer. He is able to make his audience believe that he is can solve all of their problems by a simple tweet. He carries with him the language of hyperbole because he sees things in black and white. His imagination creates the most extreme of emotions. Everything is wonderful, better, and most stupendous or evil and bad with Trump. Journalists who do not display any knowledge of history, culture, or politics have allowed him to fascinate them with his bombastic rhetoric. He is an amazing showman to many of them and they do not take him seriously even now that he is President of the United States of America.

Without steady and skilled journalists a society is left to be eaten by the hungry dogs of charismatic personalities capable of whipping up the vilest emotions in uneducated, and sometimes, educated people. Voters who have a sense of history and experience are usually able to filter out the language of hate, discrimination, and white nationalism. One reason the black voter is not fooled is because the black voter is a historical being having come through nearly four hundred years of dealing with people who have sought to dismiss, brutalize, and murder them. Apparently Trump does well with the uneducated white voter. This is the voter who probably has limited knowledge of the world and operates or speaks from a position of racial animus toward other people. This voter is fearful, not so much about physical harm, but about something deeper, collective salvation in the midst of the rising populations of Mexicans, Africans, and Asians in the United States (Mazama, 2016).

Reporters and journalists who do not see how Trump plays this card will never understand his pull on the ordinary white, mainly, male voter. However, one must be careful here to analyze the data given the fact that Trump also got 54% of the white women voters! The collapse of the white women voters, the feminist instinct, the turn toward white nationalism stunned many progressives. We had all predicted that there was no way for the white population to gain the kind of political control that it once held during the last century without courting some Mexicans and African Americans. Scholars believed this as well as journalists who had covered the last three presidential elections. Journalists thought they understood this and some tried to take note of Trump's empty rhetoric as demagoguery.

### *The Narcissist and the Admirer*

Something exists in human society that causes people to accept the narcissist as an extra powerful individual largely because the narcissist says that he is extra powerful. Gullibility on the part of the masses is the coin upon which the narcissist is able to operate and to pay for his actions. It is not so much that people allow tyrants to rule; they often place the tyrants in positions to rule them. In the case of Trump who has not seized power, the Republican establishment voted him into the position as their representative for president; the American people voted him into power. Trump displayed the elements of narcissism throughout his run for the White House. Some of the characteristics of narcissism are an extreme selfishness, a projection of one's self as an external object, a vain sense of one's capabilities and talents, and a sick craving for the admiration of the voters. Most often the narcissist thinks that he is better than the ordinary voter whose support he seeks. In the case of Donald Trump it is clear that he believes that he alone is capable of handling the politics of the American nation. In fact, his personality is so vain he does not believe anyone else is able to do so. I believe that at the core of his narcissism was the success of Barack Hussein Obama as the President. Trump could not take it that a man of African descent was the President of the United States and did everything he could, being out of political office, to cripple the president, often by using those who were in partisan politics. The birther movement, provoked and maintained by Trump, was about the supposed idea that Obama was not born in the United States.

What are the tools of a narcissist when it coms to the masses? I think that the narcissist will use shame and guilt of the masses. The narcissist says that he is "the best" negotiator or whatever and that the masses and their representatives have been "outsmarted by others" and look like "chumps" around the world. This line of rhetoric is to make the masses feel that they are dumb and have no idea of how shameful they seem to others. However, the narcissist must step in and say that he is the one who can change things and make them feel less shame. In fact, he can make them "great again" and then bring them to the position where they will not have to drag their heads because they have been beaten in the game of life by others. They are made to feel guilt that they could not prevent their weakness from showing and since they have been represented by less intelligent people than the narcissist, they should feel bad about it. Their guilt ought to make them realize that there is only one way to be redeemed and to make themselves feel better; they have to vote for the narcissist. In Greek mythology, Narcissus fell in love with his own reflections in a pool of water; it is the epitome of self-gratification by the pursuit of a determined and relentless egotistic admiration. When the narcissist is defeated he retreats into insults feeling that the very people he wanted to save have betrayed him. In the case of the election of Trump to the presidency, the narcissistic spirit sees the victory as confirmation of his superior knowledge and skill. Indeed, he even believes that he does not need the CIA and FBI to give him information.

## SECOND PART

Africa provides us with the first example of persuasive eloquence in world history. Around 2025 BCE, a peasant farmer named Khun-anup, married to Marye, was on his way to sell his goods when his donkey accidentally transgressed the property of a rich man, Rensi, who had a stern guard of the land named Nemtynakht. Whereupon Nemtynakht accosted the poor man and took his donkey, and all of the goods that he had amassed to take to the market. When Khun-anup was left with nothing because of this transgression, not even of his own making because Nemtynakht had tricked him by placing a sheet on the ground so that the donkey would have to go over the cliff or through the crops to avoid the sheet across the path, he was very distressed. Now he would not have food for his family. Now as destitute as he was he was even more miserable. He vowed to find Rensi, the nobleman whose land he had violated, so that he could make his case directly to the proper judge.

Of course the elegance of the arguments in the text speaks to a reflective and studied concentration of the nature of human relationships, greed, honor, respect, authority, power, poverty, generosity, and punishment. The tension between the rhetorical artifice and skill of Khun-anup and the silence of Rensi, the magistrate and owner of the property, gives Khun-anup's rhetoric a strong contemporary message in achieving justice. It is always difficult to bring the strong before the bar of justice because power builds on power and only the moral will and determination of the weak can overcome, if ever, the position of the strong.

Kemet remains for us the model civilization in antiquity because it provides more than any other civilization at a comparable time, information, documents, scripts, sculptures, and other accounts of its prodigious creations. Here we are confronted with the very evidence of the emergence of our consciousness, and hence, our use of the artifice of communication, but it is used to achieve justice. There are few examples more precise about the nature of maat in human relationships than the story of Khun-anup, a peasant, who appeals for justice in a case where he was robbed and beaten. The appeal of Khun-anup is one of profound speech, divine speech. Khun-nup spent many days making his appeal but because he was a poor man had a difficult time convincing the noble Rensi. However, after Khun-anup's last appeal, Rensi was impressed and ordered the donkey be returned, that Khun-anup be compensated with all his property plus the property of Nemtynakht, making Nemtynakht as poor as Khun-anup had been.

Among Africans reverence for the word, based as it was on the future life, was the source of the Egyptian's concern with Maat and precision in language. You could not just say anything for emotional response; one had to speak truth as clearly as one knew how to do so. The appeal was not vile and obscene; it was measured and tempered with the quest for justice.

The implications for rhetoric in this situation where the political future is staring you in the face with the necessity for getting it right now are enormous. One could say that the reverence for the word reverberated throughout everything that the ancient African society constructed and led to stability that was a major force in maintaining Maat. When we are confronted with Maat we are confronted with the possibilities of establishing truth, harmony, righteousness, justice, order, balance, and reciprocity, for these are the elements that construct our response to the universe. But yet it is at the heart of what we think when we imagine the nature of the ancient African society as one of divine speech. As I reflect on this it reminds me of the Native Americans' concept and understanding of speech, the sacredness with which they held the word, their insistence, as among the Iroquois, that you allow for a period of silence of maybe three minutes after a person spoke to permit her or him to change their minds after reflecting on what was just said. Well, the Africans had a similar idea in the ancient times and it went by the term Maat as a comprehensive concept including balance, harmony, order, righteousness, truth, justice, and reciprocity. Obviously this is something outside of the purview or view of Donald Trump. Stuck in the Greek myth of Narcissus he is unable to see himself as others see him.

Here are the principles that we learn from Khun-anup and other African sources of speech and rhetoric.

1. Criticality: the ability to distinguish good from evil, and right from wrong.
2. Devotion: Consecrating oneself by vow to Maat..
3. Control: Regulate and exercise power over the mind.
4. Discipline. Training that develops self-control, orderly behavior
5. Tolerance: Allowing and permitting others to express their views
6. Forbearance: Possessing freedom from resentment
7. Stedfastness: Holding firm to one's beliefs and ideas
8. Faith: An expression of optimism
9. Spiritual Desire: Showing the will to achieve the victory over present circumstances.
10. Initiation: Achieving the mastery over self through renewal of devotion.

Needless to say, Trump's speech is based on a much more dismal assessment of the public than an ethical rhetoric would insist. He is hampered by a lack of moral vigor and an assertive arrogance that claims his superior knowledge, wealth, and ability. In the end he is a fraud and a racist bigot with a monumental ego as expressed in his language of uniqueness. His persuasive appeal is based squarely on the minority of whites who support the idea of a white America. Trump advocates an extreme nationalism that has strong racist and discriminatory cadences.

History is one of the best teachers about the possibilities of a megalomaniacal narcissist using the people's feelings of weakness and fear to rise to power. Trump provides bombast, virulent anti-immigrant rhetoric, vile Islamophobia, hardcore bluster about "Black Lives Matter" proponents, and anti-Latino diatribes that stir the feelings of race pride in the misguided white base that drives his campaign.

Just as Adolf Hitler saw himself as indispensable to the German nation Donald Trump now insists that he is indispensable to the American nation. Neither narcissist got it right; there are no indispensable people. Trump seeks the biggest political hustle on a modern state since Hitler by using the same playbook of stirring up and stoking the fears of immigrants among the low-class of whites who need somebody to tell them that they "remain" the kings of the universe. Thus, we witness nasty and obscene bigotry couched in rhetoric of narcissism by a person seeking to become the leader of the Free World.

Like Hitler who edged out all other German political speakers in the 1930s because no one would speak so brazenly against Jews, immigrants, Roma, and others with such venom as Hitler, Trump dominated the Republicans to win the primary by the same bold tactics and went on to win the presidency with the same appeal to the basest values of the white American population. While no one credits Trump with the Hitlerian rhetorical gift they do see the Hitlerian appeal to the white masses that feel threatened by difference and the demographic facts. By 1921 Hitler had marginalized his enemies and was well on his way to becoming the master of his political futures. By January 30, 1933 when President Paul von Hinderburg handed him the position of Chancellor, Germany had seen the quickest political rise of one party in its history although the Nazis did not have complete majority in free elections, and no German party had such majority during the Wiemar Republic, the Nazis were the most dominant. Hitler gained his power legitimately (Kershaw, 1998).

Hitler was no tyrant who rode into power on military wings. German historian Friedrich Meinecke, said Hitler "is one of the great examples of the singular and incalculable power of personality in historical life" (Meinecke, 1950). Now the rise of Donald Trump might be added alongside Hitler as the second example of a surprising weakness in the white psyche to succumb to the election of one who promises uniqueness but who eventually will deliver disappointment.

In fact, in American society we have rarely if ever seen the likes of Donald Trump. He has made his own rules, created his own philosophy, and completely raided the Republican Establishment and in the process smashing the political careers and interests of the party politicians. The party has become a tool in his hands whether for good or evil. In actuality, there are those who believe that Trump could kill it or transform the Republican Party. The fact that his election victory over Clinton came as a surprise to many Democrats who had argued for immigration openness makes Trump a funnel for the most severe rhetoric of nationalism for decades.

Some people who heard Adolf Hitler early in his campaign wanted to dismiss him as an idiot. The German people, however, went on and supported him because he appealed to their need for a powerful leader who could return Germany to greatness. He was probably a more conscious orator than Trump but the latter's appeal is more in his bombast.

After Barack Obama's effective campaigns to win the presidency many white people felt that they had lost their country. Of course, it was no more their country than it was Obama's country. It is these "weakened" and worried white people that find Trump's boastful rhetoric attractive just as some Germans found Hitlerian rhetoric the narrative that they wanted to hear.

What did Hitler do to influence his audiences that he was tough, strong, and the great hope of the German people? He did the same thing that Trump is doing now. As a demagogue you have to use glittering generalities about other people. Trump says things like "I have many Muslim friends," or "The Mexicans people like me" or "African Americans will love me." These are jelly beans to get voters; these are not serious policy discourses, but Trump does not believe he needs to lay out in policy positions because those who will vote for him because they believe he is talking to whites will still vote for him.

The second strategy is to trash talk other people by accusing them of being weak, criminals, idiots, rapists, and gangsters. Trump asserts that those who are against him are really anti-American because the only thing he wants is to "make America great again." Actually this is called "name-calling" in a negative way to break down the moral ground of an opponent.

Trump uses testimonials of other people to support him. He will say anything to gain the support of others. He calls upon members of his audience to stand up say that they love him or that they believe his hair is real or that they want to look like him. Ordinary audiences are swayed by this everyman approach to any topic or subject. They do not care that the man cannot hold a clear narrative on any issue because for them he is a plain guy like they are. He may even be the savior for which they are waiting. Was not this the belief of Hitler? This idea that he and only he can resolve the issues of weakness and the feeling of the loss of power that grip many white voters.

No modern American politician has used the bandwagon concept any more effective than Trump. He asserts almost every day that he is leading the pack, that no one gets as many people to come out to events as he does, and that he will always be at the top. People like a winner and he tells them that he is the winner for which they have waited.

Trump knows how to get people to feel like they are just like he is. Of course, he is a billionaire who has nothing in common with 99% of the white people who flock to his rallies. A man who lives in a 30,000 square feet house eighty floors above Manhattan is not like the rest of us, no matter how he sounds. What he has that his followers like is a bold assertion about how to make them feel better about their lives. He has learned how to take their pain, their defeats, and their hopelessness, and to give them his energy and power. This transference is the key to demagoguery.

One other technique that Trump uses effectively is what communicationists call card stacking where the speaker manipulates the information about a product or idea to make it seem better than it is. Trump has mastered the idea of quoting from some report that few people have ever heard of or interpreting negative information as being in support of him. The bigger the lie the more the people think that Trump must be telling the truth because why would a political candidate tell such horrendous lies?

As Joseph Goebbels, Hitler's propaganda minister understood, the masses are willing to believe anything if you say it enough and then double down on it when you are questioned about its veracity. It is time for reporters and commentators to be trained in rhetorical analysis, history, Africology, and political science, otherwise we will continue to have politicians speak nonsense, stupidity, lunacy, and racism; neither politicians nor journalists should be able to get away with uncritical examination in a democracy regardless to who is the President of the United States.

**REFERENCES**

Asante, Molefi Kete. *Egyptian Philosophers*. Chicago: African American Images. 2001.

Kershaw, Ian. *Hitler: 1889-1936, Hubris*. New York-London: W.W. Norton & Company, 1998

Mazama, Ama. "Demographic Trends: Political Implications and The Future of White Supremacy." *The Asante*, June, 2016, 4:2

Meinecke, Friedrich. *The German Catastrophe: Reflections and Recollections*. Cambridge, Mass., 1950.

Tillotson, Michael. *Invisible Jim Crow*. Trenton: Africa World Press, 2013.

# Chapter Two

## *Rhetoric and the Whispers of Race*

### We Can Hear You: Dog Whistles, Blaring Trumpets and Race Language in the Obama-Trump Era

#### Clarence Lusane

*"I have a great relationship with the blacks. I've always had a great relationship with the blacks."*
DONALD TRUMP[1]

*"We won. America belongs to white men."*
RICHARD SPENCER, FOUNDER OF WHITE SUPREMACIST GROUP ALT-RIGHT[2]

In the aftermath of the Donald Trump election victory on November 8, 2016, the Southern Poverty Law Center documented more than 1,000 incidents of hate targeted at African Americans, Latinos, Muslims, immigrants, and others who had been targets of his rhetoric during the campaign. In many of these cases, Trump's name was evoked either through written or spoken language. The SPLC documented that at least 37 percent of the cases directly reference Trump in one fashion or other.[3] While Trump would claim that he did not direct or even support these incidents, it can be argued that his vitriolic language during 18 months of campaigning and since the November election certainly played a role in inspiring these outbursts. Despite his claim of innocence, he does not get to escape the consequences of his provocations. As writer Toni Morrison noted, "Oppressive language does more than represent violence; it is violence."[4]

Victories won by the Civil Rights Movement and the Black Power Movement usually evoke thoughts of key legislative, policy, and political gains such as the 1964 Civil Rights Act, 1965 Voting Rights Act and mid- to-late 1960s black electoral accomplishments. Virtually overnight, after the passage of the VRA, African Americans began to win local, state and federal offices in record numbers.[5] Equally important, an energized and mobilized black community was poised to punish electorally any white officials who refused to address the interests of the black community. These were highly visible concrete gains.

There were also cultural triumphs as well. One area in which change occurred was the transformation in the national political discourse that found it no longer acceptable to use explicit racist language publically. Prior to the black uprisings in the 1950s and 1960s, white officials, particularly but not exclusively southern politicians, regularly used overt racist language, including the "N-word," in speeches, interviews, rallies, and elsewhere. The objective of this venom was to not only tap into the racism of white supporters but to insult and demean African Americans and other people of color in every way possible including employing dehumanizing language. However, demands and resistance by communities of color shutdown, for the most part, those crude expressions of racism. This was not done because white leaders had suddenly become anti-racist. Self-interest drove most racially conservative or racist political figures to use coded language, a strategy that came to be known as a "dog whistling."

That is until the election of Barack Obama and now the Trump era. In this article, I argue that the norm of "dog whistle" language used to convey in coded but easy to interpret phrases and words a political affinity to the racist views of white voters and constituents has been shattered. Starting from the surge in public displays of racism in the wake of the 2008 presidential campaign and election of Barack Obama, the unadulterated and brazen use of blatant racist language has moved to center stage with the campaign and subsequent victory of Donald Trump for president of the United States. The destruction of this norm has several implications not the least of which is the placement of heretofore fringe white supremacist elements to not only a higher visibility but to even being viewed as politically legitimate by mainstream politics. Trump's appointment of white nationalist promoter Steve Brannon as his White House chief strategist and senior counselor only generated a short ripple among major media outlets. Brannon was the chairman of Breitbart News Network and provided a media outlet for white nationalists on the website.

Furthermore, Trump's political talk comes very close to what scholar Susan Benesch has called "dangerous speech," i.e., speech that is perceived to be a call for violent political action.[6] When speaking of public policy, Trump usually uses deliberate ambiguity in what is thought of as either an effort to not commit himself to a particular policy or to hide his ignorance. However, when discussing non-white political groups, his speech often transforms into more provocative racist and inciting speech.

How did the nation go from twice electing the first African American president to selecting an inexperienced, ill-tempered, ill-informed, racist, misogynist, xenophobic bigot? The language of race was key.

## The Transformation

By the early 1970s, it was taboo in mainstream politics and media to use vulgar racist phrases and words. As the late Republican strategist Lee Atwater said in an infamous 1981 interview, "You start out in 1954 by saying, 'Nigger, nigger, nigger.' By 1968 you can't say 'nigger'— that hurts you, backfires. So you say stuff like, uh, forced busing, states' rights, and all that stuff."[7] It is debatable, of course, how much this reluctance to use racist language existed in private speech. There is little doubt though that public discourse changed.

As a shrewd student and practitioner of U.S. racial politics, Atwater recognized the need for a transformation in political language brought about by the successes and gains of the black liberation movement. His admonition to Republicans was not to argue that the party should change its views on race to a more progressive position, but rather than it should change its tactics to accomplish the same objective: the realignment of whites, southern whites especially, to the party that was more sympathetic to their racial beliefs. The future of the GOP relied on converting them from Democrats to Republicans using strategies that now required a more nuanced appeal to their racial proclivities.

Thus, beginning in the early 1970s and for more than three decades, public officials and political leaders, north and south, Republican and Democrat, employed coded language in addressing issues of race, particularly in seeking to exploit white racial fears. As noted by scholar Ian Haney Davis, they spoke in what he coined "dog whistle" language. He defined dog whistle vernacular as "coded talk centered on race."[8]

In particular, appealing to white racial alarms, confusions, resentments and anger, words and phrases such as "law-and-order," and "states' rights" were relatable signals of alliance and understanding. The terms provided enough elasticity, ambiguity and generality to allow plausible deniability for officials who clearly understood the taboo nature of certain words. It also allowed for whites to locate themselves outside of what is normally thought of as racist behavior and beliefs, i.e., they were not the hood-wearing, cross-burning, N-word shouting segregationists that tends to define our popular images of racists.

Anti-racist forces consistently called out the "wink wink" nature of the use of these words and often forced apologies (mostly insincere) and walkbacks. Overall, a change unfolded that created a less racist national discourse among political leaders and opinion makers even as racial disparities were maintained and worsened in some instances.

Reagan used this strategy to great effect. In a well-known incident, he opened his 1980 presidential campaign following the Republican National Convention at the Neshoba County Fair outside of Philadelphia, Mississippi. The area was infamous as the site where the bodies of three murdered Civil Rights activists – James Early Chaney, Andrew Goodman, and Michael Schwerner – were found in 1964. In his speech to the thousands of whites who gathered, he delivered the line, "I believe in states' rights," the term used by southern racists as their legal and constitutional justification to establish and maintain Jim Crow segregation.[9] Before and during his presidency, Reagan would also dog whisper about "welfare queens," "young bucks," "busing," and "affirmative action."[10]

It should be clearly understood that it was not just Republicans who used dog whistles. In 1996, Bill Clinton used this strategy in his rise from governor of Arkansas to winning the White House. His call for "welfare reform" and support for the "death penalty" were meant to be seen as signs that he had broken with post-1960s Democratic Party racial orthodoxy and was more than willing to feed racist perceptions about these issues to win white voters.

While coded language was used when it came to African Americans, one group in which there were few filters was the Muslim community. From the Iranian hostage crisis of the late 1970s to the September 11th attacks in 2001 to the present, the popular narrative that links Islam and terrorism has allowed politicians and much of the media to feel little obligation to use dog whistles or softening language when discussing the Muslim community. Following September 11th, it became acceptable or at least tolerated to use anti-Islam language even in public settings. In December 2015, Trump's call for a "total and complete shutdown of Muslims entering the United States" stunned many in the political class but was joyously received by the Republican base of voters.

When challenged and criticized about the use of inflammatory, racist, or sexist language, conservatives cried they were being victimized by the tyranny of "political correctness." This ill-defined term was generally meant to convey, by conservatives, that their freedom of speech rights were being denied or policed in unfair ways by a political left with Stalinist-like tendencies. Appropriated from the left by the right in the 1990s, it would become the catchall term to pushback against charges of racism, sexism, homophobia, and discrimination in general. In the 2016 race, Trump would use the term frequently not only against the Democrats, #blacklivesmatter movement, and women's rights movement, but also traditional Republicans who did not support him. As writer Moira Weigel noted in *The Guardian*, "Trump consistently blasted political correctness, blaming it for an extraordinary range of ills and using the phrase to deflect any and every criticism."[11] He said on a number of occasion to rousing cheers from his supporters that "I think the big problem this country has is being politically correct," a view shared by surgeon Ben Carson, Sen. Ted Cruz, former Gov. Mike Huckabee, and other Republicans who ran for the presidency, as well as their constituencies in the Republican Party.[12] Weigel maintains that "We should not underestimate how many Trump supporters held views that were sexist, racist, xenophobic and Islamophobic, and were thrilled to feel that he had given them permission to say so."[13]

To a significant degree, however, Trump was an outlier. Despite the notable embrace of the political correctness defense by some well-known figures, for the most part, very few national Republican (or Democratic) leaders broke from the practice of dog whistling and continued to avoid the use of incendiary language. Dog whistling had been successful in realigning white southerners to the GOP so there was little reason, it appeared, to abandon a strategy that seemed to be working fine. Then the unthinkable happened.

## The Obama Game-Changer

In 2004, Barack Obama surged into the political limelight in a speech he gave at the 2004 Democratic National Convention. In his speech, he memorably stated, "There's not a black America and white America and Latino America and Asian America; there's the United States of America."[14] Some party leaders saw in this then-unknown but gifted speaker state legislator, who was running for the U.S. Senate, a potential presidential candidate who was black but preached a politics of inclusion. For many, including some Republicans, he was not seen as divisive in a way that Rev. Jesse Jackson had been perceived to be back in the 1980s when he twice ran for the nomination on a progressive and strong racial justice agenda, or Rev. Al Sharpton, who ran for president in the 1990s and was perhaps the nation's best known and most visible black leader.

This hope was realized when in 2007 Obama announced his intention to run for the nomination in the upcoming 2008 presidential election. He would eventually vanquished his Democratic rivals and, in the general election, defeat the hapless Sen. John McCain. His victory would be hailed as a historic step forward in the nation's racial saga. Many whites hoped, though few African Americans believed, that the nation had moved into a post-racial era.

However, a significant number of whites, specifically a core of Republican voters, immediately linked Obama's rise with their ever-increasing dread of demographic doom where whites would no longer be the majority racial group. A black president, even one as moderate as Obama, crystalized all of their fears, and a highly racialized anti-Obama movement quickly grew and metastasized among Republicans and conservatives.

The Obama-haters, as researcher Algernon Austin has called them, felt little compulsion to play nice or mollify their views through dog whistles.[15] The fact that Obama's father was from Kenya further fed the racist anti-Obama hysteria. Rumors began to fly and quickly gain currency that he was a Muslim and/or a non-citizen giving rise to the "birther movement."[16] These explicitly racist campaigns were, for the most part, rejected by mainstream Republican leaders, at least publicly and certainly by those who had presidential ambitions. McCain famously corrected a McCain Campaign volunteer named Gayle Quinnell at one of his rallies who called Obama an "Arab," by which she meant Muslim. He responded by saying Obama was a "citizen, that I just happen to have disagreements with on fundamental issues."[17]

Behind the scenes, however, local Republican leaders were feeding these rumors. Quinnell, for instance, claims she received her information about Obama being "an Arab" came from information she received at her local Republican/McCain campaign headquarters. During the campaign a number of Republican officials were forced to resign or apologize after emailing or distributing racist materials about Obama.[18]

While McCain avoided racist language and even dog whistles, his vice presidential running mate, then-Alaska Gov. Sarah Palin, emboldened the racists in the party with her inciting language and pandering to the most reactionary wing of the party. Her rallies became places where racists of all stripes found a welcome space. Reportedly, her events became so toxic the Secret Service spoke to the McCain campaign about the issue noting the spike in death threats to Obama and his family that were perhaps linked to the fanaticism she was causing.[19]

Early on aspersions began to circulate about Obama's birthplace being outside the United States. Republican voters especially felt that he was not constitutionally eligible to become president because they firmly believed he had been born in Africa, Indonesia or some foreign nation. In fact, after he became president, the number of Republicans who believed Obama was foreign-born actually increased over time, i.e., from 2010 to 2011, Republican birthers grew from 32 percent to 45 percent according to a CBS/*New York Times* poll.[20] Questioning Obama's birthplace in public forums and the media crossed the line from subtle racial innuendos to full-blown racist assertion. In 2011, one of the individuals who would tether himself to this racially poisonous movement and emerged as perhaps its most famous advocate was reality star and real estate mogul Donald Trump. As outlined below, Trump spent several years questioning Obama's birthplace as part of his effort to ingratiate himself to that part of the Republican and conservative base most antagonistic to the president and willing to embrace racist memes to deny his legitimacy to the presidency.

In 2010, hatred of Obama, in part, gave rise to the Tea Party movement. The movement began as a rant against the federal bailout to the banks, the stimulus package, and aid to the auto industry but quickly became a forum on Obama. The Tea Party movement consolidated the anti-Obama forces and the shift by many of its members away from dog whistles to blaring trumpets in public discourse about race. From elected officials to Republican Party leaders to their base voters, any attack on Obama, racial or otherwise, in any form was deemed acceptable by most Tea Party supporters.[21]

## From Dog Whistle to Trumpet

As noted, dog whistling had been successful for decades so why change? Trump, Palin and others recognize fairly quickly as Obama ran for the presidency that there is a base of voters who were being ignored by mainstream Republican leaders and whose racial resentments needed a champion who did not parse words, or damper the furor and victimization they felt. Inevitably, Trump rose from the pack of outside Republican aspirants to play that heroic role. He rode in on a white nationalist horse so to speak.

At the core of Trump's white nationalist project is the thesis that American whiteness in all of its cultural, political, social, economic, and even genetic forms is under existential threat from people of color, immigrants of color, and Muslims who are being protected by the ideology of political correctness and multiculturalism. White Americans are victims of this reverse racism that is furthered daily by inexorable nonwhite demographic trends. Trump's campaign theme of "Make America Great Again" – a shameless theft of Reagan's 1980 campaign theme of "Let's Make America Great Again" – promised a return to a mythical era in which white men ruled a prosperous, world-dominating unified and great America without challenge or opposition from pesky racial or religious minorities or women. The narrative of white nationalism hovered just under the surface of the campaign's ubiquitous slogan.

Trump's history of racism – his refusal to rent to African Americans during the 1970s and his near fanatical demand for the death penalty for five black and Latino youth falsely accused of rape and a beating – were noxious but alone did not have the impact or ability to propel him to the national political spotlight as did his decision to claim Obama was not born in the United States.[22] His presidential ambitions were growing and he had begun to test the election waters for a 2012 presidential run. As the *New York Times* noted, "The more Mr. Trump questioned the legitimacy of Mr. Obama's presidency, the better he performed in the early polls of the 2012 Republican field, springing from fifth place to a virtual tie for first."[23] Whether he actually believed it or not, his birther campaign allowed him to emerge as a leader of the most racially radical elements of the GOP and served his broader purpose of positioning him to compete to be the party's presidential nominee. "Trump recognized," writes *Times* reporters Ashley Parker and Steve Eder, "an opportunity to connect with the electorate over an issue many considered taboo: the discomfort, in some quarters of American society, with the election of the nation's first black president. He harnessed it for political gain."[24] He would go on Fox News, ABC's "The View," and other programs to raise the issue and sow doubts about the legitimacy of Obama's nationality and the grand conspiracy that was hiding the truth behind his questionable birth. He claimed that he had sent investigators to Hawaii to look into the matter and they were finding documents to back him up, however, he never produced any documents and few believed he dispatched investigators as he stated.

The birther language and movement was racially derived and driven. Obama's blackness was an opportunity for racists to delegitimize his campaign and then his presidency. Two white presidential candidates, Sen. John McCain in 2008 and Sen. Ted Cruz in 2012, were both born outside of the United States, in Panama and Canada respectively, but were never subjected to the suspicion and venom and vitriol that Obama faced. Neither was "othered" or seen as an outsider. Facts mattered little to these voters. An August 2015 poll found that while only 29 percent of Republican voters believed that Obama was born in the United States,

40 percent erroneously believed that Cruz had been.[25] Obama, in April 2011, would eventually be forced to produce the long form of his birth certificate although that did not satisfy his most fervent opponents.[26]

While not taking any responsibility whatsoever for the politically tainted atmosphere that he helped to create or offering an apology, Trump would belatedly and half-heartedly state in September 2016 that he finally did believe that Obama was born in the United States. His followers, unsurprisingly, were not so convinced. A September 18-19, 2016 YouGov poll found that while 71 percent of Americans overall thought Obama was U.S. born, only 58 percent of Trump voters thought so.[27] This disparity, as glaring as it is, should not obscure the unsettling fact that the birther campaign had succeeded to the point where even some Democrats who supported Obama thought he was foreign born.

There were many other examples of racist, explicit blaring language from Trump during the campaign. He opened the campaign calling Mexican immigrants to the United States "rapists;" he accused Gonzalo Curiel, an American judge of Mexican heritage of being bias against him because of his Mexican background; and in his call to ban all Muslims from entering the United States, he racialized the entire global Islamic community. On more than one occasion, he retweeted tweets from white supremacists including a chart with false information claiming Blacks were responsible for 81 percent of the homicides against whites. Politifact and other fact-checking organizations quickly proved that information wrong. The FBI stated that the number was actually about 15 percent. Researchers also found that the original graphic Trump tweeted came from a neo-Nazi source yet Trump used it anyway to make a racist point about African Americans and crime.[28]

Trump is also notorious for using distancing language when referring to people of color as shown in the epigraph used at the beginning of this article. He referred to African Americans as "the African Americans" or "the Blacks," and similarly to Latinos as "the Latinos." As late as the second debate on October 9, 2016, he employed this vernacular when he stated, "I'm going to help the African-Americans. I'm going to help the

Latinos, Hispanics."[29] His spoken awkwardness is disturbing in a number of ways as some linguists argued that Trump's language served to reinforce racist marginalization and outsider status for people of color and others. First, use of the article "the" to precede a group serves to create a distance between that group and both the speaker as well as for the audience who hears it. Conservative writer Kathleen Parker calls the "the" as used by Trump "a separatist term."[30] Linguist Eric Acton argues that it was "a way of highlighting the group's otherness."[31] Trump's othering of African Americans fed the prejudices of his overwhelmingly white supporters at his rallies as it was combined with either ad hominem attacks on those groups or condescending assertions.

Second, Trump's "the" language also lumped all individuals in a particular sub-group to an undifferentiated mass. "The" African Americans becomes one body without gender, class, talent, education, or any other meaningful distinctions. Linguist Sali Tagliamonte calls it "drawing a circle around a certain group of people."[32] For communities that are already marginalized, this phrasing furthers their outsider status.

Trump is consciously employing these language patterns. As a celebrity and then a reality TV star, he spent much of his adult life engage in image-making and selling narratives. More likely, he is reflecting a lifelong habit and experience of very limited quality engagement with African Americans and Latinos beyond those who are employed by him. His inability to see African Americans outside of his own narrow interests emerged time and again during the campaign. Another example of this and his racialized and insensitive wording is when he said at a June 2016 rally in Redding, California, *"Look at my African-American over here."*[33] As was the case at virtually all of Trump's campaign rallies, there were very few Blacks in attendance. During his remarks, Trump was being defensive about charges of racism against him and his campaign. Earlier, he had spotted a black man in the crowd holding a "Veterans for Trump" sign, and perhaps as an ill-advised joke called him out to the crowd to demonstrate that he did indeed have black supporters. For not the first time, Trump was wrong. The man in question, Gregory Cheadle, was not a Trump supporter as it turned out and had been holding the sign to block out the sun. He was, however, a Republican candidate running for California's 1st Congressional district, but eventually lost.³⁴

More broadly, when Trump spoke about the black community it was in dystopian terms. In an effort to pushback against the unrelenting accusations of racism, a response most felt was aimed at skittish white educated female voters reluctant to vote for an outright, unfiltered racist, in the last weeks of campaign Trump spoke of why black voters should support him. He stated, "Poverty. Rejection. Horrible education. No housing, no homes, no ownership. Crime at levels that nobody has seen. You can go to war zones in countries that we are fighting and it's safer than living in some of our inner cities that are run by the Democrats. And I ask you this, I ask you this — crime, all of the problems — to the African Americans, who I employ so many, so many people, to the Hispanics, tremendous people: What the hell do you have to lose?"³⁵ *Trump's rambling, meandering rant, rather than address the institutional and systemic racism faced by African Americans, painted a dystopic drama that reinforced stereotypes held by most whites about the black community. Most African Americans do not live in poverty, high quality as well as low achieving schools both exist in the black community, and most adult African Americans are working. He implied incorrectly and insensitively that all African Americans live in inner-city, urban hellholes believing like most of his supporters that "inner-city" and "urban" are pejoratives.*

*His campaign actually developed a written proposal for addressing these issues, a proposal cynically titled "Trump's New Deal for Black America," cynical in that every political impulse from Trump and his party is to overthrow whatever vestiges are left of Franklin Roosevelt's New Deal reforms. The document focused on using traditional conservative solutions to tackle education, employment and crime issues confronting black communities. Throughout the document, he attempts to exploit and appropriate the language of black struggle by repeatedly using the phrase "civil rights." For example, to deal with the "no good" schools found in inner-cities, he proposed "school choice," calling it the "civil rights issue of our time," meaning vouchers that undermine public education.*³⁶

*He advocates for a hard line on crime stating, "Safety is a civil right.*[37] *Trump calls for general equal justice but does not specifically mention police abuse or police killings of unarmed people of color; disproportionate arrests, prosecutions, and incarceration; or felony disenfranchisement, the criminal justice issues that have been given priority by the black community. Finally, there is an attempt to link African American and Latino interests with his onerous immigration policies. His New Deal proposal states, "We will restore civil rights of African-Americans, Hispanic-Americans, and all Americans by ending illegal immigration."*[38] *The whole statement is meaningless in that he never actually says how he will end illegal immigration or how it is tied to the status or loss of "civil rights" of African Americans and Latinos in the United States.*

### "I AM A GENE BELIEVER:" TRUMP'S EUGENICS HABITS

Trump's deeply held racist views manifest in other ways as well. Though given little attention, Trump often uses the language of eugenics to describe himself and others. Eugenics is the faux science that emerged at the end of the 19th century that argued that intelligence, success, temperament, criminality, and other personality qualities and talents are driven primarily by the genetics one inherits. Eugenics promoters also argued that there is a biological racial hierarchy and that whites were at the top of the genetic ladder and people of color were at the bottom. Although best known to be employed by the Nazis during the Hitler era to target Jews, Roma, and African-descent peoples, other nations including the United States utilized the theory to repress and victimized non-white communities.[39]

Despite being completely discredited by real science, even as late as 1994 when the controversial book, *The Bell Curve: Intelligence and Class Structure in American Life* by Richard J. Herrnstein and Charles Murray was published, eugenics theory sought academic legitimacy.[40] One of the authors, Murray, became a consultant to Republican lawmakers who used his ideas, particularly his view that a genetic or cultural predisposition to poverty cannot be ameliorated by public policy, to argue for and push through welfare reform in the 1990s.

None of the bogus nature of eugenics seems to have been accepted or understood by Trump. On numerous occasions he stated his deeply held belief in genetic superiority. In a 2010 CNN interview, he said: "Well I think I was born with the drive for success because I have a certain gene. I'm a gene believer."[41] In celebrating his genetic blessings, he dismisses the wealth he was born into, the opportunities that that wealth provided, and the startup funds of millions he received from his father as irrelevant to his success. He truly does believe in genetic destiny. On other occasions, he stated:

> "You have to have the right – the right genes."
>
> "Do we believe in the gene thing? I mean I do."
>
> "I have great genes and all that stuff which, I'm a believer in."
>
> "The fact is you have to be born and blessed with something up here [referring to his brain]."[42]

Naturally, Trump extended his views on genetics to include his children. He argued that his children had inherited his great, wonderful genes so they were destined to be successful. As *ThinkProgress* reported, he claimed his children had superior talent and skills and "don't need adversity" to develop character.[43] His children believe in their genetic luck as well. Donald Jr. once told a *Los Angeles Times* opinion writer, that like his father, "I'm a big believer in race-horse theory. He's an incredibly accomplished guy, my mother's incredibly accomplished, she's an Olympian, so I'd like to believe genetically I'm predisposed to [be] better than average."[44] The so-called "race horse theory" conjectures that breeding two superior horses will automatically produce an equally superior offspring, and, it is reasoned, this can be applied to humans.

## FROM HATE SPEECH TO DANGEROUS SPEECH

Trump's words, frightfully, go beyond fabricated science and intemperate tweets. At a rally in Iowa, Trump told the crowd, "So if you see somebody getting ready to throw a tomato, knock the crap out of 'em, would you? Seriously. Okay? Just knock the hell — I promise you, I will pay for the legal fees. I promise. I promise."[45] On February 22, 2016, at a rally in Las Vegas, he stated to the crowd as an anti-Trump protester was being removed from the event, ""I'd like to punch him in the face, I tell ya."[46] There were many such instances as these at his events.

Violence not only occurred at Trump rallies but was explicitly condoned by Trump himself. When challenged on this unprecedented behavior on his part, Trump refused to back down or apologizes. On a Fox News interview, he was asked about an incident in which a Black Lives Matter activist was assaulted during one of his rallies. Trump's response was, "Maybe he should have been roughed up, because it was absolutely disgusting what he was doing."[47] It should be emphasized that the protester was behaving peacefully and the attack was initiated by a Trump supporter.

Trump's provocations in his campaign speeches came disturbingly close to what some scholars define as "dangerous speech." As Benesch argues, dangerous speech goes beyond hate speech, which can have direct or indirect harm but without physical violence. Dangerous speech is different. "When an act of speech," she states, "has a reasonable chance of catalyzing or amplifying violence by one group against another, given the circumstances in which it was made or disseminated, it is Dangerous Speech."[48]

To measure dangerous speech, there are five variables to be considered. These are (1) the voice of "a powerful speaker with a high degree of influence over the audience;" (2) an audience that "has grievances and fear that the speaker can cultivate;" (3) "a speech act that is clearly understood as a call to violence;" (4) "a social or historical context that is propitious for violence;" and (5) "a means of dissemination that is influential in itself."[49] The more of these variable that are present, the more the likelihood that group violence will ensue. These variables are complex in their individual instances and context is of the upmost importance. Their various combinations are also critical in assessing whether hate or provocation is present or actual incitement, deliberate or not, is achieved. Benesch believes that the United States, different from pre-genocide Rwanda or pre-genocide Bosnia, has institutional, historical, and cultural factors that limit the opportunities for dangerous speech to have an impact. However, Rwanda, Bosnia, Cambodia, Nazi Germany and other states that have experienced genocide or extreme political violence evolved over time to create the conditions under which dangerous speech thrived and facilitated politically repressive authoritarian states.

Trump's rally speeches, tweets, and interviews have at moments embodied one or more of the variables listed above. A number of studies have shown that Trump supporters tend to have higher instances of racial grievances than other Republican voters.[50] The Trump campaign brilliantly exploited white grievance and white victimization thinking. Along with his supporters, he identified the targets of white rage as immigrants, Muslims, #blacklivesmatters, feminists, and ultimately anyone else who opposed him. While not directly calling for violence, or at least not consistently, he clearly excused the violence of his supporters in the moment of their actions. He did not challenge the violence while it was occurring or the hate-filled chants at his rallies aimed at Hilary Clinton such as "kill her," "lock her up," or "hang the bitch."[51] In those cases, silence could be and was read as consent.

Trump did issue a call for a political action that at a minimum was racial profiling. At his rallies and on his website, he called for his supporters to become a "Trump Election Observer" and go visit areas on Election Day where he predicted election chicanery would occur. This was widely understood to mean urban black neighborhoods where anti-Trump votes would be highest. Trump argued that he could only lose "if in certain sections of the state they cheat."[52] Perhaps due to the widespread negative response he received, it appears that few, if any at all, took him up on his offer. This time.

## Conclusion

Trump has vowed to continue his populist rallies even after taking office. In the days after the election, he went on a nation tour and held rallies in several cities where he not only repeated the main themes of intolerance that he had spoken of during the campaign, but also pledged to be aggressive in meeting that agenda once he assumed office.

The bellicose and combative nature of Trump's remarks are explosive and should not be underestimated. As Benesch contends, "[P]olitical speech that simultaneously demonizes people and legitimates violence can shift speech norms, and inspire violence by the subset of people who are easily incited to it."[53] The norms of presidential campaigning have been smashed and decimated, and the institutions to police and defend those norms have been deeply weakened.

The 2016 presidential race was embarrassing long slog of name calling, school yard taunts, and juvenile antics and, the candidate with no experience in elected office, with very limited and often wrong knowledge of critical domestic and foreign policy, with the temperament of a petulant teenager, with a history of unparalleled racism, sexism and bigotry defied the polls, party leaders, media predictions, and endless scandals, gaffes, and blunders and won. Political scientists and other researchers will spend many years if not decades attempting to understand how this set of events came about.

Certainly one factor was Trump's deft use of race language that managed to reach enough disaffected, outraged, and racially apprehensive white voters in key states to win the Electoral College jackpot and, despite losing the popular vote by nearly seven million votes, to allow him to become the nation's 45th president. Nothing breeds repetition like success. Going forward, it is likely that some candidates will follow the Trump playbook and abandon, at least in part, dog whistle tactics for trumpet ones. Whatever may be the individual benefit this strategy may bring, for the nation this is a road to perdition.

# (Endnotes)

1. Azi Paybarah, "Trump: 'Always Had a Great Relationship With the Blacks,'" *New York Observer*, April 14, 2011.
2. Robert Mackey, "'America Belongs to White Men,' Alt-Right Founder Says," *The Intercept*, December 7 2016. https://theintercept.com/2016/12/07/america-belongs-white-men-alt-right-founder-says/.
3. https://www.splcenter.org/hatewatch/2016/12/16/update-1094-bias-related-incidents-month-following-election]
4. Toni Morrison, Nobel Lecture, December 7, 1993. http://www.nobelprize.org/nobel_prizes/literature/laureates/1993/morrison-lecture.html.
5. In 1970, there were 1,469 black elected officials nationwide. In 2016, there were over 10,000. See Khalilah Brown-Dean, Zoltan Hajnal, Christina Rivers, and Ismail White, *50 Years of the Voting Rights Act: The State of Race in Politics* (Washington: Joint Center for Economic and Political Studies, 2015).
6. Susan Benesch, "Donald Trump: Hallmarks of Dangerous Speech," December 20, 2016. Dangerous Speech website: http://dangerousspeech.org/blog/2016/8/12/donald-trump-crossing-the-line-into-dangerous-speech.
7. Carol Anderson, *White Rage: The Unspoken Truth of Our Racial Divide* (New York: Bloomsbury, 2016), p. 119.
8. Ian Haney Lopez, *Dog Whistle Politics: How Coded Racial Appeals Have Reinvented Racism & Wrecked the Middle Class* (New York: Oxford University Press; 2015), p. 4.
9. Ari Berman, *Give Us the Ballot: The Modern Struggle for Voting Rights in America* (New York: MacMillan, 2016), p. 123.
10. Greta de Jong, *Invisible Enemy: The African American Freedom Struggle After 1965* (New York: Wiley & Sons, 2010), p. 47.
11. Moira Weigel, "Political correctness: how the right invented a phantom enemy," *The Guardian*, November 30, 2016.
12. Ibid.
13. Ibid.
14. Barack Obama, Democratic National Convention speech, Boston, Massachusetts, July 27, 2004.
15. See Algernon Austin, *America is Not Post-Racial: Xenophobia, Islamophobia, Racism and the 44th President* (Santa Barbara, CA: Praeger, 2015).
16. The most notable book from the right is Jerome R. Corsi, *Where's the Birth Certificate?: The Case that Barack Obama is Not Eligible to be President* (Centreville, VA: WND Books, 2011). An excellent progressive critique of the birther movement is Martin A. Parlett, *Demonizing a President: The "Foreignization" of Barack Obama* (Santa Barbara, CA: ABC-CLIO, 2014).
17. Jonathan Martin and Amie Parne, "McCain: Obama not an Arab, crowd boos," *Politico*, October 10, 2008.
18. See John Amato and David Neiwert, *Over the Cliff: How Obama's Election Drove the American Right Insane* (Sausalito, CA: PoliPointPress, 2010).
19. Tim Shipman, "Sarah Palin blamed by the US Secret Service over death threats against Barack Obama," *The Telegraph*, November 8, 2008; and Lola Adesioye, "Palling around with racists," *The Guardian*, October 14, 2008.
20. Mark Blumenthal, "'Birther' Polls: Independents Unaffected, Republicans Remain Divided," *Huffington Post*, April 28, 2011. http://www.huffingtonpost.com/2011/04/28/birther-polls-unite-obama_n_855135.html.
21. See Kate Zernike, *Boiling Mad: Inside Tea Party America* (New York: Times Books, 2010); Theda Skocpol and Vanessa Williamson, *The Tea Party and the Remaking of Republican Conservatism* (New York: Oxford University Press, 2013); and Jill Lepore, *The Whites of Their Eyes: The Tea Party's Revolution and the Battle over American History* (Princeton: Princeton University Press 2011).

22  See Glenn Kessler, "Trump's claim that a racial discrimination suit was 'brought against many real estate firms'," *Washington Post*, September 28, 2016; Nicholas Kristof, "Is Donald Trump a Racist?," *New York Times*, July 23, 2016; and Amy Davidson, "Donald Trump and the Central Park Five," *New Yorker*, June 23, 2014.
23  Ashley Parker and Steve Eder, "Inside the Six Weeks Donald Trump Was a Nonstop 'Birther,'" *New York Times*, July 2, 2016.
24  Ibid.
25  Will Femia, "Chris Christie, Rand Paul scraping the bottom in new PPP poll," August 31, 2015. www.msnbc.com/rachel-maddow-show/chris-christie-rand-paul-scraping-the-bottom-new-ppp-poll.
26  Karen Tumulty and Anne E. Kornblut, "Obama, frustrated by 'this silliness,' produces detailed Hawaii birth certificate," *Washington Post*, April 27, 2011.
27  "Trump may recant birtherism, but many of his supporters haven't." https://today.yougov.com/news/2016/09/23/trump-may-recant-birtherism-many-his-supporters-ha/.
28  Jon Greenberg, "Trump's Pants on Fire tweet that blacks killed 81% of white homicide victims," Politifact, November 23rd, 2015, http://www.politifact.com/truth-o-meter/statements/2015/nov/23/donald-trump/trump-tweet-blacks-white-homicide-victims/; and Judd Legum, "Trump Tweeted Fabricated Murder Stats From A Neo-Nazi And This Is How The Media Reported It," *ThinkProgress*, Nov 23, 2015, https://thinkprogress.org/trump-tweeted-fabricated-murder-stats-from-a-neo-nazi-and-this-is-how-the-media-reported-it-125064da6372#.ixene6vs2.]
29  Lynne Murphy, "Linguists Explains Why Trump Sound Racist When He Says 'the' African Americans." Qz.com.
30  Kathleen Parker, "Trump can't fake love of 'the blacks,'" *Washington Post*, August 30, 2016.
31  Mark Abadi, "'The blacks,' 'the gays,' 'the Muslims' — linguists explain one of Donald Trump's most unusual speech tics," *Business Insider*, October 17, 2016.
32  Ibid.
33  Nick Corasanitijune, "'Look at My African-American Over Here,' Donald Trump Says at Rally," *New York Times, June 3, 2016.*
34  Brakkton Booker, "Trump's African-American: 'I Am Not A Trump Supporter,'" NPR, June 5, 2016. http://www.npr.org/sections/thetwo-way/2016/06/05/480864303/trumps-african-american-i-am-not-a-trump-supporter.
35  Jenna Johnson, "Donald Trump to African American and Hispanic voters: 'What do you have to lose?,'" *Washington Post*, August 22, 2016.
36  *Trump's New Deal for Black America: With a Plan for Urban Renewal*, Trump campaign. https://www.donaldjtrump.com/press-releases/donald-j.-trump-announces-a-plan-for-urban-renewal1.
37  Ibid.
38  Ibid.
39  See Edwin Black, *War Against the Weak: Eugenics and America's Campaign to Create a Master Race* (Washington, DC: Dialog Press, 2012); Daniel Kevles, *In the Name of Eugenics: Genetics and the Uses of Human Heredity* (Cambridge, MA: Harvard University Press, 1998); and Stefan Kuhl, *The Nazi Connection: Eugenics, American Racism, and German National Socialism* (New York: Oxford University Press, 2002).
40  Richard J. Herrnstein and Charles Murray, *The Bell Curve: Intelligence and Class Structure in American Life* (New York: Free Press, 1996).
41  Caroline Mortimer, "Donald Trump believes he has superior genes, biographer claims Republican nominee follows 'racehorse theory' of genetics," *The Independent* (London), September 30, 2016.
42  Marina Fang, "This May Be The Most Horrible Thing That Donald Trump Believes," *Huffington Post*, September 28, 2016.
43  Alice Miranda Ollstein, "Donald Trump's veiled signals to white supremacists," *ThinkProgress*, August 12, 2016.
44  Michael D'Antonio, "Donald Trump believes he was born to be king," *Los Angeles Times*,

December 3, 2015. http://www.latimes.com/opinion/op-ed/la-oe-1203-dantonio-trump-race-horse-theory-20151203-story.html.
45 Philip Bump, "Donald Trump reverses course on paying legal fees for man who attacked protester. But could he do it?," *Washington Post*, March 15, 2016.
46 Michael E. Miller, "Donald Trump on a protester: 'I'd like to punch him in the face,'" *Washington Post*, February 23, 2016.
47 Ibid.
48 Susan Benesch, Dangerous Speech: A Proposal to Prevent Group Violence, February 23, 2013. http://dangerousspeech.org/guidelines.
49 Ibid.
50 German Lopez, "Polls show many — even most — Trump supporters really are deeply hostile to Muslims and nonwhites," *Vox*, September 12, 2016. http://www.vox.com/2016/9/12/12882796/trump-supporters-racist-deplorables.
51 Ibid, Benesch, "Donald Trump: Hallmarks of Dangerous Speech."
52 Ari Berman, "Donald Trump is Encouraging Intimidation and Racial Profiling at the Polls," *The Nation*, August 15, 2016.
53 Ibid, Benesch, "Donald Trump: Hallmarks of Dangerous Speech."

# THE WALL STREET JOURNAL.

WEDNESDAY, NOVEMBER 5, 2008 - VOL. CCLII NO. 108    ★★★★ $2.00

# Pres. Trump Tweets German Leader Merkel is Smelly "Fat Pig"

### Protests and Outrage from Berlin as US Ambassador summoned to emergency meeting in early hours of Saturday

BY JONATHAN WEISMAN
AND LAURA MECKLER

WASHINGTON—Sen. Barack Obama was elected the nation's first African-American president, defeating Sen. John McCain decisively Tuesday as citizens surged to the polls in a presidential race that climaxed amid the worst financial crisis since the Great Depression.

The culmination of the epic two-year campaign marks a historic moment in a nation that since its founding has struggled with racial divisions. It also ushers in a period of dominance for Democrats in Washington for the first time since the early years of President Bill Clinton's first term. With Tuesday's elections, Sen. Obama's party will control both houses of Congress as well as the White House, setting the scene for Democrats to push an ambitious agenda from health care to financial regulation to ending the war in Iraq.

In becoming the U.S.'s 44th president, Illinois Sen. Obama, 47 years old, defeated Arizona Sen. McCain, 72, a veteran lawmaker and Vietnam War hero. Despite a reputation for bucking his own party, Sen. McCain could not overcome a Democratic tide, which spurred voters to take a risk on a candidate with less than four years of national political experience. Sen. Obama is the first northern Democrat elected president since John F. Kennedy in 1960.

Also elected: Joe Biden of Delaware as vice president, the veteran senator who has promised to help Sen. Obama steer his

WINNING SMILE: Sen. Barack Obama became the nation's first African-American president, riding a historic turnout amid voter discontent with the economy to defeat Sen. John McCain.

agenda through Congress.

Sen. Obama's victory was built on record fund raising and a vast national campaign network. It remade the electoral map that had held fast for eight years. He overwhelmed reliable Democratic strongholds in the Northeast and West Coast. He won big in the industrial Midwest and contested fiercely in areas of traditional Republican strength. He

won Virginia, the first time a Democratic candidate had taken the state since Lyndon Johnson in 1964. And he finally wrested Florida and Ohio from the GOP, two states that had bedeviled his party in the last two elections.

The president-elect will enter office with a long policy wish list that includes ending the war in Iraq, implementing a near-universal health-insurance plan and

finding alternatives to Middle Eastern oil. All this will have to be carried out amid record budget deficits, a looming crisis in Social Security and Medicare spending as the baby-boom generation retires and fears that the nation is on the edge of a deep recession. Democrats have touted the prospect of a big sweep not just as a partisan conquest but as an ideological turning point, one

that could reverse the last great shift in 1980, when Ronald Reagan ushered in a period dominated by tax-cutting conservatism and muscular foreign policy.

It's a startling turnaround from just four years ago, when Republicans controlled Congress and the White House, and benefited from a conservative majority on the Supreme Court. The
*Please turn to page A6*

### Secretary of State Sarah Palin says Trump's latest gaffe "Lamestream" Media Conspiracy

BY GREG HITT
AND BRODY MULLINS

WASHINGTON—Democrats strengthened their majorities in both houses of Congress and moved close to a level of domination in the Senate that could enable them to push through major legislation.

Combined with Sen. Barack Obama's victory in the presidential race, the congressional results gave Democrats broad power in Washington that they haven't enjoyed in decades.

The Democratic gains represented the final repudiation of the Republican revolution of 1994, marking the second straight strong showing for Dem-

## Democrats Expand Majorities In Congress

BY GREG HITT
AND BRODY MULLINS

WASHINGTON—Democrats strengthened their majorities in both houses of Congress and moved close to a level of domination in the Senate that could enable them to push through major legislation.

Combined with Sen. Barack Obama's victory in the presidential race, the congressional results gave Democrats broad power in Washington that they haven't enjoyed in decades.

The Democratic gains represented the final repudiation of the Republican revolution of 1994, marking the second straight strong showing for Democrats in congressional elections. The results return the balance of power that prevailed on Capitol Hill for much of the 20th century, when Democratic con-

## What's News—

**Business & Finance**

The Dow Jones Industrial Average soared 305.45 points, or 3.3%, ahead of election results. The value of 9626.38 was the highest in nearly a month. Oil prices rose, back above $70 a barrel. Rallies continued early Wednesday in Asia, with the Nikkei up 1.2% in midday trading after Tuesday's 6.3% gain. C1, C9.

● The benchmark yield curve in major government bond markets has steepened

**World-Wide**

■ Obama was elected the first African-American president. The Illinois senator decisively defeated McCain as citizens thronged to the polls amid the worst financial crisis since the Depression. Obama's victory was built on record fund raising and a vast campaign network. He captured reliable Democratic strongholds in the Northeast and West Coast, won big in the industrial Midwest, prevailed in Virginia and wrested Florida and Ohio from the Republican Party. A1-A14

■ The presidential race entered a critical three-day period in September, when the economic cri-

### The New Landscape

■ Gerald Seib on challenges for Democrats ...............A6
■ A battle for the soul of the Republican Party ...........A8
■ A momentous day for African-Americans ...............A8

■ See WSJ.com for full state-by-state election results.

## As Economic Crisis Peaked, Tide Turned Against McCain

BY MONICA LANGLEY

The presidential race entered a critical three-day period in September when the economic cri-

Obama asked his staff on the trail, according to aides. At a news conference in Florida, he said, "It's going to be part of the president's job to be able to deal

his car: "I've never seen anything like this," he said, according to several aides. "Some of the Republicans are clueless. Bush and I were trying to convince

# Chapter Three

## *Misogyny on the Campaign Path*

### Political Terrorism against Women: Analyzing Trump's Campaign Tactics Designed to Scare the American Public into Supporting White Male Leadership

#### Marquita Pellerin-Gammage Ph.D.,

American politics have long been laced with misogynistic and sexist judgments against women, especially Black women. From the inhumane enslavement of African women, the writing of the American constitution centered in white male privilege, to the backlash against the women's suffrage movement and Roe v. Wade, American politics have historically categorized women as inferior beings not worthy of equal treatment in society. (Chisholm 1973; Davis 1981; Dallard 1990; Ransby 2003; Hudson-Weems 2004; Giddings 2008) Therefore it comes as no surprise to find historical and contemporary political figures have resorted to political tactics based in female subjugation. However, with the gains of the Civil Rights Movement, the ratifying of the Equal Rights Amendment, and the increase number of female elected officials, to name a few, American politics began to move away from blatant attacks on women. (Bonilla-Silva 2001; Shapiro 2004) Instead, gender neutral discourses emerged, which at times achieved the same outcome as anti-women campaigns with less offensive language. Ironically, however, in the 21$^{st}$ century American politics and political figures, Donald Trump in particular, have returned to century old assaults on womanhood as a political strategy designed to scare the American public into supporting white male leadership and in turn white male chauvinism. The American public is now witnessing a departure from the previous gender neutral discourse and a reoccurrence of racist and sexist politics as the American way.

Since the announcement of Donald Trump's bid for the presidency in June 2015, he has wedged a campaign against Blacks, minorities, and women. Campaign speeches, social media posts, and news media interviews have been use as a venue to advance political terrorism against minorities and women. Countless numbers of unsupported claims against Blacks, Hispanics, Muslims, and women in general have crowded Trump's speeches, to the point where he has not established a definitive political agenda but have been applauded for promoting racism and sexism. Trump's campaign slogan "Make American Great Again" is predicated on the idea that that America has somehow become dysfunctional given its advancements towards equal rights for minorities and women. This theory completely ignores the continued presence of institutional racism and sexism in American society, not to mention the persistence of cultural and personal racism. Thousands flock to Trump's campaign events in support of a return to the American political and social order of the 1950s. During the 1950s African Americans and women were treated as second-class citizens, although to different degrees. (Lewis 1993; Marable 2007) During this time period it was also socially and politically accepted to use racist and sexist derogatory statements against women and minorities. (Lewis

2000) In fact, many laws were established to restrict and control the Black population and women. (Chisholm 1973; Davis 1981) The Civil Rights Movement put an end to this era of Jim Crow. However by the end of the Civil Rights Movement a new era was birthed, an era of race and gender neutral discourse was unleashed. (Alexander 2010) For minorities and women, this meant that the previous overt political targeting was disguised and made-up of new race and gender neutral terminology carrying the same mission as the pervious era. Hence, Trump departs from this era of race/gender neutral politics and instead adopts a political strategy that embodies a terroristic approach to American politics grounded in racism and sexism.

The misogyny in Trump's political speeches is no accident, instead given the emphasis on white masculinity within American politics, women are destined to be portrayed as subordinate to their male counterparts. Moreover, because of this emphasis, the American political system markets racist and sexist political terrorism against women globally as the singular American political lifestyle. As Trump entered into the final stage of the presidential election, this positioning of women as subordinate objects captured the attention of the American public and a larger international audience. Thus, an Afrocentric analysis of Trump's misogynistic campaign tactics is needed to detail the legacy of American political terrorism against women in order to lay the foundation for Trump's adoption of this political approach, and why this approach was so successful. Also, a critical analysis of Trump's rhetoric on women during his campaign for presidency will be offered as evidence of a sexist based political campaign.

## A Brief Legacy of American Political Terrorism against Women

The treatment of women in American society as inferior and subordinate human beings is long standing. In fact, women within American society have historically been objectified, hyper-sexualized, and commodified. Such exploitation practices can be traced to the systematic objectification of Black women during enslavement. From the early 1600s America directly participated in the commodification of Black womanhood and African humanity by forcing enslaved Africans to provide a free labor supply, treating them as non-human, and subjecting them to sexual marketing and abuse. To rationalize such inhumane actions, political rules and laws were established to justify and validate the subjugation of African people and women. Although, Africans resisted this inhumane system of servitude at all times, the founding of America was established and based in racist and sexist political ideologies. (hooks 1981; Dubois 1999) Cementing these ideas and practices, on September 17, 1787 the U.S. Constitution was signed granting White men rights and privileges of citizenship based on their gender and race. For Africans, including Black women, this meant that they were not citizens nor did they possess any rights of citizenship. The implementation of the constitution carried with it privilege based on gender, or one's physicality on maleness, and of course paired with whiteness. Thus, not even white women possessed the same citizenship rights, such as the right to vote, as white men. Although, white women were considered humans and citizens. (hooks 1981; Dubois 1999) Political campaigns were launched and laws were enacted that prohibited white women from exercising the same rights and privileges as white men. (Chisholm 1973; Davis 1981; Hudson-Weems 2004; Giddings 2008) For Black women, this meant that they were hit with a double edged sword, dehumanized because of their race and objectified because of their gender. According to Gammage (2015) in *Representations of Black Women in the Media: The Damnation of Black Womanhood*, during enslavement African women experienced a terroristic form of objectification which "valued them based on their physical bodies, working strength, and reproductive ability" (22). As noted:

African women were employed as breeders and the traditional role of mother was removed. The customary treatment that African women experienced in their indigenous societies was not adopted in enslaved communities. Instead, women continued to work and did not receive proper nourishment throughout pregnancy. The results of forced conception, abuse, and overwork led to increased miscarriages, and stillbirths. Given this oppressive employment, African women were valued on their ability to provide additional generations of laborers. The younger the female the more fertile she appeared and thus a higher monetary value was placed. For older women who had passed child-bearing age, they were considered less valuable and sold for a reduced price. These sexually oppressive conditions fostered an environment where African women would forever endure a legacy of a damned womanhood.

Not only were African women subjected to non-marital sexual encounters with enslaved men, they also endured the burden of sexual assault by White male enslavers. These acts were not considered rape by White society, as African women were seen as property with no human rights. Nonetheless, African women saw these acts as non-consensual and unwarranted. But, the laws of the land did not grant African women protection and they were prohibited from testifying against White men in the court of law. (Gammage 2015, 23)

Major resistance ensued against enslavement and women's suffrage. With the ending of enslavement a new social order was introduced, frequently referred to as the era of Jim Crow. During this era, Blacks were treated as second class citizens and were once again subjected to laws and political campaigns that called into question their humanity. (Alexander 2010) Governmental entities and intellectuals also participated in the political targeting of Black, and Black women in particular. In 1965, Daniel P. Moynihan was commissioned by the U.S. Department of Labor to study the status of the Black family. In "The Tangle of Pathology," he reported that the Black family was pathologically dysfunctional because it departed from the norms of white American culture and the middle-class white family structure. More specifically, he argues that because the Black family is not based in male leadership and Black women are contributing earners with degrees, the family structure is problematic, and creates and prohibits African Americans from achieving the American dream. Hence, Moynihan advances white cultural hegemony and promotes white male privileges as he sees it rewarded by American society. According to Moynihan:

There is, presumably, no special reason why a society in which males are dominant in family relationships is to be preferred to a matriarchal arrangement. However, it is clearly a disadvantage for a minority group to be operating on one principle, while the great majority of the population, and the one with the most advantages to begin with, is operating on another. This is the present situation of the Negro. Ours is a society which presumes male leadership in private and public affairs. The arrangements of society facilitate such leadership and reward it. A subculture, such as that of the Negro American, in which this is not the pattern, is placed at a distinct disadvantage. (Moynihan 1965)

Here, Moynihan categorizes the Black family structure into a matriarchy because Black women and men share in household responsibilities, the women earn degrees, and have secured corporate employment. This misclassification of the Black family has been used to inform public policies that target and limit the Black family and woman's social, political, and economic power.

The Civil Rights Movement waged a war against the era of Jim Crow, the unjust targeting of Black women and men, and the unequal treatment of Blacks as second-class citizens. (Lewis 1993; Bonilla-Silva 2001; Shapiro 2004; Marable 2007) Following suit, the women's movements such as Black women's movement and the feminist movement began a national campaign advocating for women's rights to full citizenship. Gains were won across the board, from the passing of the civil rights legislation, to the ratifying of the equal rights amendment. However, backlash to the Civil Rights Movement and the white women's feminist movement resulted in political campaigns once again aimed at restricting the citizenship rights of minorities and women. In the 1980s politician Ronald Regan launched his campaign for presidency, entitled "To Restore America," the idea of returning to the American political and social order of the 1950s. Regan classified strategies of the Civil Rights Movement, namely civil disobedience, as the leading cause of crime in America, fabricated tails about Black women, and coined the term welfare queen without any evidence supporting his claims. These scare tactics used, worked like a charm. Regan was elected president in 1981, and for eight years maintained systematic targeting and attacks on the Black community and Black women. As noted in my text on representations of Black womanhood:

The political and economic attack on Black womanhood continued with the mislabeling of Black women as welfare-queens, matriarchs and baby-mommas. Scholars have accurately credited both republicans and democrats for the political alienation and devaluing of Black womanhood. Although both political parties have misrepresented Black women as the face of welfare, the reality is that there is no statistical data to support the claim that Black women are criminal abusers of the welfare system. If Regan's creation of the term "welfare-queen" (1976) wasn't enough, then surely Clinton's (1996) display of Black women and children on stage as he announced his plan for welfare reform, hammered the idea that Black women were the primary fraudulent recipients of government aid. These policies classify Black women as get-overs, meaning that they falsify their actual need, and are unworthy of governmental assistance. To validate these claims Black motherhood was alleged to be unauthentic and illegitimate. Fabricated stories of Black women having children just for a check, spending aid on their hair and nails, and abandoning their children while they go to clubs, all have been used to further delegitimize Black women as suitable mothers. These approaches institutionalized the damnation of Black womanhood and have been made into public policies that punish and damn Black mothers. (Gammage 2015, 27)

This is just another illustration of the systematic political targeting of Black women. Unfortunately, such practices have yielded high reward. Reagan's campaign to restore America, i.e. promote white supremacy and restrict Black advancement, resulted in him serving two terms as president. The political tactic of terrorism against minorities and women is used to protect the all-white boys club in American politics. It is also designed to preserve white-male privilege and the legacy of white domination in America. In the same way that we saw Reagan's attack on Blacks and Black women as a backlash to the Civil Rights Movement, it is not surprising that after the first African American president, President Barrack Obama, we once again find this tactic used to reset the American political system to privilege Whites.

## Trumps Hate Speech against Women as Political Terrorism

In the 21st century, political figures have once again turned to scare tactics aimed at the white American public, designed to invoke fear of minorities and women. The election of President Barrack Obama carried with it the hope for a change in the racial climate of America. While idealistic, that a single man could change the state of racial affairs in America, many believed in this possibility. This assumption resulted in many Americans backlashing against the ideas of racial equality. In fact, the President and first family were subjected to an immense amount of racial assaults, the Black community experienced increased targeting and killing of Black men, women and children, and intuitional racism did not cease to exist. Yet, a fuel was burning in America, an eagerness to return to a social order where white privilege was clear and definite. Enter Donald Trump, previous democrat and supporter of the Democratic Party, and businessman. Similar to Reagan, Trump switched political parties before running for office and adopted the same political scare tactics, which plays on the concerns and fears of the white American public. Although Trump has a history of racism and sexism, in running for president he has rooted his campaign on the fears of minorities and women; thereby resulting to the same terroristic scare tactics as Reagan. More specifically, given that Trump's primary competition was from a woman, he engaged in systematic assaults on womanhood in order to validate the assumption that the office of presidency is designed for white males. In analyzing Trump's speeches, interviews, and social media posts, we find that he has classified women into four categories that deem them ill fit and unqualified to serve in political offices and should not have influence on political decisions.

## Women as Biologically Inferior

In discussing women, Trump has historically and contemporarily classified women as biologically inferior to men. Trumpshas made vague references to women's reproductive systems, their weight as link to their level of competency, and hormonal instability. In the beginning of his campaign during the GOP debate, Trump stated that Megyn Kelly from Fox News' had:

"blood coming out of her wherever." (Trump, CNN August 7, 2015)

In another instance, Trump referred to Hillary Clinton as:

"unstable." "short-circuited" "She took a short-circuit in the brain." "She's got problems." (Trump, CNN August 6, 2016)

According to Alicia Machado, a former Miss Universe, Trump referred to her as overweight and a house servant. Trump responded by confirming his assessment of her work ethic was based on her weight. Trump's sexist assaults on women's biological makeup, illustrate a devalued understanding of womanhood and is used to justify his belief that women are unfit to run the oval office. This approach appeals to the historical American ideology on women, which previously prevented women from political participation and the right to vote. This approach also validates the sexist assumption that women's gains in education, politics, and the workforce have somehow contributed to hardships in the American economy and political functioning.

## Women as Unfeminine

Trump's assaults against women do not end with his assumptions that women are biologically inferior,.he also classifies certain type of women as unfeminine. In an interview with Rolling Stone magazine in fall 2015, Trump attacked a potential female competitor, Carly Fiorina, by stating that her physical appearance, a female and in his assessment unattractive, makes her unqualified to run for office.

"Look at that face!"

"Would anyone vote for that? Can you imagine that, the face of our next president?!" (Trump, September 9, 2015)

Once again attacking Clinton, in December 2015 during a debate, Trump refers to Clinton as disgusting. Trump's emphasis of women's level of attractiveness is simply a return to the subordination of women based in beauty. This century old idea is that women are meant to be pretty, based in European standards of beauty, and are not expected to offer much else. And yet, when women, white women in particular, do not fit within European standards of beauty they are classified as worthless and unfeminine. Trump's had adopted this idea, symbolizing his advancement of a sexist American society that values women based on their level of European beauty. These illustrations paint a picture of Trump's view of women, and may portend his treatment of women once sworn as president.

### Women as Politically Inferior

On several occasions, Trump has suggested that women are politically inferior and are unqualified to serve in political office. In an interview with ABC News, Trump argued that Clinton was less qualified to serve as president based on her physical appearance.

"I just don't think she has a presidential look,"

"And you need a presidential look."

"She doesn't have the look. She doesn't have the stamina." (Trump September 26, 2016)

Trump has no problem attacking women who challenge him, but when the father of a fallen soldier, Khizr Khan, challenged Trump at the Democratic National Convention, Trump instead attacked his wife Ghazala Khan during an interview with ABC. Trump suggested that because of her religion and gender Ghazala did not speak to the public. Here, Trump suggests that Muslim women are restricted from speaking openly in public and their husbands dominate over them, which is another false assumption, not rooted in fact. Yet still, Trump makes no apologies and continues to insult specific women and womanhood in general. During summer 2016, Trump once again called into question Hillary Clinton's ability to uphold the duties of the president. He argued that Clinton was ill-fit to nominate a Supreme Court justice, and if elected the American public would suffer the consequences. Trump later implied that gun holders may want to put an end to Clinton whether by vote or violence. Although Trump's political advisors argued that Trump's suggestion was for Americans to take to the polls to prohibit Clinton from assuming office, the suggestion of violence and murder had already entered into the public sphere. This was not the only time Trump suggested murder against Clinton, however. In a later statement, Trump advised that without bodyguards Clinton would be defenseless. One has to wonder, is this because of her gender? Absolutely, Trump's political campaign is largely predicated on sexist and racist ideas in order to advance the call for a return to overt white male supremacy. By attacking and misrepresenting women as unable to serve in political offices, Trump reinforces the assumption that only white men are capable and competent enough to lead America.

### *Women as Sexually Subordinate*

A final illustration of how Trump has taken a derogatory stance against women can be noted in his remarks about women as sexually subordinate to men and therefore unqualified to serve in political office nor should women have any rights or influence on laws. Taking a stance on abortion, Trump's interview with MSNBC in March 2016 revealed his belief in criminal punishment against women who chose to have abortions. In addition, Trump advocates for women, even his daughter, to undergo punishment for experiencing sexual harassment in the workplace. In an interview with USA Today, Trump suggests that if his daughter experienced sexual harassment while at work she should bear the burden and punishment by losing or quitting her job without any consequences for her violator.

"I would like to think she would find another career or find another company if that was the case." (Trump August 1, 2016)

This type of victim-blame mentally is often displayed by Trump. In 2013, Trump commented on Twitter that military sexual assault is a part of the culture of the military, and that it should be expected. Never once did Trump mention policies to protect women from such practices and he essentially argued that if women are to serve in the military, they should expect to be sexually assaulted. He states:

> "26,000 unreported sexual assaults in the military-only 238 convictions. What did these geniuses expect when they put men & women together?" (Trump May 7, 2013)

Trump has not altered his opinion. Instead he continues to attack women when they have conflict with men, in particular sexual conflict with men. On April 16, 2015, Trump once again took to Twitter to attack women and render them sexually subordinate to men. Trump writes that Hillary Clinton is not suitable for presidency because she will not 'satisfy' the American public as she presumably did not satisfy her husband. Trump states:

> "@mplefty67: If Hillary Clinton can't satisfy her husband what makes her think she can satisfy America?" @realDonaldTrump #2016president" (Twitter post April 16, 2015)

Here, Trumps suggests that Hillary Clinton is unqualified to serve as president because her husband had an affair, in which Trump essentially blames her for. The sexual subordination of women by Trump is used as a political tool to ostracize women for being violated by men. By not holding men accountable for their actions, Trump is validating the all-boys club mentality and is directly advocating for male privilege and white male leadership.

## Conclusion

Critics have argued that political strategies rooted in female subjugation play a major role in influencing the political trends in America. The racist and sexist rhetoric represented in Trump's campaign speeches may become integrated into the conscious and unconscious minds of the American audience. Through the politicizing of racist and sexist notions conveyed in the form of campaign speeches, political organizations manipulate the reality and lifestyle of women. This political strategy concerns the reliance on scare tactics as a political frame for understanding the needs of the American society. Therefore political terrorism against women aids in the construction of race and gender biases in American politics and gives credence to the systematic subjugation of women and minorities. The historical legacy behind this political targeting of women reveals the continued presence of a call for white male privilege as the face of the American political system. From the founding father, to Regan, and now Trump the history of racist and sexist political ideology continue. Once again, this political strategy has proven extremely effective. On November 8, 2016, Donald Trump was labeled president-elect and is set to become the 45th president of the United States of America. The baton has been passed and Trump has gladly accepted the task of returning America to a state of privilege for white men.

**REFERENCES**

Bonilla-Silva, Eduardo. *White Supremacy and Racism in the Post Civil Rights Era*. Boulder: Lynne Rienner Publishers, 2001. Print.

Chisholm, Shirley. *The Good Fight*. New York: HarperCollins, 1973. Print.

Dallard, Shyrlee. *Ella baker: A Leader Behind the Scenes*. Englewood Cliffs: Silver Burdett Press, 1990. Print.

Davis, Angela Y. *Women, Race and Class*. New York: Vintage Books, 1983. Print.

DuBois, W.E. Burghart. *Darkwater: Voices from Within the Veil*. Dover Publications: New York, 1999. Print.

Gammage, Marquita M. *Representations of Black Women in the Media: The Damnation of Black Womanhood*. New York: Routledge, 2015. Print.

Giddings, Paula. *Ida: A Sword Among Lions: Ida B. Wells and the Campaign Against Lynching*. New York: HarperCollins, 2008. Print.

Hooks, bell. *Ain't I A Woman: Black Women and Feminism*. Boston: South End Press, 1981. Print.

Hudson-Weems, Clenora. *Africana Womanist Literary Theory*. Trenton: Africa World Press, Inc, 2004. Print.

Lewis, David L. *W.E.B. Dubois: Biography of a Race, 1868-1919*. New York: Owl Books, 1993. Print.

*W.E.B. Dubois: The Fight for Equality and the American Century, 1919-1963*. New York: Owl Books, 2000. Print.

Marable, manning. Race, Reform, and Rebellion: The Second Reconstruction and beyond in Black America, 1945-2006. 3rd ed. Jackson: University Press of Mississippi, 2007. Print.

Moynihan, Daniel P. "U.S. Department of Labor –History—The Tangle of Pathology." *U.S. Department of Labor—History—Chapter IV. The Tangle of Pathology*. 1965. Web. 15 May 2015.

Ransby, Barbara. *Ella Baker and the Black Freedom Movement: A Radical Democratic Vision*. Chapel Hill: The University of North Carolina Press, 2003. Print.

Shapiro, Thomas M. *The Hidden Cost of being African American: How*

*Wealth Perpetuates Inequality*. New York: Oxford University Press, 2004. Print.

Trump, D. (2013, May 7). Donald Trump Defends his Awful Claim about Military Sexual Assault. Interview. Retrieved October 4, 2016, from http://www.huffingtonpost.com/entry/donald-trump-military-sexual-assault_us_57d0b947e4b03d2d45985347

Trump, D. (2015, August 7). Trump draws outrage after Megyn Kelly remarks. Interview. Retrieved October 4, 2016, from http://www.cnn.com/cnn/2015/08/08/politics/donald-trump-cnn-megyn-kelly-comment/

Trump, D. (2015, August 16). If Hillary Clinton can't satisfy her husband. Retrieved October 4, 2016, from Twitter.

Trump, D. (2016, August 1). Trump says he hopes Ivanka would quit if she got harassed: Kirsten Powers. Speech. Retrieved October 4, 2016, from http://www.usatoday.com/story/opinion/2016/08/ 01/ailes-trump-sexual-harassment-fox-news-women-gretchen-kelly-greta-news-column/87915454/

Trump, D. (2016, August 6). Donald Trump on Hillary Clinton: 'She took a sort-circuit in the brain.' Interview. Retrieved October 4, 2016, fromhttp://www.cnn.com/cnn/2016/08/06/ politics/donald-trump-hillary-clinton-short-circuit/

Trump, D. (2016, September 9). Donald Trump Insults Carly Fiorina's Appearance. Interview.

Retrieved October 4, 2016, from http://www.cbsnews.com/amp/news/donald-trump-insults-carly-fiorinas-apperance/

Trump, D. (2016, September 26). Donald Trump: Hillary Clinton Doesn't Have a Presidential Look. Interview. Retrieved October 4, 2016, from http://time.com/4480541/donald -trump-hillary-clinton-look-presidential/

# The Boston Globe

Sunday, April 9, 2017

# DEPORTATIONS TO BEGIN

President Trump calls for tripling of ICE force; riots continue

**Curfews extended in multiple cities**

PRESIDENT TRUMP has set in motion one of his most controversial campaign promises, calling on Congress to fund a "massive deportation force" by tripling the number of federal Immigration and Customs Enforcement agents.

The president made the announcement to a carefully selected address last night from the Old Post Office building in Washington, D.C., now a Trump International hotel. In a surprise move after the speech, Trump unveiled Attorney General Chris Christie to stand right next to him at the podium to field questions. "was_side_eye for Christie this time," tweeted Fox News Channel reporter Megyn Kelly, who was covering the speech from a sports bar near Rockefeller Center because she has been placed on a White House blacklist.

Although Trump reiterated his promise to eject some 11.2 million illegal workers on a two-year timetable — "so fast that your head will spin" — he also promised to "do it humanely." He did not immediately offer details but said he intends to flesh out the policy with special adviser George Papadopoulos, just as soon as the 2009 college grad returns from a preplanned Model UN session in Geneva.

The $400 billion deportation program promises to be one of the most

LIVE NOW: PRESIDENT ADDRESSES THE NATION

BREAKING NEWS — TRUMP: DEPORT ILLEGALS 'SO FAST YOUR HEAD WILL SPIN'

the White House. Singing and chanting have been audible inside the executive mansion day and night for weeks. The scent of tear gas pervades

take the MBTA's #1 Bus across the Charles River to an alternate site in Boston.

Already in California, armed ICE

"Sishango unraided in the kitchens of San Francisco restaurants and ever $9 billion strawberry crop is ultimately left to rot."

## Markets sink as trade war looms

WORLDWIDE STOCKS plunged again Friday completing the worst month on record as trade war with both China and Mexico seem imminent.

Markets from the Dow to the FTSE to the Nikkei have sunk on speculation that China's dumping some of its US Treasury holdings after the Trump administration announced tariffs as high as 45 percent for all Chinese imports and 35 percent for some Mexican goods.

"I don't mind trade war when we're losing $58 billion a year," the president said last year. But Chinese officials have made it no secret that they will not let tariffs go unanswered. The Asian giant is the largest holder of US debt, moving news

Dow declines at record pace

# Chapter Four

## *Feeding the Trump Base*

### Police Culture: A Socio-Epistemological View

#### Kọ́lá Abímbọ́lá

For many years, criminologists, psychologists, anthropologists, legal theorists, and philosophers have been studying police culture. Police culture refers to the world-outlook of police officer1s—it is a description of how those who put policing into practice conceive of the world and their role in it, and how this world-outlook governs (or at least shapes) day-to-day police inferential tasks. Although scholars such as Jerome Skolnick, Robert Reiner, and many others have supplied significant insights into the values, norms, and social organization of the police, these scholars did not analyze the cognitive impact of these values and norms on police inferential tasks. The contrast is between sociology and epistemology.

This paper argues that the social organization of policing has an important cognitive or epistemological dimension that is often overlooked in standard accounts of policing. Following Peter Tillers (1986), I describe this cognitive dimension of sociation as *practical belief-logics* (or practical beliefs). For police officers, practical belief-logics are intimately related to generalizations. Hence, to fully understand the inferential tasks of police officers, we need to understand the nature and types of the generalizations they assume. In a democracy where the ruling Party has a significant majority, the official generalizations and world-outlooks of politicians will of necessity directs policing, irrespective of the legal rules.

In what follows, I will describe the standard sociological view of police culture and then outline what I describe as the epistemological view. My argument is that the epistemological view of police culture provides some new insights into our understanding of the processing of argument and evidence by police officers during the pre-trial stages of criminal investigation. My contention is that sociology is not enough. Before we can fully understand the cognitive manner in which police officers reason from evidence and fact to conclusions, we need to pay serious attention to the roles of unstated background assumptions in the inferential tasks of police officers.

## POLICE CULTURE: THE SOCIOLOGICAL VIEW

Many commentators and scholars have observed that legal rules and regulation are often marginal to how the police in fact operate. The point is not merely that police officers find it easy to disregard regulation and the law. Rather, the point is that the legal rules and regulations are sufficiently permissive in the sense that the police officer has too much discretion. There is a substantial gap between the letter of the law and how police officers choose to enforce it. This gap ranges from issues such as the decision to arrest an offender, through the decision of whether to charge or caution the offender, to the decision to investigate. Moreover, as James Q. Wilson aptly observed, 'the police department has the special property ... that within it discretion increases as one moves down the hierarchy.' (Wilson 1978: 7)

The general point then is that legal rules and regulations do not, and cannot, completely determine police practice because police officers have too much discretion. It is precisely because of this that studies on police practice urge that, in relation to any police force, we need to distinguish between three types of rules: working rules, inhibiting rules, and presentational rules.

When police officers internalize and make use of legal rules as the guide to their behaviors, they become "working rules" that serve as heuristic action-guiding principles for the regulation on their conduct and behavior. When legal rules as perceived as impediments to investigation, police officers take them to be "inhibiting rules," and they will develop "presentational rules" that they will use as acceptable glosses that mediate between their working rules and the legal rules.

Legal rules and regulations often function as *presentational rules* for police officers. They may even view some legal rules as inhibitory to police investigation. And, often, legal rules are *presentational* in the sense that, having carried out their actions on the basis of their own working rules, the police would, after the fact, use legal rules to justify their initial actions. In short, if we truly seek an understanding of police practice, we need to understand their *working rules*, how these *working rules* are formed, maintained, and sustained over time.

Jerome Skolnick gives one good account of the working rules of police officers. According to Skolnick, the policeman's 'working personality' is a function of "two principal variables, *danger* and *authority*", and one constant, the "constant pressure to appear efficient" (Skolnick and Fyfe, 1993).

Policing is unique in the sense that police officers are daily being required to work under the threat of sudden and unpredictable danger. The uniqueness of this threat is not so much in high risk of physical injury; rather, it is in its unpredictability. As Robert Reiner puts it, 'the police officer faces, behind every corner he turns or door-bell he rings, some danger, if not of firearms at least of fists'.

The second variable is that of authority. The police officer represents and embodies what we may call *legitimate authority* within society. They wield a lot of power and authority within society because they are required to enforce various laws—some of which are regarded as "puritanical" by those on the receiving end. But the enforcement of these laws is by and large discretionary because police officers have some leeway on *how*, *when*, *whether to*, and, indeed, on *which* laws to enforce. As Robert Reiner puts it: 'It is because he represents authority, backed by the potential use of legitimate force, that the police officer faces danger from those who are recalcitrant to it'.

The third main characteristic of the policeman's working personality is 'the pressure put upon individual policemen to "produce"—to be efficient rather than legal when the two norms are in conflict'.

Danger and authority are variables in the sense that the amount of danger each officer is subjected to, or the precise amount of authority each individual officer has, varies. The amount of danger a police officer in New York, NY faces is considerably different from that faced by the Amherst, MA police officer. The type of authority the police officer on patrol has is different from the type of power the Sheriff has. Moreover, the specific type of danger faced, and the specific type of authority wielded, by two police officers from the same force, varies. But the "pressure to produce results" is a constant in the sense that all police officers are subject to both internal pressures from their superiors, and to external political and social pressure to solve and control crime.

Sociological accounts of police culture maintain that these main environmental characteristics of policing gives rise to a unique set of beliefs, principles and attitudes, on the basis of which police officers conduct their day-to-day activities. These beliefs and attitudes include: a sense of mission, which is coupled with solidarity; the attitude of suspicion; conservatism; and racial prejudice. These attitudes are ingrained into police practice in the sense that they are brought about by the nature and environment of policing itself. Specifically, these attitudes are the product of the danger, authority, and the pressure to produce results, which are characteristics inherent in the structure of policing any modern society.

The sense of mission 'is the feeling that policing is not just a job but a way of life with a worthwhile purpose.' Police officers, it is claimed, do not conceive of their work simply as that of enforcing the rule of law. Central to their attitude to, and motivation for, work is a sense of purpose—a sense of doing something that is not merely legally required of them, but which is also morally imperative for 'the preservation of a valued way of life and the protection of the weak against the predatory'.

Policing also breeds the general attitude of suspicion in police officers. Unlike most other occupations, policing is unique in the sense that the police officer constantly deals with situations that are highly unpredictable, uncertain and risky. Because the threat of sudden danger is constant, a police officer is generally a "suspicious person". One policeman described this attitude as follows:

> You drive along and you see things, or read things differently to your wife or friends. And invariably matchboxes and cheques are covered with car-numbers and this sort of things. You go to the football, and you tend to be more aware, to keep your eye on the yobs. Or you notice odd things, like the old chap standing by a school.
>
> **(REINER, 1992, p.114.)**

Due to the combined influence of authority, danger, and the pressure to produce results, suspicion becomes inevitable for any police officer that wants to produce results.

The police are regarded as the symbol of cohesive authority, and people are generally nervous around them. The presence of police officers immediately sharpens the sense of peoples' awareness (even those who have done nothing illegal). The result of this is that it is often difficult for police officers to mix with the ordinary civilian in social life. In their social life, the police are often isolated from the general public, and as a result they form a solidarity unit amongst themselves. Of course, the need for police officers to rely on their colleagues in their dangerous day-to-day activities also heightens the solidarity amongst them.

According to Reiner, in orientation, police tend to be politically and morally conservative. There are various reasons for this. One is the nature of policing itself. Policemen are very often pitted against radicals and those of the left, especially in demonstrations and riots. Given the hierarchical structure policing, officers conservative outlooks are more likely to fit in.

It is also suggested that the police are generally more hostile to, and more prejudiced against, Blacks. In fact, researchers such as Robert Reiner have confirmed that hostile and suspicious views of Blacks were openly uttered by the police during interviews he conducted at police stations. Reiner suggests that the crucial question is not merely whether the police are prejudiced; rather, the question is whether they are more prejudiced than the general public. For it could well be that the evidence of police prejudice says nothing distinctive of the nature of policing: society itself might be generally racially biased, such that police officers are merely manifesting the general level of societal bias.

The central claim of sociological account of police culture is therefore the following: The two variables, *authority* and *danger*, and the constant, *the pressure for results*, are unique elements of policing in any contemporary society. These elements in turn give rise to the policeman's 'working personality', namely: mission, suspicion, isolation/solidarity, conservatism, and racial prejudice.

### *Police Culture: An Epistemological View*

The sociological accounts of police culture undoubtedly supply significant insights into the nature of policing, and indeed, into the policeman's working personality. At the very least, these sociological studies suggest that the standard responses to police malpractice are deeply flawed. I think I am correct in maintaining that there are two standard approaches to police malpractice and misconduct. One is to lay down new laws and rules of conduct; the other is to attempt to make examples of specific police officers by trying them in a court of law. As the distinction between 'working', 'inhibitory', and 'presentational' rules suggest, new rules may not succeed in changing police practice. And as cases such as that of

Amadou Diallo suggest, criminal prosecution may not change anything. The question then is this: how can we make use of our understanding of police culture in an effort to change police practice? The answer I think lies in elevating our study of police culture from sociology to psychology.

My point can be put differently. Criminologists such as Reiner and Skolnick often discuss police culture without acknowledging its importance on the processing of evidence in pre-trial criminal procedure. For if understanding police behavior requires an understanding of how they view the world, the next question we ought to ask is that of how police officers' perceptions of the world affect their day-to-day inferential tasks.

The answer to this question lies in the fast that human beings are cognitive agents with a variety of background assumptions and beliefs. These background beliefs and assumptions shape, mold, or at least direct the processing of fact in law. The background beliefs and assumptions of police officers are to a large extent the product of policing itself. Generalizations form one important class of these background beliefs. Although there are various types of generalizations, I will discuss only three types of generalizations, viz.; Case-specific generalizations; scientific generalizations; and General knowledge generalizations.

Case-specific generalizations are those that are assumed and relied on by individuals in a particular case. For example:

- "In most matters concerning their relationship, John abused Mary".
- "The workers at the asbestos manufacturing plant were mostly illegal aliens".
- "The employer regularly discriminated against ethnic minorities in its employment practices".

These are case-specific generalizations in the sense that they are specific to individual cases. They may be held by fact investigators and fact finders (i.e. police officers, lawyers, judges, or jurors) involved in the specific cases in which they arise. They may be explicitly upheld by these investigators, but they could be tacit and as such operate as background assumptions. There may be concrete evidence in support of some of these generalizations. (For instance, the generalization that workers on the asbestos plant were illegal aliens). But they may become operative because the investigator interprets fact and evidence on the basis of established beliefs. And indeed, case-specific generalizations could be the product of both evidence present in the case, and pre-established beliefs of the fact-investigator.

Scientific knowledge and research establish scientific generalizations. These would include statements such as 'smoking causes cancer'; 'if the force exerted on a particle of mass $m$ is $f$, then that particle's acceleration is $f/m$'; 'A fingerprint identification is valid if there are at least 16 points of comparison between the print recovered from the crime scene and the suspects' prints (as long as there is no point of disagreement)'. An expert witness usually testifies to a scientific generalization in court.

General knowledge generalizations are information-based claims accepted as true or reliable. They are often founded upon cogent and coherent evidence. Consider for instance, the following generalizations quoted from Anderson and Twining: 'Palm trees, rain, and high humidity are common in Miami, Florida; transactions in securities traded on the New York Stock Exchange are accurately summarized in the Wall Street Journal; most pubs in England are affiliated in some manner with a brewery.' Even though we may not be able to state off-hand the justification or authority for these generalizations, they are all founded upon cogent and well-founded evidence of some sort.

But general knowledge generalizations may also be founded upon introspection, indoctrination, moral education, religious beliefs, etc. When they do, they may not be based upon evidence at all. Thus, many may accept the general knowledge generalization that anyone seen running away from the scene of a stabbing with the bloody knife in his hands is likely to be guilty of murder, but I doubt whether there is any hard-statistical evidence in support of this generalization. It is more likely than not that this generalization is based upon introspection and general beliefs about the behavior of humans.

General knowledge generalizations are of crucial importance to evidential reasoning. For lawyers, judges, juries, police officers, and everyone involved in the legal process all make use of generalizations in the analysis of evidence. Examples of the three types of generalizations I have identified can easily be identified from the investigation into any crime. Consider for instance a burglary in which the police were able to recover some fingerprints believed to be that of the burglar from the crime scene. Suppose further the house owner, call her Mrs. Jones, actually saw the burglar (call the burglar Elliot) as he was taking flight from the house. In carrying out their investigation into this burglary, the police would first ascertain whether they have a corresponding print on record. If they do not, then the police might implicitly rely on case-specific generalizations about burglars who are indifferent or careless enough to leave their fingerprints all over the crime scene. One such generalization could be that: in cases of this kind, we do not have a seasoned professional burglar. Another could be that, say, in cases of this sort, we have an individual who has a somewhat respectable social standing and who therefore does not envisage himself ever getting into trouble with the law.

Moreover, in relying upon Mrs. Jones's description of the burglar, the police are relying upon a general knowledge generalization. For the police would intuitively assume that house holders who give descriptions of burglars are unlikely to deliberately mislead officers. Also, they could rely on the general knowledge generalization that individuals (such as Elliot) who are seen fleeing from crime scenes are very likely to be guilty of an offence.

It should, however, be pointed out that the classification of generalizations into three types is primarily for the purposes of analysis. In real life, it might be difficult to pigeon-hole a generalization into one and only one group. Consider for instance the role of generalizations in the identification of firearms. According to Bonfanti & Kinder:

> Firearms identification has relied on the hypothesis that there is a unique signature left by a firearm on the elements of the fired round, i.e. the striation marks on the bullet or [a number of] marks on the cartridges. The hypothesis assumes a unique combination of striation lines or other impressions so that the probability of finding two identical sets of marks is practically zero. These traces originate ei-

ther from the close contact of the bullet or the cartridge case with one or more parts of the forearm, or from the dynamic processes during the firing. During this contact, an imprint is made of the imperfections of the firearm, resulting from either its manufacture or its continual use. (1999, p.4.)

Bonfanti & Kinder point out that, despite the fact that striation marks on gun barrels are caused by the process of manufacturing, firearms identification is predicated upon the assumption that even guns from the same manufacturing batch (i.e. consecutively-manufactured firearms) leave different striation marks on bullets and cartridges. Bonfanti & Kinder evaluated over fifty different studies in which this generalization was put to test. And in all of them, the researchers claimed that the generalization was confirmed. Conclusions such as: "The traces left by each barrel are individual"; "Each barrel has a distinctive and separate individuality"; "The striation marks on the bullets allow the identification of the weapons which shot them", etc. were reached by each of these empirical tests.

On the basis of the conclusions reached by these empirical tests, the generalization that 'a unique "signature" is always left by a firearm on the bullet or cartridge case', is regarded as justified. Hence in identifying bullets, firearms investigators assume that there is a unique one-to-one mapping between guns and bullets (or cartridges) fired from each gun.

This generalization is clearly a scientific generalization. As the Bonfanti & Kinder report indicates, this claim has been subjected to test after test by researchers in numerous experiments. But the claim also functions as a general knowledge generalization. Firearms investigators, police officers, and everyone interested in ballistics accept the generalization as true and reliable, thereby making use of the information in their inferential tasks—without caring much for how the scientific generalization was established. Until there is a need to question a conclusion arrived at on the basis of a scientific generalization of this sort, it will simply be an essential part of the culture for fact investigation.

Practical belief-logics form another important class of this background information. Practical belief-logics are individuated beliefs, convictions, and principles on the basis of which human beings operate. These beliefs and principles affect our practical decisions, actions and in-actions, and consequently our relationship with other humans. But most importantly, we often make use of these individual-specific beliefs in our interpretation and understanding of others. Following Tillers, I will refer to the action-guiding principles and beliefs as *practical belief-logics*:

> Human beings have various systems of beliefs, principles, and sets of mental operations and activities that they often use to regulate and control their conduct. Believing this, many of us implicitly believe that making good guesses about human beings often requires an understanding of actors' practical belief-logic—the principles and other conceptual matters by which human actors regulate their activities. In sum, many of us believe that human beings are self-regulating actors—i.e., we use a practical belief-logic to regulate our activities—and that guesses about the activities of human actors often require an understanding of that practical belief-logic. These beliefs are not unreasonable or unwarranted. (Tillers, 1986, p.927.)

Practical belief-logics are really mirror images of generalizations because anyone who *acts* on a generalization is *ipso facto* operating on the basis of a practical belief-logic. Differently put, practical beliefs supply us with an internal perspective for understanding others: they are about beliefs and principles on the basis of which humans regulate and conduct their activities. These beliefs are those which affect practical affairs in our day-to-day lives. Consequently, understanding someone requires making reasonable guesses about their practical belief-logics. Practical belief-logics play important roles in inferential reasoning. Indeed, they supply a perspective that is often left out of most analysis of legal reasoning.

Consider, for instance, the so-called *battered women syndrome*. Traditionally, English law accepted provocation as a defense to murder only if there was a 'sudden and temporary loss of self-control'. Hence 'slow-burn' cases, in which women reacted as a result of years of abuse and humiliation, were initially rejected as candidates for the defense of provocation. This was so until *R. v.*

*Ahluwalia (1993) 96 Cr App R 133 Court of Appeal* when the courts accepted that a delayed reaction *might* still amount to killing as a result of provocation.

One could analyze the legal position in these slow-burn cases by claiming that what the traditional approach left out was the defendants' practical belief-logics. In most of these cases, the actions that culminated in the killing would have been brewing for years. And during those years, the battered woman would have operated under the earnest belief that there was no way out of the abusive relationship. Very often, the woman in question would also have no independent income or means of subsistence, and might also have serious concerns about the welfare of her children if she were simply to pack their bags and leave.

But after *R. v. Ahluwalia,* the courts accepted an explanation of human action that had been obvious to psychologists all along: namely that human action has internal perspectives that are not often captured by generalizations. These internal perspectives include: beliefs, principles and cognitive assumptions that regulate and control human conduct. In short, in slow-burn cases the abused individual might operate on the genuinely held belief that there is no practical solution to the abusive relationship, until ultimately, she snaps, and decides to take the law into her own hands.

The practical belief-logics we uphold are often based on facts. Thus, in slow-burn cases, the defense will have to adduce clear-cut evidence of abuse. The defense will also have to establish that this unique set of beliefs and principles regulated and controlled the actions of the accused. But often times, these practical beliefs are based on false generalizations, stereotypes, propaganda, and, indeed, alternative facts.

Understanding why an individual acted in one particular way is not just about analysis of fact, it is also about understanding and interpreting the facts in light of what the interpreter (and the subject') practical belief-logics. Once a practical belief-logic is formed, it functions as a background assumption for the interpretation of human actions on the basis of evidence. Consider again slow-burn cases. There are many fact-based movies in which defendants use the defense of slow-burn provocation to cover-up elaborate premeditated murders. These cases indicate that practical beliefs are fact-based devices we use in our understanding and the interpretation of the actions of others. A defense of provocation in slow-burn cases succeeds only if the court accepts that the abused woman operated on a set of beliefs and convictions that truly regulated and controlled her conduct.

My general point then is this: when an agent's actions and conduct are regulated and controlled by a generalization, or by a particular set of practical belief-logics, we can also say that these generalizations and practical beliefs operate as *inferential warrants* which, in effect, *license* or *permit* the decisions and conduct of the agent. Epistemically speaking, generalizations and practical belief "authorize" the steps in the network of beliefs (and conclusions) held by fact investigators in the legal process. This, they do, by permitting or licensing the move from one item of evidence to another in arguments from premises to conclusions. In preliminary fact investigation, the sorts of conduct we are interested in are those that arise within evidential contexts. Conduct such as: charging suspect $X$ with the murder; taking the jewelry box back to the police laboratory for fingerprint enhancement instead of applying the grey fingerprint powder on in at the crime scene; etc. In this respect, the type of "conduct" we are talking about are activities requiring action on the basis of evidential fact. We are in effect talking about evidential inference.

## THE CASCADED NATURE OF INFERENCE

What exactly do we mean by "inference"? John Henry Wigmore discussed at length this very question and his answer was dual: the one general, the other technical. In its general sense, inference is 'the *process* of thinking about a piece of evidence, not the *result*.' Here the term signifies the thought process by which we extract information or conclusions from evidence. It does not describe that piece of evidence, (which is the basis for our thought processes). Nor does it describe the end result (i.e. conclusions) we arrive at from our evidence. Rather, it simply describes the mental act of drawing conclusions from items of information.

Wigmore's technical definition of inference takes it offshoot from the fact that reasoning within the legal context always involves more than one step; it is cumulative. It will typically involve a series of steps in which a latter step is inferred from an earlier one. Consider, again the evidential circumstances of the burglary analyzed above (p.9). Suppose that Elliot (the burglar) was later arrested for the offence. The evidence presented by the prosecution includes testimonial and forensic science evidence. Elliot was seen running out of the Jones' house by Mrs. Jones just as she was returning home. When Mrs. Jones reported this crime to the police, she gave them a detailed description of the burglar. Moreover, the crime scene examiner (call him Ian Williams) was able to recover fingerprints, and other DNA material corresponding to that of Elliot at the crime scene. Suppose further that Police Constable Brown arrested Elliot on the same day as he was patrolling a neighboring street. Brown arrested Elliot because he (Elliot) fitted the description of the burglar given by Mrs. Jones.

If Elliot is charged with the burglary and the case eventually proceeds to trial, the prosecution's case will be that Elliot committed the crime in question. The prosecution will argue that Elliot was at the scene of the crime. But to show that he was indeed at the scene of the crime, the evidentiary fact that Elliot's fingerprints match those recovered at the crime scene will be advanced. The prosecution will rely on the testimony of Ian Williams, the Scene of Crime Examiner. Ian Williams will present items of evidence (such as exhibits of the recovered prints) in his testimony. Williams' testimony thus becomes the basis for drawing the inference to the claim that the fingerprints are those of Elliot's.

As David Schum has emphasized, we need to distinguish **E** (the occurrence or non-occurrence of an event) from **E\*** (someone's testimony that event **E** did or did not occur). So, suppose we designate Ian Williams' testimony as: **E\***. Williams' testimony to event **E** is not the same as event **E** itself. For the mere fact that Williams testifies to **E** *does not provide conclusive evidence* of the occurrence of event **E**. Perhaps Elliot's fingerprints were not recovered at the crime scene at all and Williams in collusion with the police had simply planted the evidence. Or perhaps Williams is mistaken in his identification of the fingerprints. Simply put, **E** (the occurrence or non-occurrence of an event) is distinct and distinguishable from **E*** (someone's claim that event **E** occurred).

The foregoing has an important implication that should not be overlooked. If we cannot equate **E** with **E***, then, in evidential reasoning, whenever we move from *evidence proffered* to a *conclusion*, there is at least one intermediate stage of reasoning involved within this process. This intermediate stage is here supplied by the fact finder when s/he infers **E** from **E***. For the fact finder must be able to make a chain-of-reasoning connection between the testimony to the event and the occurrence of the event itself if s/he is to conclude (on the basis of the testimony) that the event did in fact occur.

In other words, in the legal process, we are always being urged to infer **C** (the conclusion) from **E,** and **E** from **E***. This is what we mean by *cascaded, catenated, hierarchical or multistage* reasoning.

**FIGURE 1:** The Cascaded Nature of Evidential Reasoning

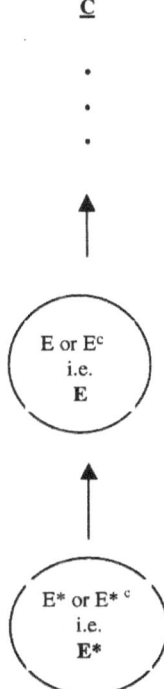

C: Conclusion (e.g. verdict of trial, decision to arrest, etc.)
E: Occurrence of event.
$E^c$: Non-occurrence of event.
E*: Witness testimony that event did occur.
$E^{*c}$: Witness testimony that event did not occur.
**E**: {E or $E^c$}
**E***: {E* or $E^{*c}$}

But how do police officers perform the mental act of moving from one link in the chain to another before we arrive at the judgement **E** or **C**? What provides the warrant, support or justification for the inference from one stage of reasoning to another? What makes the mental process of drawing a conclusion **C** from certain items of information justified? The answers to these questions lie in the role of generalizations and practical beliefs in police culture.

## GENERALIZATIONS, PRACTICAL BELIEF-LOGICS AND PRE-TRIAL CRIMINAL EVIDENCE

I will use one concrete example from English criminal justice to illustrate my point about the twined role of generalizations and practical beliefs in pre-trial criminal evidence.[1]

Stephen Lawrence and his friend Duwayne Brooks were on their way home about 10:30pm on 22 April 1993. As they approached the bus stop in Well Hall Road, Stephen went ahead of his friend to see whether a bus was approaching. As Duwayne Brooks called out to his friend to ask him whether he saw the bus coming, someone from a group of five or six white youths on the other side of the road (who must have heard Duwayne) called out: "What, what nigger?" The whole group then crossed the road, engulfing Stephen. Duwayne turned and ran, and he also called out to Stephen to run. But Stephen was stabbed twice—once in the chest and

---

[1] See Abímbọ́la 2002 for a more detailed analysis of the Stephen Lawrence case. Further implications of generalizations are also identified in that article.

once in the arm, as he was in the process of flight. Both wounds on either side of the body were about five inches deep. Both stabs severed axillary arteries, and blood was pumping into and out of Stephen's body as he ran for about 130 yards before he fell.

Duwayne Brooks ran across the road and away from the scene. There were three eyewitnesses at the bus stop. Stephen died a few minutes after he fell (and before the arrival of the ambulance). Indeed, according to Dr. Shepherd, the pathologist who examined Stephen's body: 'It is surprising that he managed to get 130 yards with all the injuries he had, but also the fact that the deep penetrating wound of the right side caused the upper lobe to partially collapse his lung.'

Although we have no official statement of the police's initial assumptions about the sequence of events, it is quite obvious that they adopted a different story in their investigation of the murder. This is because their initial investigation was carried out on the assumption that the death was the result of a failed drug deal. The police's prime suspect was in fact Duwayne Brooks and it was not until a month after the incident that the police decided that Brooks was not a conspirator in the killing of Stephen Lawrence.

The police's initial assumptions about the series of events leading to the death of Lawrence can be regarded as a product of their understanding of the problems and questions that confronted them. For in their initial response to the crime, the police did not define the crime as a racial incident. Thus, in carrying out their inquiry, the presuppositions of their initial inquiry did not include racial motives for the attack.

Part of the problem has to do with the identification of a "racist incident". The Macpherson Report defines a racist incident as follows:

> A racist incident is any incident which is perceived to be racist by the victim or any other person. (London: HMSO, 1999, para 1.7.)

This definition is itself based upon a definition proposed by the Association of Chief Police Officers:

A racist incident is any incident in which it appears to the reporting or investigating officer that the complaint involves an element of racial motivation, or any incident which includes an allegation of racial motivation made by any person. (London: HMSO, 1999, para 45.16.)

Supposing we set aside the numerous problems with the subjective nature of this definition of 'racist incident', a more important problem is the gap that exists between formal definitions and police practice. For despite the testimony of Brooks, the police's initial investigation was carried out on the assumption that the death was the result of a failed drug deal.

It is plausible therefore to conjecture that until Brooks was eliminated as a suspect, the police accepted a different story. For despite the fact that various persons from the general public volunteered information to the effect that the five individuals were responsible for the crime, the police did not take this information seriously. Stephen Lawrence was killed on 22 April. On the 23$^{rd}$ of April, a letter giving the names of these suspects was left at a phone box. On that same day, various people made statements to the police about the attacks. The names of these five suspects were prominent, but most of these informants wished to remain anonymous because the whole neighborhood was terrified of the gang. The information given to the police also indicated that stabbing an innocent individual was part of the gang's initiation ceremony.

Someone referred to as "James Grant" supplied very important information to the police. (The informant was given this pseudonym to protect his identity.) James Grant went to the police station on two occasions—on the 23$^{rd}$ and 24$^{th}$ of April. As stated in the Macpherson inquiry:

> The most important information of all to reach the team during the first weekend came from a man whose identity was in fact established from the start, but who was for obvious reasons given a pseudonym, namely "James Grant." At 19:45 on Friday 23 April,

this young man, later described by DS Davidson as "a skinhead," walked into Plumstead Police Station. Detective Constable Christopher Budgen had been recruited on that day as a member of the AMIP team. He was sent to see the young man, and the information received was vital and illuminating. The information (as necessarily edited) ... is known as Message 40:

"A male attended 'RM [Plumstead] and stated that the persons responsible for the murder on the black youth, are Jamie and Neil Acourt of 102 Bournbrook Road SE3 together with David Norris and 2 other males identity unknown. [He reported] that the Acourt Brothers call themselves 'The Krays'. In fact, you can only join their gang if you stab someone. They carry knives and weapons most days. Also, David Norris stabbed a Stacey Benefield a month ago in order to prove himself. ... He then went on to say that a young Pakistani boy was murdered last year in Well Hall, that Peter Thompson who is serving life was part of the Acourts gang. That in fact one of the Acourts killed this lad. They also stabbed a young lad at Woolwich town centre called 'Lee.' He had a bag placed over his head and was stabbed in his legs and arms in order to torture him." (London: HMSO, 1999, para 13.25.)

Despite the fact that the police were able to corroborate some of Grant's claims, the police did not take any action on this information until 26 April—3 days later. The police did not arrest any of the suspects, nor did they request a search warrant. Rather, Detective Superintendent Crampton (who was in charge of the case) arranged for surveillance of the suspects—even though he knew that surveillance evidence of this sort was inadmissible in court. But in fact, the surveillance was bungled. The full surveillance team did not arrive on time, and the team's researcher and photographer were simply watching when (alleged) vital evidence (the clothes worn by the Acourt brothers on the night of the murder) was taken out of the house and away in a car to be destroyed.

One could conjecture that the information about the gang was not initially regarded as crucial by the investigating team because they were pursuing the theory that the killing was a failed drug deal in which Brooks was also involved. This conjecture gains some support from the fact that while all this information about the gang was coming into the police station, the police were in fact busy investigating the background of Stephen Lawrence and Duwayne Brooks.

To understand why the initial investigation pursued this line of inquiry, we need to place the investigation in the wider context of police culture. Studies by Reiner and Holdaway have shown that the police routinely rely on generalizations about black youths as criminals. Reiner, for instance, claims that:

> Cain's and Lambert's studies of city forces in the early and late 1960s show a clear pattern of rank-and-file police prejudice, perceiving blacks as especially prone to violence or crime, and generally incomprehensible, suspicious and hard to handle. ... My own interviews in Bristol in 1973-4 found that hostile and suspicious views of blacks were frequently offered quite spontaneously in the context of interviews concerning police work in general. ... One uniform constable summed up the pattern: 'the police are trying to appear unbiased in regard to race relations. But if you asked them you'd find 90 per cent of the force is against coloured immigrants. ...' (Reiner, 1992, p. 125-126).

Stereotypical generalizations which seemed to have informed the police investigation of the murder would include:

- All/most/many black male youths are involved in criminal activities.
- All/most/many black male youths are unreliable witnesses.
- All/most/many black male youths are involved in drug-related crimes.

In the case of Brooks, these three generalizations can be converted into case specific generalizations because despite the facts that: Brooks had no criminal record; he was not known to the police as a criminal; and that there was no evidence to doubt his version of events, the police nonetheless conducted their initial main investigation along the lines of a failed drug deal. The police's initial inquiry is therefore consistent with an assumption of the sort of stereotypical generalizations Reiner and others talk about in their research on police culture.

In his evidence to the Macpherson inquiry, Holdaway identified another sort of generalization. According to Holdaway, in investigating the incident:

> The officers were 'colour blind,' denying the relevance of racial status of the victims, the racial motivation of the assailants and, therefore, the need for a particular approach to the investigation of the Lawrence murder. The failure of the police officers dealing with the Lawrence case to recognize and accept 'race' as a central feature of their investigation is in my view central to the deficiencies in policing identified by Kent Police. (HMSO, n 16, para 11.2.)

Holdaway's generalization is case specific. For what he is in effect claiming is that 'in all matters concerning their initial investigation, the police failed to recognize or accept race as a central feature of this particular investigation.'

In short, two sorts of case specific generalizations adversely affected the investigation of the crime. One has to do with the victims (Lawrence and Brooks); the other has to do with the assailants. Because the victims were black, the police assumed, without any evidence, that the incident was a drug-related crime. And because of this assumption, the police adopted assumptions about the assailants' motives. As Holdaway puts it: 'The officers [denied] ... the racial motivation of the assailant.'

The generalization identified by Holdaway also functions as a practical belief-logic governing the police in their interpretation of the assailants' motive. Since the police did not accept Brooks' story of the events, they also operated on the assumption that they understood the assailant's motive—a dispute in a failed drug deal. This in turn affected the sorts of questions they regarded as germane to solving the crime. For the sorts of questions, they were asking from witnesses were all directed at discovering evidence that could implicate Brooks and Lawrence in criminal activities.

The role of generalizations in this case also illustrates the point that generalizations are necessary, but dangerous. They are necessary because all arguments from fact to conclusion rely upon at least one background general assumptions. But they are also dangerous because they are often unsupported by evidence, and are often based upon prejudices. In the case of Stephen Lawrence, the role of stereotypical generalizations in police inquiry hampered the investigation of a serious crime.

The response of the black community to the police investigation also highlights the role of practical belief-logics in the analysis of fact. Within the first few days of police inquiry, individuals from the black community had begun alleging racism on the part of the police. Most of these initial criticisms of the police inquiry were not founded upon fact; they were based upon beliefs about how police forces in Britain usually operate. For having taken it for granted that the police hold stereotypical images of black youths, some early criticisms of the investigation were based on beliefs about the usual operation of police investigations. In short, two sorts of practical belief-logics can be discerned from some of the criticism:

First, we have practical belief-logics about the actions of the police. The general public assumed a generalization such as the following: 'officers in charge of this particular crime made stereotypical guesses about the actions of Brooks and Lawrence.' So, even though there was initially no evidence to sustain the belief that the officers who investigated the homicide were being stereotypical in this particular investigation, this generalization was transformed into a practical belief about the action-guiding principles that informed the police investigation. Specifically, assumptions about police culture led many individuals to make guesses about how the police were likely to conduct the investigation.

Second, this same generalization ('officers in charge of this particular crime made stereotypical guesses about the actions of Brooks and Lawrence') generated practical belief-logics on the basis of which the black community regulated their response to the police investigation. That is, the general assumption that the police were likely to be stereotypical in their investigation affected the practical conduct of many individuals and organizations. Thus, guesses about the practical belief-logics of the police itself generated another set of practical beliefs (namely, those of conscious antagonism and distrust) on the basis of which many individuals regulated their response to the police investigation.

It is important to be precise about the claims being made in the points above. At the beginning of this paper, I outlined how attitudes and beliefs which arise out of the structure of policing could become ingrained into police culture, and thus become part of the *modus operandi* of day-to-day policing. The case of Stephen Lawrence provides two clear-cut examples of generalizations which engendered practical beliefs of this sort. Stereotypical beliefs about blacks and drug-related crimes coloured the police's initial investigation of the death of Stephen Lawrence. And because black pressure groups themselves operated upon a stereotypical image of police officers as prejudiced and racially biased, many of these groups began an outcry of racism against the police even before the line of investigation taken by the police became apparent. In short, what we had in the investigation of the killing of Stephen Lawrence was not simple reasoning in which one premise leads directly to a conclusion. It's was a cascade of reasoning in which generalizations, theory, political prejudice, stereotypical assumptions, and real evidence constrain and confine the process of thought. At the base of all reasoning from fact and evidence to conclusion, therefore, are generalizations.

In human inferential tasks, the generalizations and practical beliefs we rely on are unspecified and are therefore relied on intuitively in inferential tasks. Nonetheless, if we examine our reasoning processes closely, they would almost always rely upon some generalization or the other.

But as sociological studies in police culture have shown, the variables (danger and authority) and the constant (pressure to produce results) lead to specific character traits in police officers. As already mentioned, one of these traits is that of suspicion. Sociological studies of cop culture emphasize the point that, suspiciousness is a natural response to the nature of policing. But as my analysis of the Stephen Lawrence evidence has shown, such attitudes are also generalized. Hence to function effectively in their day-to-day tasks, the police might operate intuitively on generalizations about which individuals are suspicious enough to be questioned, detained, or arrested. And because of the other attributes of police culture, namely, conservatism and racial discrimination, some individuals are more predisposed to the direct effects of police power and authority.

In short, the attributes of police culture are not just sociological traits, they are psychologistic attributes of the police mid-set, some of which are generalized, and some of which operate as action-guiding principles governing the drawing of inferences from fact and evidence.

## Conclusion

While sociological accounts of police culture view attitudes such as suspicion and racial stereotyping as inevitable characteristics of policing, the epistemological account of police culture adds to this. Specifically, the epistemological account maintains that these traits, attitudes, and beliefs form the basis of generalizations and practical beliefs on the basis of which police officers conduct their day-to-day inferential tasks. In reasoning from evidential fact to conclusion, police officers rely on stereotypical generalizations, and other practical belief-logics as inferential warrants that justify the move from one item of evidence to another in inferential tasks. Unfortunately, most of the generalizations and practical beliefs relied upon in police practice are implicit, and, therefore, operate as background assumptions. Consequently, until these generalizations and beliefs are explicitly identified and brought to the forefront, the standard response to police malpractice is doomed to fail. Until police training fully comes to grips with the symbiotic roles of sociology and epistemology in policing, creating new legal rules and making examples of specific police officers by putting them on trial, will not change the policeman's working personality. We need to ensure that police officers have the socio-epistemological background that is congenial to policing a multi-cultural society.

## REFERENCES

Abímbọ́lá, K. (2013). Reason and Proof in Forensic Evidence. *J Forensic Res S*, *11*, 2.

Abímbọ́lá, K. (2004). Twining and Monk: Evidence and Inference in History and Law: Interdisciplinary Dialogues. *The Modern Law Review*, *67*(3), 527-530.

Abímbọ́lá, K. (2002). Questions and answers: the logic of preliminary fact investigation. *Journal of Law and Society*, *29*(4), 533-559.

Abímbọ́lá, K. (2000b). Abductive reasoning in law: Taxonomy and inference to the best explanation. *Cardozo L. Rev.*, *22*, 1683.

Ackroyd, J. E. (1974). *The Investigator: A Practical Guide to Private Detection*. Muller.

Anderson, T., & Twining, W. (1991). Analysis of Evidence: How to Do Things with Facts Based on Wigmore's Science of Judicial Proof. *Little, Brown: Boston, MA*.

Anderson, Terence, David Schum, and William Twining. *Analysis of evidence*. Cambridge University Press, 2005.

Bonfanti, M. S., & De Kinder, J. (1999). The influence of manufacturing processes on the identification of bullets and cartridge cases–a review of the literature. *Science & justice*, *39*(1), 3-10.

Bridges, L. (1999). The Lawrence Inquiry–incompetence, corruption, and institutional racism. *Journal of Law and Society*, *26*(3), 298-322.

Holdaway, S. (1998). Statement to the Inquiry into the Matters Arising from the Death of Stephen Lawrence. HMSO: London.

Holdaway, S. (1989). Discovering structure. Studies of the British police occupational culture. In M. Weatheritt (ed.), *Police Research: Some Future Prospects*. Avebury: Aldershot.

Macpherson, W. (1999). The Inquiry into the Matters Arising from the Death of Stephen Lawrence. *CM4262-1 http://www. archive. official documents. co. uk/document/cm42/4262/sli-pre. htm (accessed 12/01/10).*

Jackson, J. D. (1988). Theories of truth finding in criminal procedure: An evolutionary approach. *Cardozo L. Rev.*, *10*, 475.

Kuhn, T.S. (1962). *The Structure of Scientific Revolution*. University of Chicago Press.

MacCormick, N. (1994). *Legal reasoning and legal theory*. Clarendon Press.

Reiner, R. (1992). *The politics of the police*. Oxford University Press.

Reiner, R. (1982). Who are the police? *The Political Quarterly*, 53(2), 165-180.

Reiner, R. (1981). Black and Blue-Race and The Police. *New Society*, 57(983), 466-469.

Schum, D. A. (1994). *The evidential foundations of probabilistic reasoning*. Northwestern University Press.

Schum, D. A. (1987). *Evidence and inference for the intelligence analyst* (Vol. 1). Univ Pr of Amer.

Skolnick, J. H., & Fyfe, J. J. (1993). *Above the law: Police and the excessive use of force* (pp. 43-48). New York: Free Press.

Tillers, P. (1988). The Value of Evidence in Law. *N. Ir. Legal Q.*, 39, 167.

Tillers, P. (1986). Mapping inferential domains. *BUL Rev.*, 66, 883.

Twining, W., & Miers, D. (1999). *How to do things with rules: a primer of interpretation*. Cambridge University Press.

Twining, W. (1999). Narrative and generalizations in argumentation about questions of fact. *S. Tex. L. Rev.*, 40, 351.

White, P. (2010). *Crime scene to court: the essentials of forensic science*. Royal society of chemistry.

Wigmore, J. H. (1913). *Principles of judicial proof* (p. 16). Little, Brown.

Wilson, J. Q. (1968). Dilemmas of police administration. *Public Administration Review*, 28(5), 407-417.

Wilson, J. Q. (1978). *Varieties of police behavior*. Harvard University Press.

# President Trump fills world leaders with fear: 'It's gone from funny to really scary'

Most of the world seems to agree a Donald Trump presidency is a disturbing possibility

# CHAPTER FIVE

## *The Art of the Rhetoric of White Nationalism*

Yurugu Rhetoric: Psychopathy and Savagery

KenZoe Brian J. Selassie, Ph.D.

The most critical aspect of any peoples' existence is their culture. According to Daryl Harris, "Culture really does matter" (2011, p. 1). Marimba Ani (1994) uses the African term *asili* (seed) to explain culture in its most fundamental essence, representing the germination of philosophical and spiritual origins of a civilizations' way of being. "The concept of "asili"–a Kiswahili word, is used in several related ways to mean: beginning, origin, source, nature, essence, fundamental initiating principle, germ–is introduced" (Ani, 1994, p. 3.) Similarly, Harris (2011) offers an equally significant perspective suggesting, "It [culture] is the womb, the central organizing site for developing and promulgating the interpersonal and societal aspects of human experience. Accordingly, culture (which really is a euphemism for philosophy) contains the formative stuff—values, concepts, and ideas—that gives substance, direction, and purpose to all manner of theoretical and ideological formations and their attendant political, socioeconomic, and religious institutions, processes, and practices" (p. 1). In both respects, understanding the psychology of culture prompts context about how it works, including communicatively (Ani, 1994; Harris, 2011; Selassie, 2016). Understanding that culture is a critical component to any peoples' context of civilization and nationhood, it becomes equally important to consider how culture is communicated. It is equally worth mentioning that in as much as culture varies from one civilization and nation to another, the same variations of communication exist.

Often, there is an assumption that communication, otherwise rhetoric, is a social function possessing the same meaning to all people. However, research (Hecht, Jackson II, & Ribeau, 2003; Jackson II & Richardson, 2003; Asante & Mazama, 2002; Cummings & Roy, 2002) suggests it is not. The very existence of intercultural communication (Ting-Toomey & Chung, 2005) suggests different cultures throughout the world experience, conceptualize, and value rhetoric in a variety of ways that differ as much as they are similar. This becomes the fundamental basis for addressing the conceptualization of *Yurugu rhetoric*. Borrowing from Marimba Ani's (1994) conceptualization of Yurugu, Yurugu rhetoric examines the specific lineage and origins of White rhetoric that values, celebrates, and promotes persuasion by any means necessary and creates what is synonymous with Yurugu rhetoric as chaos rhetoric.

Imaginably, if rhetoric/communication is tied to culture, it is a part of the asili/seed/womb and thus, chaos rhetoric is likely found at the essence of the people otherwise considered White/Yurugu. While some may argue that Africans assisted in the development of linguistic form and function of verbal utterances upon the engagement of Whites/Yurugus, this research argues that long before the assistance from African people, the behavioral/performative aspects of White/Yurugu rhetoric were oriented in savagery stemming from chaos. Further, Amanishakete Ani

(2015) maintains, "The struggle, referring to the fight against racism and all forms of oppression creating chaos in the lives of African people, must become more discursively and methodically scientific" (p. 65). Accordingly, oriented in the findings of historical literary and textual research, Yurugu rhetoric/chaos rhetoric emerges popularly during the Greco-Roman era, extends through time as a self-propagandized basis for all human communication through literature and political rhetoric, and orients itself presently amidst what is offered by the U.S. President Donald J. Trump, in one of American popular cultures' most notable social media platforms: Twitter.

## Framing the Conceptualization of Yurugu Rhetoric

Marimba Ani's (1994) conceptualization of Yurugu is focused on a West African cosmological understanding of the Universe. It lends itself to the belief that Yurugu is the God of chaos and incompleteness, and thus produces discord, misperceptions, imbalance, maladaptive components, and paranoia. As such, Yurugu rhetoric is conceptualized as written, verbal, and behavioral (performative) chaos. What is more, this chaos rhetoric stems from the same incompleteness that fosters and encodes within its messages, elements of discord, misperceptions, imbalance, maladaptive components, and paranoia; thus producing a rhetoric of hatred and vileness echoing the characteristics of psychopathy and savagery.

The danger of Yurugu rhetoric, particularly in mass media and among national leaders, is that the national-level social discourse is presented as a standard of strength, certainty, and righteousness, but is usually unveiled over time as psychopathic delusions, fallacies, intentional falsehoods, maladaptive components, and an underlying intent to engage in oppression through savagery. The Greco-Roman (eventually becoming Eurocentric) era of rhetoric, through philosophical schools (Stoics, Epicureans, Cynics, and Skeptics) each orient themselves in Yurugu rhetoric. For example, the philosopher, Diogenes, aimed to live like a dog in an effort to accept all of humanity and animal-kind, an attempt at a sense of connection to nature and the cosmos that resulted in maladaptive behavior whereby he behaved more like a canine than human; hence the word *cynic* has etymological roots associated with the word, *canine* and *doglike*. The example of Diogenes and what is more, the Eurocentric philosophical schools, further affirms the spiritual incompleteness that reveals the anti-nature and anti-cosmos essence of Yurugu. Furthermore, the close observation and consideration of these accounts of evidence related to Yurugu, reveal the desperate necessity to savagely steal from the legacy of Africa as described by George James' (1954) *Stolen Legacy*.

Extending from this savagery then reveals the psychopathy that aims to proclaim the knowledge and achievements that were stolen as their own. Such claims as being the originators of rhetoric, arithmetic, chemistry, medicine, astrology, and so forth all become akin to the underdeveloped perspective, intelligence, and understanding of a petulant child—except Yurugu, irrespective of how they age physically, are eternal petulant children psychological orientations of reality steeped in psychopathy and savagery. This is the characterization of Yurugu incompleteness, chaos, psychopathy, and savagery in thought. However, from the thought comes the verbalized, written, and behavioral expressions that characterize Yurugu rhetoric.

The literary era of English Renaissance produced Shakespeare's (1985) MacBeth, lending itself to the characteristics of Yurugu rhetoric when Lady MacBeth laments as a result of blood stained hands as an utterance of her psychopathy riddled in guilt. As her chaos rhetoric is revealed in thought, word, and behavior, the evidence of Yurugu alongside Yurugu rhetoric is evident. What is more, *is* Shakespeare's Moor, Othello. Saturated by Greco-Roman/Eurocentric chaos rhetoric (Yurugu rhetoric), Othello slays his wife suspecting her unfaithful to him; a type of psychotic act performed primarily due to paranoia. Despite Othello's being a Moor, a term linked to a social identity that creates distinction from Whiteness, thus presuming his African-centeredness, his susceptibility to Yurugu rhetoric and the tactics of his comrades' agenda, through their use of Yurugu rhetoric- given their own psychopathy and savagery, suggests that although Yurugu is not the innate orientation of African and African-descended people, they are susceptible to it when saturated by the social norms and major venues of Yurugu. Thus, Othello's experience echoes the very definition of the theoretical conceptualization of *centric saturation*, proffered as, "the absence of identity negotiation resulting from an ethnocentric posture of the dominant culture as supreme; thus causing a person or group of people to become inescapably saturated by the dominant culture's social and societal norms as a secondary *origin of being-asilli* functioning as the conflicting co-primary source of a person or groups' culturally centered identity; thus creating identity confusion and disorder" (Selassie, 2016, p 2).

Transitioning further toward the present-day, the likes of national leaders such as Adolf Hitler characterize Yurugu rhetoric in psychopathic and savage statements such as, "Any alliance whose purpose is not the intention to wage war is senseless and useless" (Holmes, 2011, p. 57). Such a statement is an indication of Eurocentric values such as individualism, terrorism, and power through oppression. However, this is not isolated to Hitler as a national leader as much as it is the cultural legacy of Yuguru-true to the definition of the people who are incomplete spiritual beings and purveyors of chaos and discord. As such, Sam Page and Jason Dittmer (2016) suggests, "Like Andrew Jackson and George W. Bush, Trump's swaggering white capitalist presence asserts a masculine authority that Palin was never able to achieve" (p. 77); albeit the lack of achievement does not negate the sincere undertaking of the effort by Sarah Palin as well as Hillary Clinton, alongside many other Yurugu White women. Thus, the evidence of Yuguru and Yurugu rhetoric are not new to the existence of humankind in as much as the conceptualizations have become framed in educational philosophy in the same way that Donald Trump's particular style of chaos rhetoric is also not new. Page and Dittmer (2016) affirm this understanding stating, "Trump is therefore not entirely new; he is the most recent and vehement mutation for this resonance machine's racist ethos of existential revenge" (p. 77). Continuing in this legacy, is U.S. President Donald J. Trump.

Donald J. Trump's communication style and delivery are consistent with Yurugu rhetoric in a series of examples produced through social media's Twitter. For example, in reference to Mexico, Trump (2015) states, "….likewise, billions of dollars gets brought into Mexico through the border. We get the killers, drugs & crime, they get the money!" Other tweets about Mexico from Trump (2015) include, "I love the Mexican people, but Mexico is not our friend. They're killing us at the border and they're killing us all on jobs and trade. FIGHT!" Trump's fear of appearing weak and compromised, lends itself to the similar Yurugu rhetoric offered by Hitler, Diogenes, Lady MacBeth, and Othello in their various expressions of psychopathy.

In other twitter posts related to the United States of America, Trump (2016) states, "Our country is totally divided and our enemies are watching. We are not looking good, we are not looking smart, we are not looking tough!" This twitter post articulates a heighten sense of paranoia that is also associated with the psychopathy embedded in Yurugu rhetoric. These examples echo the misperceptions, paranoia, and maladaptive components of psychopathy and savagery associated with the chaos and incompleteness traditionally linked to Yurugu and extended to Yurugu rhetoric.

## The Relevance of Twitter and Tweeting as a Platform for Yurugu Rhetoric

While Twitter, as a social media platform may seem insignificant as a venue for examining the evidence of Yurugu rhetoric in a modern-day context, Lee and Lim (2016) suggests over the past decade Twitter has become a premiere public relations tool. Heavily utilized in the initial presidential campaign of then Senator Barack Obama, Twitter "emerged as an essential part of political campaigning in the U.S." (Lee & Lim, 2016, p. 849). As a social media venue within the field of mass communication, Twitter is revolutionizing the dynamics of U.S. political campaigns. In the first quarter of 2016, there are approximately 310 million monthly active Twitter users worldwide (Lee & Lim, 2016; Twitter, 2016). Twitter and other social media platforms offered President Barak Obama's use of African American/Black rhetoric, consistent with its spiritual principles such as nommo (the power of the spoken word to bring forth balance, harmony, and truth), were unfiltered accessing while the world; undoubtedly contributing to his campaign victories in 2008 and 2012.

Conversely, as a technological vehicle that abides by the will of its user, President Donald Trump uses Twitter to promote Greco-Roman/Eurocentric Yurugu rhetoric. According to Lee & Lim (2016), 42.4% of Trump's tweets were original (not retweets). Among Trump's original tweets, 47.5% "were retweeted citizen supporters' messages" (Lee & Lim, 2016, p. 853). Further characterizing the nature of Trump's Yurugu rhetoric through Twitter is the comparative account of Trump's tweets "that mock or criticize other candidates, media, or government" at four times the rate of his Yurugu-oriented counterpart, Senator Hillary Clinton (Lee & Lim, 2016, p. 853). Trump's ability to promote the power of persuasion through chaos (Yurugu) rhetoric that echoes the historic communicative style of the lineage and legacy of Yurugu appears to have triggered an awakening among Eurocentric people that "political correctness" had otherwise filtered, if not muted.

As such, Trump's Yurugu rhetoric in Twitter fostered a platform for Yurugu to openly express its innermost thoughts and feelings affirming bigotry, racism, and white privilege; thus, creating a venue whereby his Twitter is an interactive playground for psychopathy and savagery to be normalized. According to Lee and Lim (2016), "Research shows that candidates who used Twitter during the campaign received more votes than those who did not, particularly when Twitter was used in an interactive way" (p. 850). Consistent with Lee & Lim's (2016) statement, Page and Dittmer (2016) explain, "What Trump actually says or does matters less than what it is felt" (p. 77). These statements reiterate the significance of the connection Yuguru have to hearing, witnessing, experiencing, and affirming Yuguru rhetoric. This may appear insignificant at face-value, however framed in an understanding of Yurugu rhetoric, what becomes evident is President Trump's use of his social media influence to elevate psychopathy and savagery as a normalized social standard.

The tactical war strategies of *divide and conquer* are replaced by Trump's *divide and other* campaign approach. Trump's Yurugu rhetoric, specifically through Twitter, offers textual retweets affirming and elevating those willing to perpetuate his psychopathy and savagery with their own. For example, the Tweet from Donald Trump stating, "MAKE AMERICA GREAT AGAIN!" (Twitter, 2016), along with its 13,377 initial retweets and 28,153 likes implies reference to a time and era celebrating White male patriarchy while subjugating all others based upon the collective prejudice, racist, sexist, and bigoted statements he has made particularly during his campaign. The *othered*, are therefore perceived as foreign expendable objects that can be treated however the white-male-privileged feel. These others are: unattractive women, attractive women who refuse, resist, or have a disdain for being sexually assaulted (hence Trump's standard for the practice and acceptability of grabbing female genitals at-will), African-centered Blacks (Yurugu-oriented Blacks such as Diamond and Silk appear to be tolerable *others* by Trump and his white followers), immigrants of color, non-heterosexuals, and the disabled. These forms of Yurugu rhetoric as psychopathy and savagery "took up a quarter of Trump's tweets including attacks on other candidates (16.9%)" (Lee & Lim, 2016, p. 853). These accounts reaffirm the dangerous nature of Yurugu rhetoric as a normalized cultural standard of communication.

## Donald Trump, Twitter, and Yurugu Rhetoric

Donald Trump's Yurugu rhetoric is situated in the "high penetration rate [through all other media noise] and information-sharing nature, political candidates' tweets can reach [among] those who would be otherwise unreachable by conventional campaign tools" (Lee & Lim, 2016, p. 850). Furthermore, Trump's utilization of Twitter to weave an image as a champion for the politically incorrect and the foremost leader of matter-of-fact truth tellers was generally originated from his Twitter post. However, herein lies the basis for Yuguru rhetoric to galvanize an audience that has been muted by political correctness and recognized Donald Trump as the relational link to their voice becoming unmuted as well as mainstream social discourse. Thus, consistent with Lee and Lim's (2016) research, "Candidates use Twitter to create favorable images, inform potential voters of their policies, and build a strong relationship with them....Twitter is increasingly functioning as a major channel for candidates to communicate with voters through which they can develop their preferred images over the course of the campaign....Twitter may be now playing the role of traditional campaign websites" (pp. 849-851). The American media and self-aggrandizement of Donald J. Trump's Yurugu rhetoric echoes and is consistent with the lineage and legacy that generally begins during the Greco-Roman era and extends throughout history and into the present-day Euro-American-centered rhetoric.

## What Is There to Understand?

While the significance of Yurugu recognizes and prompts an African-centered understanding of the cognitive underpinnings of Whiteness through asili and Africentric analysis, Yurugu rhetoric recognizes and prompts an understanding and examination of how Greco-Roman, Eurocentric, Euro-American thought is expressed and manifests through written, verbal, and behavioral communication. The conceptualization of Yurugu rhetoric serves as a basis for African-centered people to assign a name to the observation of rhetoric that is contrary to Africanisms such as nommo (the power of the spoken word to bring forth balance, harmony, and truth), and even moreso as a basis for articulating with greater precision and accuracy what is perceived as chaos rhetoric alongside all of its ill components.

The manifestation of the otherwise ill components of Yurugu rhetoric are riddled throughout history and into the present as representations of psychopathy and savagery that are often not considered as such because they have been normalized into social order of what the dominant

Euro-American culture has weaved into the development of society. The Greco-Roman-Eurocentric philosophical schools, evidence from the literary work of William Shakespeare (MacBeth and Othello), and national social discourse of political tyrants such as Adolf Hitler and Donald Trump serve as the foremost evidence of Yurugu rhetoric. Through an African-centered perspective, the critical cultural lens guiding this investigation, it reveals facts and evidence that cultural disorientation through centric saturation cannot observe. The vileness of what Donald Trump offers through Twitter as a primary communications tool, whether he believes in what he is saying or not, echoes the incomplete chaos asili/seed/origin of Greco-Roman, Eurocentric, and presently Euro-American rhetoric – Yurugu rhetoric.

The understanding of communication and the cultural attributes associated with a respective cultures' communication is relevant to present-day mass media platforms that generally frame all communication within Eurocentrism. As this scholarly undertaking dissects the rhetorical trajectories stemming from the Greco-Roman era to present-day Euro-Americanism, the necessity to distinguish types of cultural communication is as equally significant as understanding the occurrence and effects of Yurugu rhetoric as a socialized societal norm. The hate speech and rhetorical savagery, alongside the rhetorical implications for the acceptability of physical sexual assault of women, points to a psychopathy that Donald J. Trump has otherwise brought unyieldingly back to the forefront of Yurugu common social practice and engagement. The survival of those who are not Yurugu, as *others,* rest upon the ability to discern Yurugu rhetoric in its forms of verbal, written, and behavior communication through all mass media venues as it becomes yet another tool for the African survival in a Yurugu-dominated world.

## References

Ani, Amanishakete (2015). Droppin' science for the struggle: A purposeful profile of professor Sylvester James Gates, Jr. in the era of the "New Jim Crow". *The Journal of Pan African Studies.* 8(6), 64-76

Ani, Marimba. *Yurugu: An African-centered Critique of European Cultural Thought and Behavior.* Trenton, NJ: Africa World, 1994. Print.

Asante, Molefi Kete, and Ama Mazama. *Egypt vs. Greece and the American Academy.* Chicago, IL: African American Images, 2002. Print.

Cummings, Melbourne S., and Abhik Roy. "Manifestations of Afrocentricity in Rap Music." *Howard Journal of Communications* 13.1 (2002): 59-76. Web.

Harris, Daryl B. (2011). Black politic here and now: Afrocentric essays on Black thought and struggle. *Unpublished manuscript*, Department of Political Science, Howard University, Washington, D.C.

Hecht, Michael L., Ronald L. Jackson, and Sidney A. Ribeau. *African American Communication: Exploring Identity and Cultural.* Mahwah, NJ: L. Erlbaum Associates, 2003. Print.

Jackson, Ronald L., and Elaine B. Richardson. *Understanding African American Rhetoric: Classical Origins to Contemporary Innovations.* New York, NY: Routledge, 2003. Print.

Lee, J., & Lim, Y. (2016). Gendered campaign tweets: The cases of Hillary Clinton and Donald Trump. *Public Relations Review, 42*(5), 849-855. doi:10.1016/j.pubrev.2016.07.004

Pages, S. and Dittmer, J. (2016) Donald Trump and the white-male dissonance machine. *Political Geography*, 54, 76-78. Doi:10.106/j.polgeo.2016.07.003

Potter, Nick. *William Shakespeare: Othello.* New York: Columbia UP, 2000. Print.

realDonaldTrump. (2015, June 30). I love the Mexican people, but Mexico is not our friend. They're killing us at the border and they're killing us all on jobs and trade. FIGHT! [Twitter post]. Retrieved from https://mobile.twitter.com/realDonaldTrump/status/615866741994954752

realDonaldTrump. (2015, July 13). ....likewise, billions of dollars gets brought into Mexico through the border. We get the killers, drugs & crime, they get the money! [Twitter post]. Retrieved from https://mobile.twitter.com/realDonaldTrump/status/620546522556534784

realDonaldTrump. (2016, March 12). MAKE AMERICA GREAT AGAIN! [Twitter post]. Retrieved from https://twitter.com/realDonaldTrump/status/708667676768522240

realDonaldTrump. (2016, July 17). Our country is totally divided and our enemies are watching. We are not looking good, we are not looking smart, we are not looking tough! [Twitter post]. Retrieved from https://mobile.twitter.com/realDonaldTrump/status/754788362368741376

Selassie, KenZoe Brian, J. (2016). What is this all over me? Understanding centric saturation and cultural identity orientation. *Unpublished manuscript*, Department of English, Foreign Languages, and Mass Communication, Benedict College, Columbia, S.C.

Shakespeare, William, and Alan Durband. *Macbeth: Modern English Version Side-by-side with Full Original Text*. Woodbury, NY: Barron's, 1985. Print.

Ting-Toomey, Stella, and Leeva C. Chung. *Understanding Intercultural Communication*. Los Angeles, CA: Roxbury Pub., 2005. Print.

World War II: The Definitive Visual History. (2011). Retrieved August 31, 2016, from https://books.google.com/books?id=H_ginDMhCsMC

# Chapter Six

## *Us Against Them*

### Conceptions of Cultural World Order And Ethnic Nationalism: Analysis of Trump's Naïve Realism

Jude Chinweuba Asike Ph.D.

**Abstract**

This work is an analysis Donald Trump's Political Utopianism, within the realm of international relations. Trump political sarcasm is indeed exacerbated in his ontological initiatives, which is based on the euphoria of nationalism in America. His political slogan of making America great again, is indeed a retrogression to the might of American history, as the center of excellence in the world. America is the center for the comity of nations, and head of economic world. Thus, America is always great, it is the greatest nation on earth, and Trump's amnesia of nationalism in America is a disconnection of their global importance in international relations. The perspectives on his political slogans, stipulates the transformatory imagination of idea of Brexit in America. He is purged to rebuild America through the deconstruction of American greatness, by disconnecting from NATO, and other American allies, building a wall along American/Mexican borders, and reparation of immigrants from America. On the literary level, all his erudite speeches are palatably very convincing and entertaining but cannot bring objective possibility of making America great. It takes on global moral responsibilities which resonate in exclusionary agenda. The commitment to the democratic principles of an international order which promotes the welfare of individual men and women will be relegated to the background if he becomes president. Thus, I am of the opinion that globalization represents America" greatness and cannot be hampered by some hazy ideological principles and hermeneutics as demanded by Trump.

* * *

The heightened conflict of culture in world politics is seen by some as the very reason why Trump is encouraging division in America. The forces of globalization are enhancing the speed and level of contact between diverse societies around the world. Interestingly, this has helped the world a great deal in communication and technologies. It brought the system of modernization, innovations, and creativity to all the members' civilizational identities. For some, on the other hand, globalization has negative effects and impact in the world, because, it agitates the differences between people of distinct cultural backgrounds. However, to Trump, this is simply an indication of animosity, fear and resentment of those who are different. Trump conceptualizes the concept of globalization as a means to exert group dominance, that is, as "a vehicle of domination, facilitating the projection of norms and institutions of more powerful cultures on the weaker" (Jacinta O'Hogan, 2002:188). Notwithstanding that his rhetorical stances during the presidential campaign alludes to the United States taking a more insular and isolationist view—as in America first and "I want to take my country back" (Trump 2016 on Fox News August, 2016).

However, for others, such as Hillary Clinton, who support globalization phenomena, "these processes facilitate interchange, reducing the differences between cultures and providing grounds for a common modern culture" (O'Hagan, J. 2002:186). During the 2016 presidential campaign, Hillary Clinton avoided appealing to nationalist symbols and instead sought to promote tolerance and cooperation. The forces of globalization, while expanding market driven economics to all corners of the earth, do not necessarily promote idea of cultural equality, but instead contribute to its opposite, which is the notion of hierarchy among cultures and ethnicities.

The main aim of this paper is to critically examine Trump's political ideology, its divisive calls to the civilizational identity of Nationalism in America. In so doing, it also examines the assumptions about culture in the context of nationalism and globalization in the states.

## Conceptual clarifications

- **Globalization**: Globalization refers to the period of coming together of cultures and economic systems around the world. It is a form of economic cooperation between nation states. It involves multinational corporations and improved media networks that facilitates business activity. In America, globalization brought tremendous advantages to their economic development.
- **Development**: Development is a relative concept, meaning different things to different people, but in the general sense, it relates to the idea of getting better, fuller and stronger in a society. It relates to the advancement of individuals, groups, or states via enhancements in skill, capacity, creativity, and freedom. Trump sees development in the sense of exclusiveness of non-related factors, like the deportation of immigrants, and disconnections of the allies from America.

- **Cultural Nationalism**: Cultural Nationalism is a socio-political philosophy of development that favors self-help activities for its respective group. Like democracy, it is an attitude of mind which propelled groups or citizens to live together as one. But it has the potential to be a hegemonic force of conflict among groups, whether within a nation state or across state boundaries and identity politics in any nation.

* * *

The heightened salience of culture in world politics is seen by some as a function of broader processes of change in world politics. The forces of globalization are bridging the gaps between different civilizational identities, and between diverse societies around the world. It brought a lot of innovations, creativity and modernization of cultures across the globe. Globalization is a culture of unity among nations, a cultural world order that comprises time and space; it reduces differences between cultures and providing grounds for a common modern culture. It is a convergence of potential coexistence of the world civilizational identities.

The nature of culture and its relevance to contemporary world order is deeply contested by trump in his presidential race campaign 2016. He sees culture as distinctively different from others and therefore needs to be immune with all the principles of exclusiveness. According to Trump, America needs to exclude themselves from others, under a cultural nationalism. Thus, in the very word of Trump, he says: "I want to take my country back" (Trump 2016, Fox News) He literally, wants to remove America from the other cultures without knowing that the United States is made up of coalition of states and immigrants across cultures. America is the greatest and cannot exclude itself from others.

What has prompted this resurgence of interest by Trump? Why have cultural factors become so prominent and appealing in explaining and understanding world politics? Fritz Gaenslen (1997) opined that:

When stable orders become unsettled and the grounds for collective identities are undermined or disturbed, issues relating to identity politics become pronounced.

Perhaps, Trump is capitalizing on this as the unsettled business of Globalization in which world politics has been undergoing a period of rapid flux and uncertain transformation. It is not clearly defined as a system of order when the political order or the bipolar system has been threatening by conflict and terrorism, from those who wish to dwell on civilizational identities politics. In considering this, Trump as well as Brexite set the pace for going back to cultural nationalism. Culture, as expressed through civilizational identities, structures relations between nation states of sovereignty. This perspective shifts the focus away from states as the foundation of the international and world order toward broader, culturally based communities. It shows that their interests are increasingly defined along cultural lines.

Despite the confidence shown by Trump in the homogenizing effects of the process of 'Independent Nationalism', his acknowledgement of the role that the concept of Americanization of Nationalism will play in shaping, if not ultimately determining, development indicates some tensions in this position. This raises the question of whether the concept of a single traditional identity could sustain the overall economic growth and industrialization in America. A vision of world order is drawn from the democratic structure of globalization in which Hilary is determining to build. According to Martin Wright (1966), asserts that:

> it is pluralistic, the correct world order is characterized by global international society that encompasses a variety of civilizational identities. It is multi-civilizational in membership ... and it has created a single, global political system and the context within which all civilizations function and interact.

Indeed, Trump's political naïve realism hinges on the fact that, he failed to realize the importance of the American state in relations to the comity of nations. Much of what provides the descriptive content of world order narratives appear to be happening in America. Increased interaction at the global communities is taking place in the states as well. United States is the center of the world economic community and cannot re-model its national policy from the global concerns to consolidated cultural nationalist ideology.

## CONCLUSION

The questions which are posed by the analysis of this work on civilizations and their symbolic frontiers are relevant to other forms of international relations. The extent to which interaction between conceptions of civilizational identities and broader assumptions about the nature of the cultural world order is important for studies of world politics as we enter a new millennium. It suggests the perceptions of possibilities for global political interactions, a policy of consolidation and homogenization within broad cultural communities. Presumably, assumptions of strong Universalist tendencies in civilizational interaction should be very imminent in the democratic structure of the United States of America, in which Trump wants to truncate in the act of cultural identities nationalism. His presumed policies are based on nationalistic ideology. It is retrogression to the development of America, and the world in general, because, it is feasible, and desirable, to establish a cultural world order that is pluralist. It is a culture of dialogic of a social construction rather than essentialized as fixed to be controlled by authoritarian head of superman.

Thus, the conceptual framework in which this paper is based is within the differing potentials for tightening the social bond within bounded communities and for exercising control over more extensive forms of political organization, is key elements of my inquiry into the supports of globalization as one world community. On this argument, Linklater corroborated as thus:

> It is possible to extend this further by arguing that liberal society ought to be open to the outside world because a commitment to

diversity and to a plurality of cultures is inherent in its character, but that it is not obliged to admit those who are hostile to its political beliefs or bound to absorb large numbers of outsiders without regard for the economic and social consequences (Linklater, 1998:80)

Here, proposition stands that the insiders and outsiders must be culturally or politically compatible, and there is no need to be unnecessarily hostile to the outsiders as depicted by Trump.

# REFERENCES

Fritz, G. (1997), "Advancing Cultural Explanations", in Valerie Hudson, eds. Culture and Foreign Policy (Boulder, Co: Lynne Rienner).
Hagan, J., (2002), Conflict, Convergence, or coexistence? The Relevance of Culture in Reframing World Order, edited by Falk R., Ruiz EJ, and Walker R.B.J, "Reframing the International" New York: Routledge
Huntington, S. (1993). Political Order in Changing Societies, New Haven: Yale University Press.
Linklater, A., (1998). The Transformation of Political Community, United States: University of South Carolina Press Columbia.
Martin, W. (1977). Systems of States, Leicester: Leicester University Press
Trump, D., (2016), "I want to take my country back" Campaign Slogan of Trumps in Fox News, USA, July 20, 2016.

# Chapter Seven

## *Islamophobia and Anti-Immigration*

### Capitalizing on Fear: Donald Trump's Immigration Policy in a Nutshell

#### Luqman M.I. Abdullah

When Donald J. Trump first announced his candidacy in 2015, most of the political elite, presidential scholars, and general public dismissed his bid as yet another shameless attempt at promoting his brand. Fast-forward one year, and Donald Trump has successfully managed to become the 45th President-elect of the United States of America, silencing nay-sayers and astonishing the international community. One reason for the widespread bewilderment at Trump's win is his long history of making outlandish, off-the-cuff statements that have made him both the object of public ridicule and support, but never before have his statements served as the potential basis for American domestic and foreign policy. What may be even more astonishing is that his meteoric political rise can be largely attributed to his controversial proposed policies concerning immigration.

Donald Trump's immigration policy proposals have been at the center of his rise to political power and a key feature of his presidential campaign. He has declared that the lack of secure national borders is a primary reason average Americans are "losing" and can't secure gainful employment. He has vowed to solve America's financial woes and bolster domestic job production by cracking down on illegal immigration and "putting America first." More often than not Trump's appeals to secure America's borders have entailed demeaning and degrading references to the Mexican immigrant community. Donald Trump's campaign rhetoric and policy statements regarding Mexican immigrant populations in the United States have often characterized them as criminal and violent. A prime example of this can be seen in is his depiction of Mexican immigrants in his presidential announcement speech on June 16, 2016:

> "When Mexico sends its people, they're not sending their best. They're not sending you. They're not sending you. They're sending people that have lots of problems, and they're bringing those problems with us. They're bringing drugs. They're bringing crime. They're rapists. And some, I assume and good people."[1]

Trump's broad characterizations of Mexican immigrants as criminals and deviants has served two primary purposes: It has stoked racially-based fears within the White community that their traditional socio-political dominance is in jeopardy due to an increasing minority presence in the country; and it has made an entire minority community the scapegoat for the American economic downturn initiated by the 2008 housing market collapse.

---

1   Donald J. Trump, Presidential Announcement Speech, June 16, 2016.

## The Brown Boogeyman: Manufacturing Fear

Sponsored initiatives vital to Trump's proposed immigration policy and "making American great again" are the construction of a massive border wall that would span the length of the southern U.S. – Mexican border and the deportation of an estimated 11 million undocumented Mexican immigrants. Mr. Trump's campaign website lists a Ten-Point Plan to "put America first" and tackle the problem of illegal immigration. The first point of the Plan is to "begin working on an impenetrable physical wall on the southern border, on day one. Mexico will pay for the wall."[2] The Mexican government has not agreed to any arrangement where they would pay for the construction of a border wall nor has there been any indication of forthcoming support. Actually constructing a massive physical barrier along the southern border of the United States harkens to mind images of previous containment efforts utilized by foreign governments and the desperate humanitarian conditions associated with them (i.e. Berlin Wall, Israel and the Palestinian West Bank, Apartheid South Africa, etc.).

The border wall would assumedly keep out all the dangerous and violent Mexicans who seek to wreak havoc in the US. Pandering to the fears of his audience remains a mainstay of Trump's tactical playbook. His campaign has harped on the few instances where immigrants have committed criminal acts upon US citizens to amplify and promote fear associated with immigrant populations. Such was the case with Juan Francisco Lopez-Sanchez, an undocumented immigrant who shot and killed US citizen Kate Stein on July 1, 2015 in San Francisco. Lopez-Sanchez had been deported several times in the past, but managed to return to America every time—a fact the Trump campaign highlighted as a glaring failure of US immigration policy and enforcement.

While this instance is unfortunate, it is far from representative of the vast majority of undocumented immigrants living in America. The Trump campaign's causal connection between increased immigrant levels

---

2 "Immigration," Donald J. Trump for President, accessed September 9, 2016, https://www.donaldjtrump.com/policies/immigration/.

and higher crime rates have been proven to be fallacy; in fact since the 1990's the trend has shown that as immigration levels have risen, overall crime levels have actually dropped.[3] A study conducted by the Congressional Research Service refutes the racially charged claims from the Trump camp:

> The Congressional Research Service found that the vast majority of unauthorized immigrants do not fit in the category that fits Trump's description: aggravated felons, whose crimes include murder, drug trafficking or illegal trafficking of firearms. CRS also found that non-citizens make up a smaller percentage of the inmate population in state prisons and jails, compared to their percentage to the total U.S. population.[4]

The American Immigration Council found similar results with its analysis:

> An analysis of 2010 Census data in a report from the American Immigration Council, a pro-immigration group, shows that 1.6 percent of immigrant males 18 to 39 years old were incarcerated, compared to 3.3 percent of native-born males. That disparity in incarceration rates has been consistent in the decennial Census since 1980, according to the report.[5]

Evidence shows that undocumented immigrants do not commit more violent or illicit crimes than their US citizen counterparts. Trump has

---

3  Michelle Ye Hee Lee, "Donald Trump's False Comments Connecting Mexican Immigrants and Crime," *The Washington Post*, July 8, 2015, accessed September 8, 2015, https://www.washingtonpost.com/news/fact-checker/wp/2015/07/08/donald-trumps-false-comments-connecting-mexican-immigrants-and-crime/.

4  Marc R. Rosenblum and William A. Kandel, "Interior Immigration Enforcement: Programs Targeting Criminal Aliens," *Congressional Research Service Report*, accessed October 3, 2016, http://fas.org/sgp/crs/homesec/R42057.pdf.

5  Walter Ewing, Daneil Martinez, and Ruben G. Rumbaut, "The Criminalization of Immigration in the United States," American Immigration Council Special Report, July 2015, accessed October 1, 2016, https://www.americanimmigrationcouncil.org/research/criminalization-immigration-united-states

been using this false-connection in order to stoke racialized fears of Latino immigrants "taking over the country" and displacing White Americans.

## LAST HIRED, FIRST FIRED: ECONOMIC SCAPEGOATING

Racial stereotyping of Mexican immigrants as "illegals" and "rapists" acts to dehumanize and criminalize an entire group of people and fosters and environment in which abuses of civil and human rights can easily occur. Such abuses have been documented throughout history. There are even cases of Presidentially sponsored programs seeking to get rid of undocumented Mexican nationals, primarily for political convenience. One such notorious program, codenamed "Operation Wetback" no less, has been praised by Donald Trump as a model of good immigration policy:

> "Dwight Eisenhower, a great president, moved 1.5 million illegal immigrants out of this country, moved them just beyond the border. They came back. Moved them again beyond the border, the came back. Didn't like it. Moved them way south. They never came back. The moved 1.5 million out. We have no choice."[6]

Throughout American history, during economic downturns popular White angst has been channeled into political activism by scapegoating communities of color as the culprits responsible for collective White economic grief and dissatisfaction. "Operation Wetback" serves as a prime example of this phenomenon. In response to an influx of immigrants coming from Latin America in the early 1950's and the growing perception that illegal immigrants were taking away employment opportunities from *deserving* Whites, the Immigration and Naturalization Service (INS) launched a deportation program entitled "Operation Wetback" in 1954. Under the leadership and design of INS Commissioner Gen. Joseph Swing, "Operation Wetback" was implemented with a coalition

---
6   Donald .J Trump, Republican Debate, Milwaukee, Wisconsin, Nov. 10, 2015.

of Border Patrol agents, local law enforcement, and the Mexican government to deport Mexican nationals who had entered the US without being processed.[7]

The operation was nationwide, spanning from Illinois to Texas and from Los Angeles to San Francisco, remaining in effect for 3 years. During just the first year of implementation, over one million arrests were made and several thousand other Latino immigrants returned to Mexico and Latin America for fear of persecution and prejudice faced in the United States.[8] An estimated 3.7 million Mexicans, many of them US citizens, were deported between 1954 and 1957.[9] Author Mary Romero weighs in by exclaiming, "an example of structural inequality, migrants in these circumstances are easy targets for manufactured racial panics and for the reinforcement of moral reform, regulation and social control."[10] The Trump campaign's admiration and open endorsement of such a policy should be alarming to anyone who supports the human rights of all people, regardless of immigration status. Donald Trump has embraced the tactic of racial fear mongering in order to 'manufacture' racial panics among his base of supporters in hopes that that fear will be enough to propel him into the White House.

The justification for inhumane treatment of Latino immigrants revolves around not only the hyper-accentuation of criminality being associated with these populations, but also the promoted view that their presence is a drain on the US economy, which is supported by hard working, "taxpaying" American citizens. Trump makes claims that "illegal" immigrants drain vital public resources such as social welfare aid, public education and

---

7   Erasmo Gamboa, *Mexican Labor and World War II: Braceros in the Pacific Northwest 1942-1947* (Austin: University of Texas Press, 1990).
8   Mae M. Ngai, *Impossible Subjects: Illegal Aliens and the Making of Modern America* (Princeton: Princeton University Press, 2004); Juan Ramon Garcia, *Operation Wetback: The Mass Deportation of Mexican Undocumented Workers in 1954* (Westport: Greenwood Press, 1980).
9   Steve Bender, *Greasers and Gringos* (New York: NYU Press, 2005).
10  Mary Romero, "Not A Citizen, Only A Suspect: Racialized Immigration Law Enforcement Practices," in *State of White Supremacy: Racism, Governance, and the United States,* eds. Moon-Kie Jung, Joao H. Costa Vargas, and Eduardo Bonilla-Silva (Stanford: Stanford University Press, 2011), 202.

hospital care, all without paying taxes back into the system that supports these benefits. Once again, the attacks leveled against the Latino immigrant community by the Trump campaign and his supporters are proven to be factually incorrect. Evidence shows that undocumented immigrants are far less likely than others to use expensive social services, including hospital emergency rooms. Indeed, unauthorized immigrants pay considerably more in taxes—typically through payroll withholding—than they receive in social services.[11] Ironically Mr. Trump has been embroiled in controversy surrounding his refusal to release his tax statements—a practice every presidential candidate has routinely embraced since the Great Depression. The New York Times recently acquired Mr. Trump's tax returns from 1995 and it was revealed that he had claimed losses to the tune of some $916 million that year. Reports show that by claiming a loss that substantial, Mr. Trump could have avoided paying federal taxes valued at $50 million a year for 18 years.[12] It would seem blatant hypocrisy and making continuous false statements have become defining features of his candidacy.

The Trump campaign is simply echoing the Eisenhower administration's policy and sentiment that Mexican immigrant communities are taking all the "good jobs" from otherwise *deserving* American workers and families. Trump claims that if elected he will stop the job drain from occurring and his plan would "boost wages and ensure open jobs are offered to American workers first."[13] A team of researchers took this claim to task in their 2016 report entitled, *The Economic and Fiscal Consequences of Immigration*. One view concerning the impact of immigrant labor on

---

11  Ian Haney-Lopez, *Dog Whistle Politics: How Coded Racial Appeals Have Reinvented Racism and Wrecked the Middle Class* (Oxford: Oxford University Press, 2014), 122; M. Kathleen Dingeman & Ruben G. Rumbaut, "The Immigration-Crime Nexus," *University of LaVerne Law Review* 363 (31) (2010).

12  David Barstow, Susanne Craig, Russ Buettner, and Meghan Twohey, "Donald Trump Tax Records Show He Could Have Avoided Taxes for Nearly Two Decades, The Times Found," *New York Times,* October 2, 2016, accessed October 3, 2016, http://www.nytimes.com/2016/10/02/us/politics/donald-trump-taxes.html.

13  Julia Preston, "Immigrants Aren't Taking American's Jobs, New Study Finds," New York Times, September 21, 2016, accessed October 2, 2016, http://www.nytimes.com/2016/09/22/us/immigrants-arent-taking-americans-jobs-new-study-finds.html.

native-born American workers was clearly expressed by Dr. Francine Blau, economics professor at Cornell University, "We found little to no negative effects on overall wages and employment of native-born workers in the longer term."[14]

## HYPOCRITE-IN-CHIEF?

The incredulous fact about Mr. Trump's claims against immigrants is not just that they are often false, but that his own business practices are in contradiction to his professed policy views. Trump repeatedly admonishes China for economic practices he feels undermines the American dollar and hurts American job creation. He stresses that his proposed policies will put "American workers first" and prioritize their employment, however according to a Newsweek investigation, Mr. Trump has opted to purchase the steel used in two of his last major construction projects from Chinese manufactures instead of those based in the United States.[15] Newsweek reporter Kurt Eichenwald exclaims:

> "...Trump has been stiffing American steel workers on his own construction projects for years, choosing to deprive untold millions of dollars from four key electoral swing states and instead directing it to China—the country whose trade practices have helped decimate the once-powerful industrial center of the United States."[16]

So while Trump campaigns in Rust Belt states like Wisconsin, Ohio, and Michigan, his promises of renewed investment and growth in the manufacturing sectors that made those state economies once flourish, are in direct contradiction to his very own business practices of choosing foreign labor over employing American workers. Yet another glaring

---

14 Ibid.
15 Kurt Eichenwald, "How Donald Trump Ditched US Steel Workers in Favor of China," *Newsweek*, October 3, 2016, accessed October 3, 2016, http://www.newsweek.com/how-donald-trump-ditched-us-steel-workers-china-505717.
16 Ibid.

hypocrisy found between the rhetoric and practice of Donald Trump.

Trump's denigration of immigrant groups is not exclusive to persons of Latino descent, in fact a significant part of his immigration policy is reliant upon xenophobic attitudes expressed toward an entire group of people based on their religious choice, in this case Islam. Since the September 11, 2001 attacks and the subsequent 'War on Terror' launched by the Bush administration, heightened fear of attack by extremist actors claiming allegiance to radical Islamic organizations has permeated American society. Terrorist acts in Boston, California, and New York have added fuel to the fire of debates on how to address the concern of growing attacks sponsored by foreign-born perpetrators. Mr. Trump has pounced on the opportunity to exploit the fears of his supporters by proposing immigration policies that would reverse over 100 years of American immigration progress. On December 5, 2015, following the tragic shootings in San Bernardino, California, Trump issued this statement on his campaign website:

> "Donald J. Trump is calling for a total and complete shutdown of Muslims entering the United States until our country's representatives can figure out what is going on."

His bombastic statements seek to regress our country to a time when the national immigration policy restricted acceptable immigrants to "free white persons of good moral character"[17] (in which case Trump himself may be deemed inadmissible). Closing the national borders to people simply based on their religious preference is completely against the values expressed in the Constitution of the United States. Mr. Trump has also stated that he would implement a Muslim registry database that would track all Muslims present in the country as a way to combat terrorism. His audacious statements have drawn widespread criticism from those of both sides of the political spectrum, including a statement from a former contender for Republican presidential nominee, Jeb Bush:

---

17   United States Naturalization Law of March 26, 1790 (1 Stat. 103).

"You talk about internment, you talk about closing mosques, you talk about registering people. That's just wrong. I don't care about campaigns. It's not a question of toughness. It's to manipulate people's angst and their fears. That's not strength, that's weakness."[18]

While conflagrations in Syria and the Middle East have raised concerns of 'terrorist' supporters in the US, painting an entire religious group as extremists only serves to alienate those who could be of integral assistance in defeating groups that seek to harm Americans. Although there have been cases of 'terrorist' acts being carried out by religious extremists sympathetic to groups like ISIL or Al-Qaeda, the majority of mass shootings that have taken place on American soil have been committed by American citizens who do not identify as Muslim. The Trump campaign has yet to characterize the murderous actions carried out by American White supremacist Dylann Roof as "terrorist," in spite of the fact he shot and killed nine Black parishioners in a historic Black Church after joining them for Bible study. The double standard is obvious and the hypocrisy is real—Donald Trump is using bigotry and xenophobia to lure supporters into his camp, with nothing more than racist rhetoric and false claims. A tactic that has unfortunately proved effective enough to earn Mr. Trump the title of President-elect. One can only hope the gravity and import of the office he will soon occupy impose appropriate restraint on his behavior and rhetoric, or the nation will face the consequences.

---

18  Vaughn Hillyard, "Donald Trump's Plan for Muslim Database Draws Comparison to Nazi Germany," *NBCNews*, November 20, 2015, accessed October 2, 2016, http://www.nbcnews.com/politics/2016-election/trump-says-he-would-certainly-implement-muslim-database-n466716.

## References

Barstow, David, Susanne Craig, Russ Buettner, and Meghan Twohey. "Donald Trump Tax Records Show He Could Have Avoided Taxes for Nearly Two Decades, The Times Found." *New York Times,* October 2, 2016. Accessed October 3, 2016. http://www.nytimes.com/2016/10/02/us/politics/donald-trump-taxes.html.

Bender, Steve. *Greasers and Gringos.* New York: NYU Press, 2005.

Dingeman, M. Kathleen & Ruben G. Rumbaut. "The Immigration-Crime Nexus." *University of LaVerne Law Review* 363 (31) (2010).

Eichenwald, Kurt. "How Donald Trump Ditched US Steel Workers in Favor of China." *Newsweek.* October 3, 2016. Accessed October 3, 2016. http://www.newsweek.com/how-donald-trump-ditched-us-steel-workers-china-505717.

Ewing, Walter, Daneil Martinez, and Ruben G. Rumbaut. "The Criminalization of Immigration in the United States." *American Immigration Council* Special Report, July 2015. Accessed October 1, 2016. https://www.americanimmigrationcouncil.org/research/criminalization-immigration-united-states.

Gamboa, Erasmo. *Mexican Labor and World War II: Braceros in the Pacific Northwest 1942-1947.* Austin: University of Texas Press, 1990.

García, Juan Ramon. *Operation Wetback: The Mass Deportation of Mexican Undocumented Workers in 1954.* Westport: Greenwood Press, 1980.

Haney-Lopez, Ian. *Dog Whistle Politics: How Coded Racial Appeals Have Reinvented Racism and Wrecked the Middle Class.* Oxford: Oxford University Press, 2014.

Hillyard, Vaughn. "Donald Trump's Plan for Muslim Database Draws Comparison to Nazi Germany." *NBCNews.* November 20, 2015. Accessed October 2, 2016. http://www.nbcnews.com/politics/2016-election/trump-says-he-would-certainly-implement-muslim-database-n466716.

Lee, Michelle Ye Hee. "Donald Trump's False Comments Connecting Mexican Immigrants and Crime." *The Washington Post*, July 8,

2015. Accessed September 8, 2015. https://www.washingtonpost.com/news/fact-checker/wp/2015/07/08/donald-trumps-false-comments-connecting-mexican-immigrants-and-crime/.

Ngai, Mae M. *Impossible Subjects: Illegal Aliens and the Making of Modern America*. Princeton: Princeton University Press, 2004.

Preston, Julia. "Immigrants Aren't Taking American's Jobs, New Study Finds." *New York Times*, September 21, 2016. Accessed October 2, 2016. http://www.nytimes.com/2016/09/22/us/immigrants-arent-taking-americans-jobs-new-study-finds.html.

Romero, Mary. "Not A Citizen, Only A Suspect: Racialized Immigration Law Enforcement Practices," in *State of White Supremacy: Racism, Governance, and the United States*, eds. Moon-Kie Jung, Joao H. Costa Vargas, and Eduardo Bonilla-Silva. Stanford: Stanford University Press, 2011.

Rosenblum, Marc R. and William A. Kandel. "Interior Immigration Enforcement: Programs Targeting Criminal Aliens." *Congressional Research Service Report*. Accessed October 3, 2016. http://fas.org/sgp/crs/homesec/R42057.pdf.

United States Naturalization Law of March 26, 1790 (1 Stat. 103).

# Chapter Eight

## *Radical Conservatism*

### "Making America Great Again" The Return of Conservative Political Thinking: Rhetoric that Attempts to Marginalize Black Social Movements

### Justin Gammage, Ph.D.

In light of the election of Donald Trump and the momentum of the Movement for Black Lives, it is essential to assess if the concerns of Black social movements are addressed in Trump's political platform. This research examines Donald Trump's political rhetoric and discusses how his economic strategy marginalizes the core of Black social movements. It is worth noting that the candidates for both the Democratic and Republican parties fail to accurately address the economic needs of African Americans, however special attention is given to Trump's platform given his sizeable victory and his statements about the contemporary Black Lives Matter Movement.

This chapter explores what "Making American Great Again" means for African Americans and those advancing the history of social activism for the African American communities. I will explore the political platform and the positions that Donald Trump makes on revitalizing the United States economy. This work also attempts to locate Trump's political strategy for addressing underrepresented communities. Lastly, this chapter assesses the feasibility of Trump's platform for the revitalization of the collective African American community.

## STATING THE PROBLEM

*"One of the most heated scholarly controversies in the area of racial equality and social justice over the past two decades concerns the dispute over the nature, causes, and meaning of economic changes occurring within the black community. The way in which one views these changes has enormous inherent implications for social policy."*

**(OLIVER AND SHAPIRO, 2006; 94)**

The permanent economic depression which characterizes the Afrikan American community is in good part an outcome of American social history, particularly of historical White-Black race relations. These relations have been and are such that the largest number of Afrikan Americans have been excluded from full and equal participation in the American social-economic-political system. They are deliberately excluded by White racism from equal employment, equal access to capital resources, equal opportunities to develop their economic resources, and equal opportunity to reside and work in areas where economic growth and development is advancing instead of stagnating or rapidly declining. (Wilson,1998)

African Americans have historically been engaged in social movements to preserve their humanity and protect their social, political, educational and economic rights. These movements have targeted institutions that attempt to restrict African Americans access to economic, educational, housing and political resources. The validity of these movements has been under scrutiny by those that benefit from the institutionalization of white supremacy. The aims of these movements have been to deconstruct systems rooted in oppression and construct avenues for new possibilities and equitable structures. The discourse around improving the lives of African Americans has sought to develop strategies to acquire and actualize economic and political power. While African Americans continue a legacy of activism, its best understood within the context of a Pan African liberation movement. The Haitian revolution, the creation of independent Maroon communities, the abolishment of slavery in North American, the deconstruction of Apartheid South Africa, and the contemporary Black Lives Matter movement demonstrates the global scope and continuity of this movement. There has been forward gains from this movements, however white supremacy continues to be woven in the fabric of American society and deep seeded in its international affairs. Thus, progress does not mean arrival. The current Black Lives Matter movement (BLM) is an illustration of the reoccurring issue of racism.

During the presidential campaign, Donald Trump weighed in on the plight of the African American community. Both liberal and conservative political ideology suggest that if given an opportunity, African Americans, and other marginalized communities, would achieve in the area of economics and education. While right wing politics acknowledges the influence of structural barriers limiting many African Americans, the conservative perspective suggest that those that achieve and excel in society are a reflection of their investment in their human capital. Conservative political thinking fails to recognize past and present manifestations of white supremacy and its affect on the life chances of people of African descent.

The rich history of African Americans committed to social movements begs the question; When was America Great for African Americans? While African Americans have contributed to the advancement of the United States, the social and economic ills that face African Americans are still strongly rooted in American "culture". When contextualizing African

American's economic reality, we find that the problem of poverty is staggering. More than 150 years removed from enslavement and fifty years from civil rights legislation and the proposed "War on Poverty" sponsored by the United States government, the issue of racial equality remains to be unsolved. Society still harvests a mixed legacy of racial progress (Oliver and Shapiro, 2006). Although African Americans have made invaluable progress in advancing education, intellectual discourse, civil rights legislation, innovational engineering, and political discourse, African American economics remains largely distressing. Only a small percentage of the African American population has been able to take advantage of economic opportunities now available for some (Oliver and Shapiro, 2006). It's argued by some economists that a comparative socioeconomic analysis of African American economics reveals that African American people entered the 21st century the same way they entered the 20th, impoverished, powerless, and neglected (Anderson, 2001). Currently, African Americans make up slightly more than 13 percent of the total American population but collectively control less than 3 percent of the nation's net worth and only 1.3 percent of the nation's financial assets. Even more alarming, 79 percent of African American households live with precarious resources and more than 63 percent retain zero or negative net financial assets (Oliver and Shapiro, 2006). The Survey of Income and Program Participation (SIPP), a national survey, tells us that 73 percent of all African American children grow up in households without financial resources (Oliver and Shapiro, 2006). These findings become much more significant when statistics suggest that individuals whose parents do not have financial resources are disproportionately more likely not to control wealth accumulating assets. (Chiteji and Frank, 1999)

In response to the collective economic reality of African Americans, social movements geared toward advocating a structural shift of this reality, have included a strong economic agenda. Many social movements of the past have focused on education as a means to making economic resources available for African Americas. The trend of community and economic development is still rooted in contemporary movements. A look at past and present movements that have developed demands for economic development demonstrates the centrality of access to economic resources for Black social movements.

## History of Addressing African Americans Economic Needs

Various shifts in America's political, social, and economic landscape have led to a unique approach to address African American economic development. Despite institutional racism, African Americans have organized to preserve their economic security. Even during the period of enslavement, African Americans formed cooperatives such as the Free African Society established in Philadelphia in 1787, led by Abalom Jones and Richard Allen (Ofari, 1970) to address their economic needs. By 1838, there were an estimated one hundred similar cooperatives in Philadelphia alone geared toward providing mutual aid for African Americans communities (Ofari, 1970). In 1832, free African Americans throughout the nation held the Black Convention to discuss the needs of African Americans, their security, freedom and economic stability. The philosophies of Fredrick Douglass, Henry Highland Garnet, Booker T. Washington, WEB DuBois, Marcus Garvey, Callie House etc. all contributed to a movement of resistance and African American self-sufficiency. The literature focusing on African American economic development identifies three major areas of interest: Entrepreneurial movement; community development cooperatives; and campaigns for cooperative spending. Thus, this section of the literature review explores the development of each component of African American economic development.

Among the literature reviewed, entrepreneurship played a significant role in the movement for African American economic development. Arthur Lewis identifies the functions of entrepreneurship as supplying capital; organizing production and marketing; and bearing uninsurable risks; (Lewis, 1985; 78). Robert Woodson argues that the legacy of entrepreneurship has been the backbone of the African American quest for economic development (Woodson, 1998; 6). African Americans' resistance to economic discrimination and exploitation during enslavement fostered their community with hundreds of lucrative businesses in the North and the South. According to Woodson, in the 17th and 18th centuries African Americans owned and operated inns, stables, construction firms, barbershops, tailoring and catering establishments, restaurants and taverns (Woodson, 1998; 6). At the eve of the Civil War, African American business owners had an estimated wealth of $25–$50 million in the South and $25 million in the North (Woodson, 1998; 2). At the turn of the 20th century African Americans were collectively worth $700 million (Woodson, 1998; 6).

In 1900, African American Entrepreneurship took to the forefront of economic development with the push of Booker T. Washington and the founding of the National Negro Business League (NNBL). The NNBL assisted with the growth of African American businesses. Cities such as Mound Bayou, Mississippi; Nicodemus, Kansas; and Boley, Oklahoma were all formed by way of the entrepreneurial movement among African American business owners (Woodson, 1998; 6). With booming economic enclaves throughout specific sectors of the nation, entrepreneurship was central to African American employment and wealth accumulation.

Amos Wilson also discusses the importance of entrepreneurship in regards to African American development. Wilson contends that the development of African American businesses assisted with economic stability. Like many economic scholars, Wilson regards the African American community as a separate entity (Douglass, 1852; Tabb, 1970; Anderson, 2001). He argues that entrepreneurial endeavors would help aid against the various shifts and changes in America's economy and the larger global economy. Wilson suggests that entrepreneurship and business cooperatives would assist with addressing African Americans' economic and political crisis. He suggests that without a strong network of businesses stirred by business cooperatives and entrepreneurship, the shifts of the United States economy specifically, and the global market in general, would have the ability to devastate entire communities. He refers to the effects that General Motors (GM) had on African American employment opportunities after moving its manufacturing plants to Korea. As a result of GM's contract with a Korean automobile manufacturer to produce subcompact, thousands of jobs were eliminated, thus disturbing a significant number of African American families.

While GM is only one multinational corporation, the move to outsource foreign labor has become common among corporations within the past three decades. The declining manufacturing and service sectors of the economy has left African Americans incessantly vulnerable to debt, poverty, and economic dependency (Wilson, 1998). The State of Black America, the annual report of the National Urban League, contends that African Americans rely primarily on income.

The still heavy dependence of African Americans on the manufacturing sector of the economy and on the service sectors, which are likely to decline in the near future, means that there is a "bad fit" between the current distribution of the African American work force and the reconfiguring industrial and service base (Wilson, 1993). Outsourcing has directly impacted the U.S. economy and shifted economic growth in the African American community. The literature reveals that dependence on multinational corporations at the expense of entrepreneurship has limited opportunities and competitiveness of the African American business sector.

Claude Anderson's Powernomics modal also argues that African American entrepreneurship is a vital component for economic empowerment. Although Anderson asserts that the majority of African American owned businesses are only stable enough to employ the owner, he states that business development by way of entrepreneurship would lead to an independent African American economy. Anderson stresses the need for the African American community to strive to form ethnic enclaves and a Black Nationalist ideology. He states that if Blacks had become production-oriented rather than consumption-oriented; it is quite unlikely that today they would not have a hidden national unemployment rate of 34 percent (Anderson, 2001; 74). While Anderson recognizes the need for

African American business development, he argues that without collective communal consciousness, African American businesses would serve no purpose but for individual advancement. He asserts that all functions within the African American community should be owned and controlled by African Americans. To address this concern, many contemporary Black social movements have began to incorporate initiatives that center on African Americans' economic independence.

## BLM Outlining the Concerns of African Americans

The Black Lives Matter movement is a direct extension of the Civil Rights and the Black Power movement of the 1950s and 60s. The core principles of the movement rest on a platform to address the shooting deaths of unarmed African Americans and excesses and misuse of force by law enforcement when policing African Americans. In addition, it expands its scope to critically analyze the systematic attack on Black Life and the criminalization African Americans. Cofounder of the Black Lives Matter movement Alicia Garza, states BLM is "an ideological and political intervention in a world where Black lives are systematically and intentionally targeted for demise. It is an affirmation of Black folks' contributions to this society, our humanity, and our resilience in the face of deadly oppression."

BLM is a continuum of a Pan African liberation movement that interrogates a system of thought that adopts a race-based, gender-based, sexual orientation-based value system that reinforces the normalization of European culture. In essence, it seeks to act as a venue to organize and invoke structural and transformative change to society at the federal, state and local levels. In large part, it is a grass-root force that has national and international appeal.

Of the 39 branches recognized by its official organization, 4 local branches have produced organizational demands that seek to address the needs of the African American community with respect to the organization's mission. In addition, a collaborative organization, the Movement for Black Lives, also produced demand in November 2016. Demands developed by the local branches were largely focused on reforming policing policy and addressing increasing incarceration rates of African Americans. However, of the demands not focusing on the criminal justice system, nearly 70% focused on addressing strategies for addressing African Americans' economic development. A third of the national demands focused on funding African American community development. I conclude that economics is a central concern for addressing African American needs.

To illustrate the significance of economic development, the Long Beach branch of Black Lives Matter demands "We Want Full Employment For Our People. Every individual has the human right to employment and a living wage. Inability to access employment and fair pay continues to marginalize our communities, ready us for imprisonment, and deny us of our right to a life with dignity." All demands constructed by the Cambridge branch of Black Lives Matter focus on housing and access to housing resources. The Chicago branch demands the defunding of policing entities and investment in community resources. Lastly the national demands include a platform for divestment and investment and reparations, which primarily focuses on education.

## Assessing Trump's Economic Platform

*"I have also made a center-piece of my economic revitalization plan the largest middle class tax cut since Ronald Reagan –and the largest regulatory reform in American history. That is because I know how overtaxed and overregulated the working people of this country are"*

**-Trump, 2016**

*"I am running to represent Americans – and we are going to make America Rich Again."*

**–Trump 2016**

Donald Trump's positions himself as the candidate best fit to address the nations economic challenges as well as solve the needs of African

Americans. He references Ronald Reagan's economic platform geared towards tax cuts as a means to revitalizing the domestic economy. When observing his political platform, Trump's strategy proposes to provide tax cuts for low-income and middle-income families. The four critical points of Trump's economic platform are:

- Create a dynamic booming economy that will create 25 million new jobs over the next decade.
- For each 1 percent in added GDP growth, the economy adds 1.2 million jobs. Increasing growth by 1.5 percent would result in 18 million jobs (1.5 million times 1.2 million, multiplied by 10 years) above the projected current law job figures of 7 million, producing a total of 25 million new jobs for the American economy.
- Reform policies with a pro-growth tax plan, a new modern regulatory framework, an America-First trade policy, an unleashed American energy plan, and the "penny plan."
- Boost growth to 3.5 percent per year on average, with the potential to reach a 4 percent growth rate.

It must be noted that Trump's political platform contradicts the business model that he has implemented for his own businesses. Trump's business model largely reflects economic policy produced during the Reagan administration. To place Reagan's economic plan into historical context, during his administration, the African American community took one of the hardest economic down turns in history. Some argue that the African American communities have yet the recover from the relocation of manufacturing plants overseas. As stated above, GM's, as well as other large plants relocating from urban communities, was a direct result of free-market domestic policy that primarily benefitted the wealthy elite. Yet, Trump boasts of his business success, which is rooted in Reaganomics.

Donald Trump's economic plan, much like his opponent, ignores the historical practice of white supremacy and operates with the assumption that African American economic security rests in opportunities. While this is partially true, a central issue challenging African Americans economic stability is systematic barriers that bare their access to wealth.

Moreover, a plan that fails to address the systems that help to produce poverty will fall short of addressing poverty. Trump argues, "My economic agenda is very simple: jobs, jobs, jobs. The problems we face as a country are immense, and it is going to take bold action to turn things around." Income is essential for the accumulation of wealth; however, research reveals that intergenerational transfer of wealth from one generation to the next is the single most important factor that contributes to familial wealth. Thus, the creations of jobs will not solely address poverty or African Americans' economic needs. A critical question to ask is, if African Americans have collectively only held a small portion of wealth, how can African Americans be made rich again?

Historical social movements geared toward developing new radical alternative to address African American needs have been largely ignored by political candidates and heavily criticized by Trump. Of the current Black Live Matter movement, Trump condemns the efforts of these movements and labels them terrorist activity. Trump states,

> Those peddling the narrative of cops as a racist force in our society – a narrative supported with a nod by my opponent – share directly in the responsibility for the unrest in Milwaukee, and many other places within our country. They have fostered the dangerous anti-police atmosphere in America. Every time we rush to judgment with false facts and narratives – whether in Ferguson or in Baltimore – and foment further unrest, we do a direct disservice to poor African Americans residents who are hurt by the high crime in their communities.
> -Trump 2016

While many attribute the Black Live Matter movement with the fight against police corruption, it must be acknowledged for its continuation of past movements committed to addressing economic development. The economic needs of African Americans begin with a commitment to uproot systems of oppression that devalue the lives of African Americans. This devaluation includes, but is not limited to, their physical lively, cultural space, and the value of their assets (property, businesses, degrees, etc.).

A platform that fails to address the racialized system that ascribes value based on race will never address African Americans' economic needs. To address Trump's question to the African American community, "To those African-Americans suffering in our country I say: What do you have to lose? Vote For Donald Trump. I will fix it." I say, history says different. We have seen this model before and its unfit for structural change. This is the exact mission of the Black Lives Matter movement, to force structural change in American institutions in order to bring about a radical shift in the current racial order of America. Therefore, it is imperative that any person running for the office of president, and attempts to advocate on behave of the African American, be fully vested in working to change.

## REFERENCES

Anderson, C. (2001) Powernomics: The National Plan to Empower Black America. Bethesda, MD: PowerNomics Corporation of America.

Black Lives Matter Long Beach, (n.d.). Demands: Black Lives Matter Long Beach. Retrieved December 29, 2016, from https://blacklivesmatterlbc.wordpress.com/demands/.

Black Lives Matter Chicago, (n.d.). Demands of BLMCHI. Retrieved December 29, 2016, from http://www.blacklivesmatterchicago.com/demands.html.

Black Lives Matter Cambridge, (n.d.). #AFFORDABLE 25. Retrieved December 29, 2016, from https://www.blmcambridge.org/affordable25/.

Black Lives Matter Toronto, (n.d.). Demands: Black Lives Matter Toronto. Retrieved December 29, 2017, from https://blacklivesmatter.ca/demands/

Chiteji, N. S. and Stafford F. P. (1999). Portfolio Choices of Parents and Their Children as Young Adults: Accumulation by African-American Families. The American Economic Review. Vol. 89, No. 2, May. p. 377 – 380.

Douglass, F. (1852, July 5). What to the slave is the fourth of July. Retrieved from http://www.freemaninstitute.com/douglass.htm

Garza, A. (n.d.). A Herstory of the #BlackLivesMatter Movement. Retrieved December 29, 2016, from http://blacklivesmatter.com/herstory/.

Lewis WA. (1985). Racial conflict and economic development. Cambridge, MA: Harvard University Press.

Marable, M. (2000). How Capitalism Undeveloped Black America. Cambridge, MA: South End Press.

Movement for Black Lives, (November 2016). Platform: Demands. Retrieved December 28, 2016, from https://policy.m4bl.org.

Nembhard, J.G. (2008). Alternative Economics: A Missing Component in the African American Studies Curriculum: Teaching Public Policy and Democratic Community Economics to Black

Undergraduate Students. Journal of Black Studies, May Vol. 38 No. 5 p. 758-782.

Nembhard, J.G. (2004). Cooperative Ownership in the Struggle for African American Economic Empowerment. Humanity and Society. August Vol. 28, No. 3.

Ofari, E. (1970). The Myth of Black Capitalism. New York, NY: Monthly Review Press.

Oliver, M. L. and Shapiro T. (2006). Black Wealth White Wealth: A New Perspective on Racial Inequality. New York, NY: Routledge.

Tab, W. K. (1970). Perspectives on Back Economic Development. Journal of Economic Issues, December Vol. 4, No. 4, p. 68-81.

Trump, D. (September 28, 2016) Trump Remarks in Waukesha, Wisconsin: Follow The Money. Retreived October 8, 2016 from https://www.donaldjtrump.com/media/category/speeches

Trump, D. "Economy: Donald J. Trump's Vision" *Donald J. Trump for President* (October 8, 2016). https://www.donaldjtrump.com/policies/economy/.

Wilson, A. N. (1998). Blueprint for Black Power: A Moral, Political and Economic Imperative for the Twenty-First Century. New York NY: Afrikan World InfoSystems.

Woodson, R. L. (1987). On the Road to Economic Freedom: An Agenda for Black Progress. Washington, DC: Regnery Gateway.

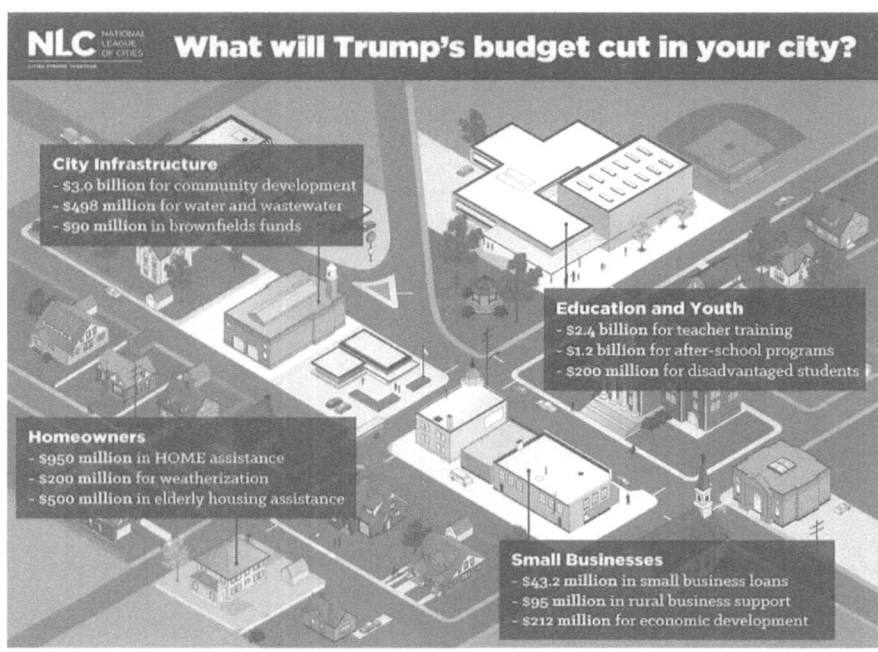
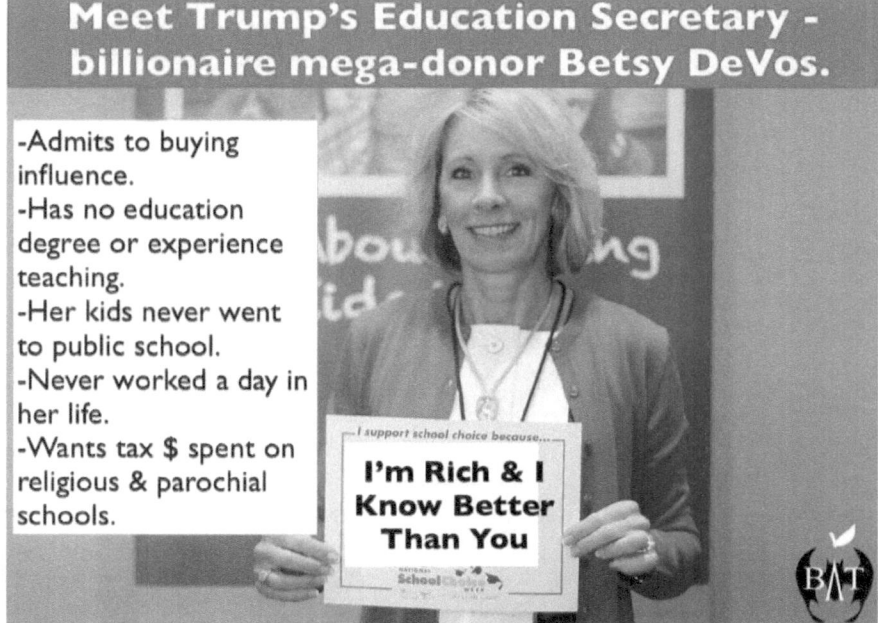

# CHAPTER NINE

## *Anti-Intellectualism and For Profit Education*

### Will Every Child Count? Exploring What Early Childhood and Gifted Children of Color Risk Losing Under a Trump Administration

#### Brian L. Wright, Ph.D.; Jemimah L. Young, Ph.D.; Donna Y. Ford, Ph.D.

Donald J. Trump's ascension to the presidency of the United States of America prompted many to see it as a stunning repudiation of the establishment and long-held ideas of American democracy, and to question what it will mean for the nation's children, especially those from underserved, underrepresented, and historically marginalized groups? Will systems, policies, and practices under his new leadership increase disparities in ways that further divide our most vulnerable citizens—children—and especially those who are low-income and/or non-White? Will every child count, regardless of her and his race and life circumstances, under Trump's administration? Or will the perpetuation of unequal and inequitable education allocations manifest more for children and families whose racial backgrounds, incomes, cultures, languages, and the like, differ from that of White, rich, and middle-class children? These and other questions weigh heavy on the minds of countless Americans, especially those on the front lines to ensure equitable, accessible, affordable, and high-quality preschool for all children, along with access to gifted education.

Rigorous educational experiences early in life lay the foundation for success in formal schooling, and also increase the likelihood that students will be advanced learners who require more challenging curriculum offered in gifted education classes. However, when students live in poverty and are Black and Hispanic, they tend not to have access to either programs, and there are long-term consequences. Under-representation in both programs, combined with the lack of teacher diversity discussed later in this chapter, raise questions regarding what is the quality of services to groups of children and families that have backgrounds, customs, languages, and pressures that are different from teachers and staff?

To effectively meet the needs of all children and families, especially those not enrolled in a preschool program, we argue that teachers not only need to understand content knowledge that incorporates language, culture, and community contexts for learning, but that they also need to understand, examine, and interrogate their own attitudes, beliefs, and values and how these manifest in their ability to construct and manage classroom activities efficiently and effectively. The latter is critical for many children because kindergarten may be their first time in a structured setting with ways of thinking, speaking, and acting that may differ from their home environments. Given these issues, we focus on some potential problems regarding early childhood and gifted education for students of color, with some attention to economic status.

Through extant research, it is evident that many children, but especially non-White children living in poverty, are disproportionately less successful in school than their White and more affluent peers (Barton & Coley, 2009) due to social and educational injustices. Despite popular discourses where the blame is placed on children and families for their academic "failure," the reality is that far too many students of color do not have access to adequate resources to thrive and be competitive in educational settings. In fact, a newly released report titled "A First Look," which is based on the 2013-2014 Civil Rights Data Collection (CRDC), highlights and details how race(ism) plays a crucial and undeniable role in limiting and denying students of color the opportunities needed to achieve at high levels in school. In addition to the CRDC, measuring student access to courses, programs, instructional and other staff, and resources, there is a focus on school climate factors (such as student discipline, and bullying and harassment), as well as representation in gifted education and Advanced Placement (under-representation) and special education (over-representation).

Hate crimes have increased dramatically in school settings during and after the election of Trump, according to the Southern Poverty Law Center (see https://www.splcenter.org/hate-map; https://www2.ed.gov/pubs/HateCrime/page1.html). Evidence of bullying and harassment came immediately following the election of Donald J. Trump. For example, graffiti messages with the words "go back to Africa" and "Trump train" demonstrate the effect of Trump's rhetoric on schools. Another example of the "Trump effect" was witnessed during lunch at Royal Oak Middle School in Royal Oak, Michigan, where a group of students chanted, "Build the wall! Build the wall!" Still other examples include a video that surfaced from a York County Technical High School in York, Pennsylvania where White students are caught chanting "White power" while holding a Trump sign. Racial hate is learned and can be unlearned; educators can and must make a difference with changes in their attitudes and curriculum. (see https://www.justice.gov/archive/crs/pubs/prevyouhatecrim.pdf)

In the wake of these disturbing White supremacist messages, following an explosive, populist, and polarizing campaign that took relentless aim at Black and Brown communities in which Trump, speaking in Dimondale,

Michigan (a predominately White suburb of Lansing), issued these words to African Americans: "You're living in poverty, your schools are no good, you have no jobs, 58% of your youth is unemployed – what the hell do you have to lose?" We are left to wonder and stress over what do communities of color have to lose during the Trump presidency? Drawing on the words and question posed by then candidate Donald J. Trump—"what do you have to lose?"—the authors of this chapter explore the implications of a Trump Administration, specifically the impact it could potentially have on early childhood education (preschool), gifted education, and teacher diversity as these relate to teaching, learning, and schooling for children of color.

## Early Childhood Education

In 2014 (see Figure 1), data on the percentage of children enrolled in preschool programs revealed a much lower percentage of Hispanic children ages 3- to 5-year-olds (32%) enrolled in preschool programs, compared to White (41%) and Black children (39%) of equal ages. These percentages are even lower when consideration is given to attendance (full or half-day preschool/ kindergarten). For instance a higher percentage of White (24%) and Asian (20%) children attended preschool half-day, compared to Hispanic (14%) and Black (12%) children. Additionally, a higher percentage of children of two or more races attended preschool half-day (20%) when compared to Black children. In contrast to children who attended preschool half-day, a higher percentage of Black children attended preschool for the full day (27%), compared to the percentages of children who were Asian (20%), Hispanic (18%), White (17%), and of two or more races (16%) (Kena et al., 2016).

The fact that all the enrollment percentages across race fall below 50% lead to other questions about accessibility and affordability that, in turn, may even point to a lack of understanding regarding the importance of what it means for all children, but especially those underserved and located in high-need, low-income urban and rural areas where high-quality preschool programs are critical to ensure that these children are ready to learn upon entering kindergarten. The unevenness of these data with respect to those children not enrolled in preschool, Head Start, and/or other high-quality structured child care programs lead to another question of how their cultural knowledge, skills, and dispositions will be recognized, engaged, and nurtured under a Trump Administration?

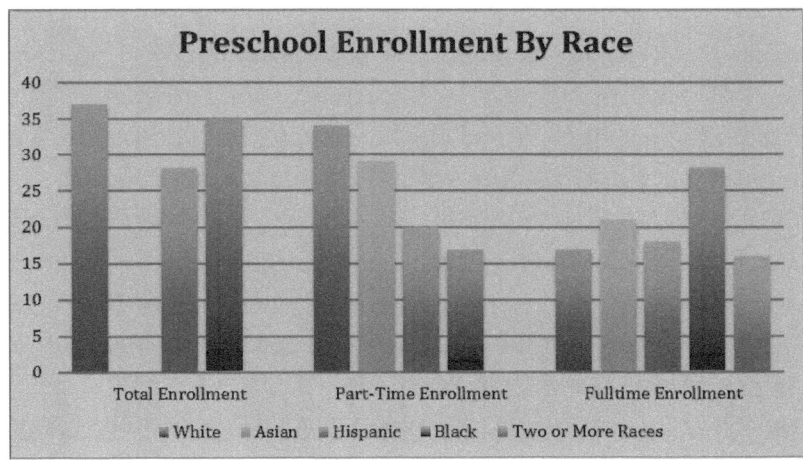

**Figure 1. Enrollment Trends for Preschool Programs by Race in the United States**

It goes without saying that quality early childhood education for all children has a long history. It is well-documented through research (e.g., The High/Scope Perry Preschool Study, The Abecedarian Project) that the early years in a child's life—when the brain is forming and most malleable—represents a critically important opportunity to develop a child's full potential and shape key academic, social, and cognitive skills that will determine success in school and in later life. Thus, the earlier we reach children, especially those from non-dominant and historically marginalized groups, the more promising the effects related to increasing their life chances. Providing every child with access to high-quality early childhood education to allow them to learn, thrive, and reach their full potential has not been without some controversy (see Tennessee's Voluntary Pre-K [TN-VPK] initiative, 2016). Despite studies like the TN-VPK initiative, which suggests participation in pre-K does not lead to long-lasting positive gains for children from low-income backgrounds, the Obama Administration declared expanding access to rigorous early childhood education as one of the wisest investments that the U.S. can make. Will the Trump administration agree?

In his 2013 State of the Union address, President Obama called upon Congress to expand access to high-quality preschool for every child in America. In 2014, the President convened state and local policymakers, mayors, school superintendents, corporate and community leaders, and advocates, for the White House Summit on Early Education, which emphasized the need for collective leadership in support of early education for America's most vulnerable citizens. The *Preschool for All* initiative was established to improve quality and expand access to preschool for four-year-olds from low- and moderate-income households. The initiative also promotes access to full-day kindergarten and high-quality early education programs for children under age four.

Betsy DeVos, a Michigan philanthropist and Trump's nominee for the position of U.S. Secretary of Education, who unlike the current secretary, John King, or the previous leader, Arne Duncan, has never lead a state education department or school district. This raises a number of questions regarding the fate of public education in general, and early childhood education in particular. Such questions include, will the progress made to ensure that children who would otherwise not have access to high-quality preschool and full-day kindergarten be in jeopardy of renegotiation under a Trump Administration, with DeVos at the helm of public education? Will Trump's Secretary of Education overhaul education and repeal the practice of universal pre-K, citing the research of Farran and Lipsey's 2015 TN-VPK study findings as justification that, although there are significant initial benefits for children living in poverty who participate in Tennessee's Voluntary pre-K program, by the time these children research the first grade, the effects begin to fade? Will DeVos, a social conservative who has funded anti-gay marriage and anti-affirmative action efforts and advocated for the concept of school choice, provided support for-profit and virtual charter schools, as well as private school vouchers, ignore the key benefits of early childhood education that include, but are not limited to socialization, cooperation, holistic development (emotional, social, physical, and intellectual development), enthusiasm for lifelong learning, self-identity, confidence/self-esteem, and more?

In addition to the aforementioned benefits, early childhood education provides exposure to diversity. Valuing differences and diversity is crucial to a child's early development. Early childhood education serves to guide children to appreciate and accept differences and, in the process, become well-rounded contributors to society. Valuing differences and diversity appear grossly absent from Trump's campaign, which was themed "make America great again" and included such promises as "Build a wall, and make Mexico pay for it," and "Temporarily ban Muslims from entering the United States," just to name a few. These campaign promises not only undermine the ideals of our democracy, but they ignore the changing face of early childhood in the United States. As of 2011, 52% of children born in the U.S. were non-White; they are now in kindergarten. Those in the field of education in general, and early childhood education in particular, are left to ponder, with trepidation, the impact of such anti-difference and anti-diversity comments on teaching, learning, and schooling for our most vulnerable and impressionable members of society.

Professionals in the field of early childhood education and all who care about accessible, affordable, and high-quality early education cannot sit idly by, in light of what is known regarding the benefits of early childhood education. They must watch and demand that the Trump administration dedicate funding and resources for early childhood education to ensure that every child matters.

## GIFTED EDUCATION AND ADVANCED PLACEMENT

Access and equity in gifted education remains a grave concern for educators, particularly those who have a multicultural focus in their work. We contend that children who are enrolled in rigorous early childhood programs are more likely to not only be prepared for formal schooling but also for gifted programs. Educators often see signs of giftedness in students within the first two years of schooling; this begins the referral process. Ample data indicate that under-referral of Black and Hispanic students is prevalent, even when such students have comparable levels of performance as White students (Ford, 2013; Grissom & Redding, 2016).

Black and Hispanic students are consistently under-represented in gifted and Advanced Placement classrooms. The Office of Civil Rights (OCR) collects data on district diversity and equity as documented in its Civil Rights Data Collection (www.ocrdata.ed.gov). The most recent OCR data indicate that Black students comprise 19% of students enrolled in public school, but only 10% of them are identified as gifted. Likewise, Latino students represent 25% of students but only 16% of the gifted population. These data indicate that a substantial discrepancy exists. Subsequently, each year hundreds of thousands of Black and Latino students combined are not identified as gifted (Ford, 2013; Ford & Russo, 2015). A similar trend exists in Advanced Placement course participation. For example, if more students attending schools with AP courses had equitable access, more than 640,000 low-income students and students of color would be enrolled in AP classes (Theokas & Saaris, 2013). These problems will most likely be magnified under the Trump administration's educational leadership.

The Trump administration's primary goal is to "Make America Great Again!" However, some suggest that this is a covert indication that the administration is charged with "Making America White Again!" (Jacobson, 2016; Sculos, 2016). Following this logic, it is likely that gifted and AP classes may return to the days of old when they were less diverse. Historically, gifted education programs have been over-enrolled by White students, taught by White teachers, and heavily guarded by White middle-class parents (Kohn, 1998; Sapon-Shevin, 1996). If state and local educational leaders embrace the many undertones of the Trump's rhetoric, gifted and AP classes may become less accessible for deserving Black and Latino students. Educators who previously have not acted on their biased beliefs may be more empowered and emboldened with Trump's administration. We anticipate that the past and current lack of teacher referrals will increase as educators act on their implicit and explicit biases regarding Black, Hispanic, and low-income students, which hinders both the recruitment and retention of such students for gifted education. Specifically, every study on teacher referral to gifted education has revealed that Black students are consistently and extensively under-referred; half indicate this for Hispanic students. Biases in the form of racial discrimination cannot be denied. Now educators, under the Trump administration, may feel free or freer to act on their biases and prejudices, with little or no fear of penalty.

Of critical concern is how access to gifted education will be regulated on public (and private) school campuses. To repeat, data indicate that Black and Hispanic students have the least access to the most rigorous educational classrooms and programs, often considered gifted and Advanced Placement. Annually, Black students at all grade levels are under-represented by approximately 50% and Hispanics by some 40% (Ford, 2013). Connecting back to early childhood, when children of color and those who live in poverty do not have access to rigorous pre-K experiences, a vicious cycle ensues, resulting in low probability of meeting requirements for gifted education identification and placement.

Increasing access and equity in and to gifted education has proven difficult in public schools, despite legal mandates that encourage educator buy-in. It is essential to note that educators and policymakers control admission and student scheduling at state and district levels because gifted education is not federally mandated. This autonomy allows schools to ignore racial disparities in gifted education. Educators and families of gifted students must be concerned about Trump's commitment to gifted education along racial and economic lines. The future looks bleak based on what we have seen thus far, relative to addressing inequities in identifying and serving gifted students who are non-White. We have witnessed little regard from Trump's pre- and post-election, along with appointments to his cabinet that gives us reason to be optimistic regarding equity and access in gifted education. Will under-representation increase? We strongly suspect so. How will federal definitions of gifted change? Will there now be a federal mandate for gifted education (as in special education)? What changes will exist in funding to support the least resourced families, schools, and communities? Will litigation and court cases increase based on discrimination (Ford & Russo, 2016)? Fundamentally, what will accountability look like in this impending administration that seems to be riddled with racism and all manner of hate that has further emboldened those with power and may not penalize those who act upon their prejudices and biases?

## Teacher Diversity

For decades, it has been clear that teacher and student diversity do not match. While student diversity is increasing, teacher diversity is not. Some 52% of students are 'minority' but some 85% of teachers are White (Kena et al., 2016). Cultural clashes are evident, as indicated above, with teachers failing to see strengths and gifts in students of color. We are not holding our breath expecting changes with the impending Trump administration; rather, we anticipate regression as America is made 'great again.' This begs the question, great for whom?

As the nation prepares (or braces itself) for Donald Trump's governance, there is division along lines of race and class. There are authentic concerns about whether he will justly execute the Office of the President of the United States, and do so to the best of his ability, preserve, protect, and defend all Americans, not a select few. This fear took root in the minds of some Americans during Trump's campaign where many immigrants and Muslims repeatedly heard declarative statements mentioned above, "Build a wall — and make Mexico pay for it," and "Temporarily ban Muslims from entering the United States," just to name a few. These statements made their way into our nation's schools almost immediately following Trump's election to our nation's highest office. Some school officials' responses to these incidences have left many families concerned for the safety of their children.

Organizations (e.g., Southern Poverty Law Center) that track and document hate crimes have witnessed a significant increase in hate-motivated incidents during and since the election. Unfortunately, there is the expectation that many more of these hate-based incidents will occur in and outside school settings. Given this prediction, how can we ensure that all children, but especially those from non-dominant and historically marginalized groups, are protected? What will a Trump Administration mean for teacher diversity? How can we ensure that every child counts in every classroom, inclusive of their of their race, class, gender, ability, or disability? The answers to these questions are of critical importance, especially since the demographic reality of U.S. schools is an increasingly diverse student population where the teaching force remains considerably homogeneous.

The demographic background of teachers in the U.S. remain 84% White and 16% non-White (Hrabowski & Sanders, 2015). This trend shows little sign of changing since the majority of students enrolled in teacher education programs continue to be White and female (Kena et al., 2016). And the percentages are similar for school administrators and counselors. As evidenced by these data, education professionals are more frequently being asked to teach students who have different backgrounds and life experiences from their own. This demographic reality, coupled with the hate-motivated incidents following the election of President-elect Donald Trump, makes it absolutely critical for teacher preparation programs to better prepare their teacher candidates for the diversity of students they will teach.

This kind of educational preparation, grounded in equity, must explore the connections between racial identities and pedagogy, with attention to poverty, since teachers and students belong to a host of multicultural and intersectional groups. It cannot be assumed that teachers with rigorous coursework to develop content knowledge, sophisticated pedagogical practices and critically examined dispositions can easily translate these funds of cultural knowledge into culturally-relevant practices. Time and time again, in teacher preparation programs across the nation there exist an underestimation of what is needed for teachers to be effective with all children, but especially those from non-dominant groups living in poverty. While teacher preparation programs can teach skills and strategies, they have not always been successful in developing appropriate and just-minded dispositions of teacher education candidates wherein they have critically examined and interrogated their attitudes, beliefs, values, and practices—and the impact on students under their charge. It is, therefore, absolutely necessary that all education professionals become aware of the many cultures they are members of and how these cultural affiliations affect, inform, and compromise their leadership, as well as their teaching and students' learning. Thus, successful teaching of students from diverse backgrounds calls for teachers from diverse racial and economic backgrounds who understand relationships between racial identity and pedagogy, and are aware of how schools can and do perpetuate inequities that exist outside of schools.

Addressing issues of teacher/educator diversity and the subsequent impact on schooling, teaching, and learning from the top down and bottom up, allows teachers to see that they are socially constructed beings and that schools and classrooms are microcosms of larger societies where hate-motivated incidents witnessed in our nation's schools following the election are a reflection, representation and, quite frankly, an enforcement of the problematic racial divides that permeate our society.

## REFERENCES

Barton, P. E., & Coley, R. J. (2009). *Parsing the achievement gap II*. Princeton, NJ: Educational Testing Services.

Ford, D. Y. (2013). *Recruiting and retaining culturally different students in gifted education*. Waco, TX: Prufrock Press.

Ford, D. Y., & Russo, C. J. (2015). No child left behind ... unless a student is gifted and of color: Reflections on the need to meet the educational needs of the gifted. *Journal of Law in Society, 15*, 213-239.

Grissom, J.A. & Redding, C. (2016). Discretion and disproportionality: Explaining the underrepresentation of high-achieving students of color in gifted programs. *AERA Open*. Retrieved from http://www.aera.net/Newsroom/News-Releases-and-Statements/Does-Student-Race-Affect-Gifted-Assignment/Discretion-and-Disproportionality-Explaining-the-Underrepresentation-of-High-Achieving-Students-of-Color-in-Gifted-Programs.

Hrabowski III, F. A., & Sanders, M. G. (Winter, 2015). Increasing racial diversity in the teacher workforce: One university's approach. *Thought & Action*, 101-116.

Kena, G., Hussar, W., McFarland, J., de Brey, C., Musu-Gillette, L., Wang, X., Zhang, J., Rathbun, A., ...Dunlop Velez, E. (2016). *The condition of education 2016* (NCES 2016-144). U.S. Department of Education, National Center for Education Statistics. Washington, DC. Retrieved from http://nces.ed.gov/pubsearch.

Kohn, A. (1998). Only for my kid. *Phi Delta Kappan, 79*, 568-577.

Jacobson, G. C. (2016). Polarization, gridlock, and presidential campaign politics in 2016. *Annals, 667*, 226-226.

Plucker, J. A., Makel, M. C., Hansen, J. A., & Muller, P. A. (2007). Achievement effects of the Cleveland voucher program on high ability elementary school students. *Journal of School Choice, 1*(4), 77-88.

Sapon-Shevin, M. (1996). Beyond gifted education: Building a shared agenda for school reform. *Journal for the Education of the Gifted, 19*, 194-214.

Sculos, B. W. (2016). Parenting for progress: Reflections on Matt Ross's captain fantastic. *Class, Race and Corporate Power, 4*(2), 6 Retrieved from http://digitalcommons.fiu.edu/classracecorporatepower/vol4/iss2/6/.

Theokas, C., & Saaris, R. (2013). *Finding America's missing AP and IB students.* Washington,
DC: The Education Trust.

# The Latin-American community unites against Donald Trump

**JUSTINE RODIER, TRANSLATED BY RODOLPHE LECLERC**
2 Décembre 2015

In the United States, the Presidential candidate Donald Trump has been forced to answer the Latin-American community over the last few months. The latter accuses him of having made repeated racist comments, especially against Mexico. Because of his speech and some of his comments about Mexico, the American billionaire now faces a unified Latin-American opposition, who is dead set

# Chapter Ten

## *Anti-Immigration and Isolationism*

### Trump, Latin America, and the Future of International Law

#### Aitza Haddad Esq. PhD.

The 45th President, Donald Trump, coined as his campaign motto the phrase "Make America Great Again." This motto became the leading voice behind the discourse that fueled his entire campaign, and secured him the election's victory, and a place in the White House for the next four years to come. However, many questioned then, and are still questioning now, the real meaning behind this motto and its actual goal. The uncertainty of the motto' meaning allowed for many to used it as an opportunity to create their own definitions and interpretations, which mainly support the demonizing of the "other," which in this case means everything that does not look like a Disney White Prince Charming, and which led to the reemergence of a hierarchy of people within the entire region, and probably, across the globe. In addition, the motto blatantly ignores that America is not just the United States but also North America, Central America and South America, and also ignores that the history of the United States itself is grounded on the defiance of governmental power, the invasion of a strange land, the near extermination of the legitimate owners of such land, and the exploitation of such land through the slavery of another group of people, which was forcedly brought here. In short, the motto seems to suggest that not only all types and dimensions of colonization were great, but that we should go back to a time in which all those practices were accepted and praised, and a hierarchy of people was not only expected, but also respected.

The hierarchy of people that reemerged out of the motto of "Make America Great Again" impacted and demonized all minority groups in United States, including the Latino and Hispanic community within United States and abroad. The motto, maybe inadvertently, not only underscored the greatness and the strength of the Latino and Hispanic community, as well as the importance of their vote to win the 2016 Presidential Elections, but also underscored the dichotomy within this community when it comes to self-identification of race and ethnicity to take advantage of the so-called "White Privilege" through the dynamic of passing, which is supported by the racial and ethnic characteristics used for demographic data collection. For example, although data collected prior to the November 8$^{th}$ election day suggests that Latinos registered to vote at higher numbers and a fast pace than even before in the history of United States presidential elections due to a fear of a Donald Trump presidency, data also suggests that 20% to 25% Latinos and Hispanics in United States, who are mainly self-identified White, actually helped Trump to secure the presidency (Reyes, 2016). This Latino and Hispanic support for Trump not only seems ironic, and for many, a betrayal to their own, it is also misguided, misinformed, and almost solely grounded on hateful definitions of Christianity, an obsessive desire and need for guns, and the fantasy of economic growth and independence.

The fear of a Trump Presidency by the remaining 75% to 80% members of the Latino and Hispanic community emerged out of a plethoric collection of Trump's negative remarks about, and characterizations of, Latinos and Hispanics throughout his entire campaign. This plethoric collection of negative remarks and characterizations of Latinos and Hispanics began in June 16, 2015, when during his speech announcing he would run for the United States presidency, Trump stated that

When Mexico sends its people, they're not sending their best… They're sending people that have lots of problems, and they're bringing those problems with them. They're bringing drugs. They're bringing crime. They're rapists… They're sending us not the right people. It's coming from more than Mexico. It's coming from all over South and Latin America, and it's coming probably — probably — from the Middle East…

Trump comments went even further when he stated that he "would build a great wall," that "nobody builds walls better than" him, that he will "build them very inexpensively … great, great wall on our southern border," and that he "will have Mexico pay for that wall." Ironically, in a "major policy address" held in Gettysburg in October 22, 2016, he admitted that under his plans, the United States would pay for the wall he wants to build, but that Mexico would reimburse the United States for it later (Colarossi, 2016). And although this was not the first, nor the last time, he changed his mind, nor retract from his own comments and promises, his supporters still considered him as honest, and as United States president material.

Trump's dislike for Latinos was further accentuated on August 2015, when he forced the removal of Mexican-American journalist Jorge Ramos from one of his rallies, on September 2016, when 1996 Miss Universe, Alicia Machado, spoke about his attacks during her time in the Miss Universe Pageant, which he used to own, and during the Third Presidential debate on October 19, when he characterized Mexicans as "Bad Hombres" (Colarossi, 2016). The fear that his hateful rhetoric produced, although increased the rate of hate crimes against minorities and other groups across the nation, and possibly the globe, it also triggered a sense of nationalism and unity in the entire region of Latin American and

Spanish-speaking countries, as well as in the 75% to 80% members of the Latino and Hispanic community in the United States against Trump, producing what could be considered as a movement against the reality show billionaire mogul (Moreno, 2015; Rodier, 2015; Cano, 2016). From prominent members of the Latino and Hispanic community, such as America Ferreira, Roselyn Sanchez, and Ricky Martin, to political figures, such as the presidents of Mexico, Venezuela, Costa Rica, and Bolivia made expressions, and some even took action against Trump's absurd and prejudicial actions, such as brilliantly comparing Trump to the late President of Venezuela, Hugo Chávez (Moreno, 2015; Cano, 2016).

If one traces Chávez's tradition to those with similar characteristics throughout the history of Latin American politics, it can be inferred that Trump's comparison to Chávez actually means describing Trump as an American caudillo. A caudillo is a post-colonial leader that although aims to rule its country by the sheer force of personality, is also "racist, narcissistic, virility-obsessed, and [a] self-aggrandizing despot" (Encarnación, 2016). In short, caudillismo is like populism, where the lines between authoritarianism and democracy become blurred. Trump's caudillist or populist rhetoric was clearly reflected in many of his remarks. For example, in April 2016, Trump delivered his first and only foreign policy speech, in which he stated that United States "will no longer surrender this country or its people to the false song of globalism" (LAA, 2016, para.1). Globalization refers to the blurring of sovereignty borders and responsibilities due to accelerating flow of people, goods, technology, and other resources and values, which makes it easier for powerful nations to extend their power over traditional sovereign borders, and thus, gain control over other nations with greater ease (Nagan & Haddad, 2012). Thus, what Trump seems to suggest is that thanks to globalization, other nations have gained control over the United States. Here globalization is the evildoer of United States, and Trump puts himself as the United States only savior.

What Trump seems to ignore is that, not only is globalization actually the product of global advances and colonization processes to facilitate trade, we are currently in the fourth epoch of globalization, called the electronic colonization epoch, which is in fact "about the mind being shaped more and more by external media" that promotes the United States taste, values, morals, history, culture, and language around the world (McPhail, 2010, p.134). In short, thanks to globalization, the United States is the one nation currently affecting other nations through neocolonial dynamics. And as a person who has expanded his businesses across the world, Trump has been part of the same process of globalization he blames as the United States evildoer himself. In fact, when in June 2016, under the same argument against globalization, he stated that as a consequence of a leadership that worships globalism over Americanism, "globalization has wiped out our middle class," he was actually talking about people like himself and his crooked business tactics (Politico, 2016, para.15). Even more, when he further explained that "[o]ur politicians have aggressively pursued a policy of globalization–moving our jobs, our wealth and our factories to Mexico and overseas [and that g]lobalization has made the financial elite who donate to politicians very wealthy [leaving] millions of our workers with nothing but poverty and heartache," he was basically describing who he is, how he does businesses, and the consequences of such businesses for those in less privileged positions (Politico, 2016, para.7-8). However, as he said in February, 2016, after winning Nevada's Republican caucuses, he "love[s] the poorly educated." And what real caudillista would not? Only through the uneducated the Caudillo can constantly and successfully impress the neocolonized and reassured itself as the perfect hero in order for the neocolonial relation to survive. In short, as Memmi (1965) explains, "[i]t is the mediocre citizens who set the general tone of the colony" (p.50). Thus, although the President of Ecuador thinks that Trump's triumph might help the progressive movement in Latin America, as a consequence of the hateful connotations of his rhetoric against Mexicans and illegal immigrants, this is not likely to ever happen.

Latin America is still recovering from the decolonization and developmental era that followed World War II and the Holocaust. The post WWII decolonization and developmental era emerged out of the international consensus and desire to help the newly decolonized countries, or

Third World Countries, and to avoid the occurrences that led to the Holocaust. These goals led in turn to the emergence of the U.N. Charter, the Universal Declaration of Human Rights (UDHR), and then the United Nations Organization (ONU), which expanded the field of international law and international relations into something more humane than just trade for profit. However, the Holocaust was not the first time the idea of Never Again emerged, and sadly, it was not the last time either. Although the Holocaust put an end to legal colonialization, it also led to the creation of new ways to control people, or neocolonization. And the ability of neocolonial practices to became part of our everyday practices without even noticing it, makes them even more dangerous than legal forcibly colonization. Latin America's history of colonialism, inequality, and class conflicts, makes the region a fertile ground for inequality, and thus, the perfect incubator for Trump's divisive agenda and caudillist populist traits. And although Mexico is the one nation State Trump as sought to stigmatized, his caudillist populist rhetoric and actions had resonated in the entire region, affecting with them the region and the entire world. For example, having what is considered to be the strongest democracy in the Americas electing a caudillist populist as President could represent the rise of like candidates in the region (Navia, 2016). Not only that, ignoring the positive effects North America Free Trade Agreement (NAFTA) has had on the economy of the region, Trump has directly attacked NAFTA stating that "is defective;" "the single worst trade deal ever approved in this country;" "one of the worst things that ever happened to the manufacturing industry;" "the worst trade deal maybe ever signed anywhere, but certainly ever signed in this country" (Collins, 2016). However, although Trump claims that "there are far fewer jobs in the manufacturing sector in the United States than there used to be ... before NAFTA came into effect ..., this change is mainly due to technical innovations that increase productivity and allow the standard of living to rise," and not due to the structural applications of the treaty (Bédard, 2016, p.2).

Although Trump has pledged to honor treaties with the United States allies, he does not see Mexico as a close friend (Hakim 2016). And under the claim that NAFTA is a disaster that destroyed America, has claimed that it needs to be renegotiated, and has even threatened to pull the United States out of the trade agreement altogether if Canada and Mexico do not agree to what he calls "better terms." If this happens, it would be the first-time the United States retreats from an international trade agreement since 1866, which has the potential to cause a trade conflict or even a currency war (Luhby, 2016). In short, in the practical sense, a retreat of United States from NAFTA could be considered as a hostile international behavior that could in turn produce a hostile international environment, pushing the region back into an era of leftist populist governments, which will end up building their own barriers against the United States This could potentially obscure the possibility of any bilateral agenda between the United States and the region on issues from "immigration to drug trafficking and law enforcement to terrorism" (Winter, 2016; Farnsworth, 2016, para.5). In the theoretical sense, a United States retreat from an international trade agreement for the first time since 1866 would raise questions of the United States commitment, credibility, reliability, and ability to engage in international partnerships, which will undermine any future initiative to engage in treaties with other nations, and any effort to promote democracy, human rights, economic principles, and leadership (Farnsworth, 2016). In short, a Trump presidency will put at stake both the future of Latin America, and the future of international law.

Possibly in recognition of this, in an ironic attempt to gain the Latino vote, and despite his divisively fascist and racially coded rhetoric, on August 20, 2016, Trump had a round table discussion with Latino leaders from almost a dozen states around the nation (Lee, 2016). Nonetheless, the focus of the discussion was the potential creation of new jobs for Latinos legally in the United States, and more "humane and efficient" ways to deal with the illegal immigrants currently in the country, and nothing was mentioned on the dangerous potential effects of his agenda on the Latin American region, and possibly the world (Lee, 2016). Nonetheless, in September 2016, under the "America First" justification, Trump expanded his original views on immigration calling for an administration that will select immigrants to legally enter the country by properly vetting them based on merit, skill and proficiency, in order to serve the national interest (NPR, 2016). Nothing within Trump's proposed immigration regime is humane nor efficient. To the contrary, it has the potential to serve as a tool to dehumanize others (Darcy, 2016). Even more, in a time "when Latin America feels more open to trade and integration than it has in 20 years," having Trump as the potential new President could represent the end of not only the illusion of a better treatment for the region, but the end of all existent relationships (Winter, 2016, para.3).

Trump's racist, bigot, and misogynists remarks were just the tip of a huge iceberg that continued to developed, and is still affecting not only Latinos and Hispanics in United States, but also the national relations between United Stated and Latin America, and the general foreign relations between United States and the entire globe as well. Nevertheless, although the above mentioned remarks, and many other erratic ones, caused for even some of the most fervent devoted conservative Republicans Latinos and Hispanics, such as Trump's former rivals to the Republican National Committee (RNC) candidate for the Presidency, Senators Marco Rubio and Ted Cruz, to distance themselves from his campaign, despite the many warnings from scholars, scientist, and leaders around the globe, many decided to put Trump's racism, bigotry, and ignorance of the law and the Constitution aside to give him a chance to make this nation "stronger, safer, and Christian." However, although Donald Trump is now the President of United States, we are far from becoming the "stronger, safer, and Christian" nation his supporters expect. Trump's campaign put at stake prior efforts to build bridges between the United States and Latin America, such as Barack Obama's 2016 negotiations with Cuba, affecting significantly nations such as Brazil, and pushing the entire region towards China (Smith & Borger, 2016). Donald Trump also revived the discourse on terrorism and turned it again into one of the new main international focuses, with Muslims as the reemergent targets of mainstream media since 9/11. With this, relationships with Latin American countries are now condemned to once again face the challenge of overcoming their historical international placement as a secondary priority, which is based almost solely on necessity of the region (Navarro, 2016).

By not recognizing the real role the United States plays within the processes of globalization and the current epoch of electronic colonization, and instead using people's lack of knowledge and understanding to demonize others and other nations through globalization in order to get his way, a Trump presidency puts at stake our democracy, the development of other nations across the globe, and the development of human rights and international law and relations. Some think that neocolonization is the last stage of the empire, and the people of United States just elected a person for president whose entire campaign was grounded on the same populist and fascist practices that brought Adolf Hitler to power in Germany, Benito Mussolini in Italy, Augusto Pinochet in Chile, Francisco Franco in Spain, Fidel Castro in Cuba, and many others around the world. Subtle messages are a thing of the past, and this last presidential race, not only created uncertainty in all Latin America about the future of the region, it also reminded the Latino community of the words of the late Simon Bolivar in an 1829 letter saying that "the United States seems destined by providence to plague America with misery in the name of liberty" (Navarro, 2016). The truth is that the relationship between the United States and these countries has already been affected, possibly without hope for restoration to the prior status quo or to one better (Cano, 2016). However, as Winter (2016) explains, after Brexit, the threat of a retirement of the United States from NAFTA, created by Trump, could have a trickle effect on other Latin American countries, and possibly the world, by setting back the global economy, and thus, delaying the recovery of Latin American, and underdeveloped countries' own economies. This is not only problematic, should be avoided at all cost because as explained by Navia (2016), given Trump's caudillist populist rhetoric, which is "aimed at building support among a discontented citizenry," predicting if the consequences of his Presidency would be simply bad or horrible is not only hard but almost impossible (Navia, 2016, para.2).

## References

Bédard, M. (2016). NAFTA: DONALD TRUMP'S CRITICISMS ARE UNFOUNDED. *NAFTA*. Available at http://www.iedm.org/files/lepoint1016_en.pdf

Cano, E. (2016). Trump y el renacer de la ira antiestadounidense en América Latina. *Univision Noticias*. Available at http://www.univision.com/noticias/elecciones-2016/trump-y-el-renacer-de-la-ira-antiestadounidense-en-america-latina.

Colarossi, S. (2016). Trump Basically Admits That The United States, Not Mexico, Would Pay For His Wall. *Politics USA*. Available at http://www.politicususa.com/2016/10/22/trump-mexico-wall-united-states-pays.html.

Darcy, J. (2016). Trump's new merit-based immigration model: Darcy cartoon. *Cleveland.com*. Available at http://www.cleveland.com/darcy/index.ssf/2016/09/trumps_merit-based_immigration.html.

Encarnación, O. (2016). American Caudillo. Trump and the Latin-Americanization of the United States Politics. *Foreign Affairs*. Available at https://www.foreignaffairs.com/articles/united-states/2016-05-12/american-caudillo.

Farnsworth, E. (2016). Donald Trump & Latin America. *Americas Society /Council of the Americas*. Available at http://www.as-coa.org/articles/donald-trump-latin-america.

Hakim, P. (2016). Should Latin America Worry about President Trump? *The Dialogue*. Available at http://www.thedialogue.org/resources/should-latin-america-worry-about-president-trump/.

Lee, K. (2016). Campaign 2016 updates: Donald Trump meets with Latino leaders from around the country. *Los Angeles Times*. Available at http://www.latimes.com/nation/politics/trailguide/la-na-trailguide-updates-1471723835-htmlstory.html.

Linares, P. (2016). Indignación en Latinoamérica por los insultos de Donald Trump a los mexicanos. *Mundiario*. Available at http://www.mundiario.com/articulo/a-fondo/indignacion-latinoamerica-insultos-donald-trump-mexicanos/20150619193830031077.html.

McPhail, T. L. (2010). *Global communication: Theories, stakeholders, and trends*. John Wiley & Sons.

Memmi, A. (1965). The Colonizer and the Colonized, trans. *H. Greenfeld, London: Earthscan*.

Moreno, C. (2015). 9 Outrageous Things Donald Trump Has Said About Latinos. *The Huffington Post*. Available at http://www.huffingtonpost.com/entry/9-outrageous-things-donald-trump-has-said-about-latinos_us_55e483a1e4b0c818f618904b.

Navarro, E. (2016). Analistas latinoamericanos a RT: "Entre Clinton y Trump hay que pensar en el menos malo". *RT Portada Actualidad*. Available at https://actualidad.rt.com/actualidad/213892-eeuu-latinoamerica-clinton-trump.

Navia, P. (2016). How bad would Trump be for Latin America? *Latin America Goes Global*. Available at http://latinamericagoesglobal.org/2016/07/bad-trump-latin-america/.

NPR (2016). Fact Check: Donald Trump's speech on immigration. *NPR.org*. Available at http://www.npr.org/2016/08/31/492096565/fact-check-donald-trumps-speech-on-immigration.

Politico (2016). Full transcript: Donald Trump's jobs plan speech. *Politico.com*. Available at http://www.politico.com/story/2016/06/full-transcript-trump-job-plan-speech-224891.

Ramirez Salas, T. (2016). Lo que le espera a Latinoamérica con el nuevo-presidente de Estados Unidos. *RT Portada Actualidad*. Available at https://actualidad.rt.com/actualidad/213412-clinton-trump-america-latina.

Reyes, R. (2016). Why some Latinos are backing Trump. *CNN.com*. Available at http://www.cnn.com/2016/11/02/opinions/why-some-latinos-back-trump-reyes/.

Rodier, J. (2015). The Latin-American community unites against Donald Trump. *Le Journal International*. Available at http://www.

lejournalinternational.fr/The-Latin-American-community-unites-against-Donald-Trump_a3409.html.

Smith, D. & Borger, J. (2016). President Trump fills world leaders with fear: 'It's gone from funny to really scary.' *The Guardian*. Available at https://www.theguardian.com/us-news/2016/apr/28/donald-trump-president-world-leaders-foreign-relations.

Winter, B. (2016). How Brexit and Trump Could Turn Latin America Upside-Down. *Quarterly Americas*. Available at http://www.americasquarterly.org/content/latin-america-brexit-and-trump-consequences.

# DEPARTMENT OF EDUCATION

The Department of Education promotes improving student achievement and access to opportunity in elementary, secondary, and postsecondary education. The Department would refocus its mission on supporting States and school districts in their efforts to provide high quality education to all our students. Also, it would focus on streamlining and simplifying funding for college, while continuing to help make college education more affordable. The 2018 Budget places power in the hands of parents and families to choose schools that are best for their children by investing an additional $1.4 billion in school choice programs. It continues support for the Nation's most vulnerable populations, such as students with disabilities. Overall, the Department would support these investments and carry out its core mission while lowering costs to the taxpayer by reducing or eliminating funding for programs that are not effective, that duplicate other efforts, or that do not serve national needs.

The President's 2018 Budget provides $59 billion in discretionary funding for the Department of Education, a $9 billion or 13 percent reduction below the 2017 annualized CR level.

he President's 2018 Budget:

Increases investment

# Chapter Eleven

## *Privatizing Education*

### President-elect Donald Trump's Rhetoric on Education

### Ann-Marie Waterman, Howard University

**Abstract**

President Donald J. Trump claims, that one of his goals as president is to "ensure that every child...will be placed on the ladder of success: a great education, and a great job" (Donaldtrump.com). However, he has not comprehensively outlined, in any definitive manner, what will be his overall education policy or specific strategy. He has addressed generic educational problems and commented on general institutional issues in his campaign speeches and his speaking/Twitter events and website offerings. Thus far, he has proffered simplistic solutions on nationally, systemic challenges that currently exist in the American educational system – in both K-12 and higher education. However, at this writing, there is no documented plan that expounds on how he, or his education cabinet selection, plan to actualize a national education vision. In the absence of a documented, comprehensive education policy, direct quotes are used as section topics and education industry commentary is provided to confirm, refute, or decry the actualization of the articulated intent, to project the kind of education policy the president-elect might offer.

*Keywords:* higher education, charter schools, education policy

\* \* \*

In September 2016, Sam Clovis, national co-chair and senior policy advisor for Trump's presidential campaign, announced that Trump would provide future details about his higher education platform which would include topics such as: federal student loans, school sharing student loans risk, and folding the Office of Civil Rights into the Justice Department. Other than his four proposals around K-12 school choice, the voting public did not see an elaboration on his higher education platform. Noteworthy of those thoughts that have been shared during the campaign is the lack of a comprehensive consideration of other factors that—directly or indirectly—impact education policy, sans funding and financial resources. Stephan J. Ball, professor of the Sociology of Education, succinctly reminds us "policies are both systems of values and symbolic systems; ways of representing, accounting for and legitimating political decisions" (Ball, 1998). Trump's expressed educational comments somewhat lack the finessed thoughtfulness that takes into account historical inequities, trending demographic shifts, legacy infrastructure deficiencies and current cultural realities – failing to define education in the broader sense of social policy and its respective framework, that encompasses the system of inputs, throughputs, outcomes, and critical adjustment feedback (Whitty, 2001). At times there appears to be sound appeasement, via furious sound bites which lack clear, understandable solutions to the complex challenges of education as an institutional structure. At other times, it appears, that President Elect Trump's proposed policies have reduced complex considerations to a simple, sometimes an inaccurate, incomplete equation. For example, Social Markets (SM)/Institutional Decentralization (ID) = Raising Educational Performance Standards (REPS) = Increased International Competitiveness (IIC) = Making America Great Again (Ball, 1998). It is timely to consider what Trump has said and then examine possible meanings and their future executions along with obvious oversights in proposed processes and implied stratagems answering resistive shortcomings and perpetual failures.

## Trump on Education and Choice

Recently, as the President-Elect, Trump spoke about his reluctance to back current education reform policy and direction. His initiatives – which some see as a Twitter rehash of current initiatives – mirror established school choice programs such as charter schools and education via voucher programs, wherein state funds are used in private school networks. Accordingly, he claims:

> Competition is why I'm very much in favor of school choice. Let schools compete for kids. I guarantee that if you forced schools to get better or close because parents didn't want to enroll their kids there, they would get better. Those schools that weren't good enough to attract students would close, and that's a good thing. For two decades, I've been urging politicians to open the schoolhouse doors and let parents decide which schools are best for their children. (Trump, 2015, p. 53)

Obviously, in that model, each school has its own curriculum and academic programs, resulting in a diverse range of quality and effectiveness in terms of overall education. Inherently, some well-established private schools have an even larger legacy problem of free-range racism to religious obstacles that are, in some cases, a departure to the past—requiring that institutes redefine their historical missions into new practices that are collaborative to support academic diversity.

Teacher rewards, for effectiveness, are another highlight of Trump's core initiatives. However, in a system fraught with already existing inequities in various forms, how will he integrate his teacher-award initiative with the individual initiatives of each state, and accommodate the regulation of programs such as the common core curricula and No Child Left Behind. Teachers who have developed effective teaching methodologies are the new core focus of many jurisdictions and have become the standard to be repeated and scaled. The challenge here is most states have eliminated any teacher tenure protocol and even if the practice had not been eliminated, the expected rise in student performance as am outcome of these masterful teachers has not materialized. As a foundation, alternate education is seemingly Trump's educational policy. As such, his overall policy foundations are rooted on the charter/private school merger to serve each location with its own best practices and local specialization in regard to curriculum, subject, personnel and standard core.

What is lacking from the education discussion entirely is the consideration of school choice availability as a factor of demographics. It is a well-known adage that human nature dictates the desire, across all demographics, to want better for one's offspring. Therefore, it is reasonable to assume that marginalized families or families with low-income still want an education system that affords them the opportunity to have educational choices that accommodate the social and cultural differences of their children. So far, Trump's proposal and communiqué have not conveyed his education concept in a reality showing of choices that systemically relate (Ball, 1993).

Variables such as social class differences, class inequalities, curriculum parody, or educational quality, have not been mentioned in print or discussion. Education policy wonks have verbalized that an education policy without consideration of the desperate differences in terms of educational facilities, instruction vehicles, instructor capacities, and other resource inequities across the nation, present a reason to be concerned about the future of education. The current configuration of public education—particularly in underserved areas—often couples zip codes to educational quality, and in doing so perpetuates the reproduction of inequalities. The concepts of school choice and parental involvement at cursory glance sound like solid, commonsense concepts. However, more delving into our educational systems reveals that the vehicles that currently deliver education reinforces rather than reconstructs class advantage and perpetuates a differentiated and stratified system (Ball, 1993).

## DONALD TRUMP ON THE BUSINESS OF EDUCATION

A big part of Trump's Alternate School Choice initiative involves competition for the student. In essence, schools would compete much in the same manner as businesses in similar industries compete for buyers share. In this model, successful schools would flourish and remain in the educational system as a result of their competitive nature and their efficient and successful school practices, standards and criteria for curricula. These schools would attract the best and the brightest because they would have the resources to do so, and conversely because the best and the brightest would want to attend the school that has the best resources. These schools would, by default, have the best test scores and most favorable outcomes across most standards.

By using the supply and demand model as the gauge, standards would become secondary because in effect the system would become self-balancing. That is, if the school scores were low and had a bad reputation no one would enroll their child in that school. There would be little demand for that school and the school would literally, go out of the business of education. Conversely, if a school was appealing and deemed effective (based on test scores and other standardized indices), then there would be an even greater expansion of the school and its resources would grow proportionate to his higher demand, thereby amounting to a version of educational survival of the fittest.

Trump has called upon Elisabeth DeVos to lead his Department of Education and to translate and formulate his policy for education. Trump has said he believes schools—particularly charter schools—should have diverse and different things to better serve educational needs. DeVos, a chairwoman for the American Federation of Children, is a supporter of school choice. She is purported to believe exceptional schools include exceptional choices via empowered parents, involved teachers and engaged local districts.

Some have called DeVos a controversial choice. Randi Weingarten, representing the American Federation of Teachers, has labeled DeVos as "one of the most anti-public education nominee" since the formation of the Department of Education (Zernike, 2016, para.10). Robin J. Lake, from the University of Washington, said, "every Secretary of Education we have had since [President Bill] Clinton at least has been supportive of charter schools – at least high-quality charter schools. The reality is the federal government has little control over education". Further, an EPI study (2016), authored by Bruce D. Baker, University of Rutgers, suggests that charter school expansion into areas where urban-based, low-income students exist in larger numbers, have produced even more poorly performing schools, deficient academic resources and learning opportunities.

Sometimes, charter schools create core inefficiencies, quality differentials and poorly prepared mission charters with little collaboration with the community they serve. The report concludes, "charter expansion may increase inequity, introduce inefficiencies and redundancies, compromise financial stability, and introduce other objectionable distortions to the system that impede delivery of an equitable distribution of excellent or at least adequate education to all children (Baker, 2016, Summary).

Trump's promise to support increased federal funding to support charter schools, sounds very familiar to Ben Carson's former plan during his run for the presidency. In a Trump/Carson war room, initiatives much like Common Core and any other federal guidance that tend to superimpose policy from a top down perspective tend to be deconstruction. Mr. Trump's belief that educational standards should be set by the federal government as opposed to the reality that individual states are already in control of curricula—with each state setting its own individual territory standards. Mr. Baker also believes that the individual teacher's status should be re-examined, especially in regards to tenure in its present form.

Critics of Ms. DeVos claim her policies illicit uneven responses in logistics and real school operation. Tony Allen, CEO of the Skillman Foundation and the Coalition to Improve Detroit Schools, concerned about the city's schools that have the lowest performing schools in the country, stated, "when I hear her name (DeVos) and I think about education, I think about choice without quality" (Ganim & Tran, 2016, para. 5). While there are strong pushes to champion charter expansions, over the last decade and a half, Michigan's educational student performance has declined when it comes to actual student performance. Fifty percent of Detroit's charters here are listed in the bottom percentile of American schools and in a stalk turnaround. Over 80% of all of Michigan's schools operate as for-profit institutes. The parallels to the prison system are striking (Ganim & Tran, 2015). In interviews about Michigan and charter schools, Allen expressed regret about the proliferation of choice and the speed at which charter schools were created, commenting in hindsight that a better approach would have been to focus on the quality of schools not the quantity. It is evident from her comments that charter schools' effectiveness, at least in Michigan, is more complex in terms of logistics, operationalization, and environment than commonly thought.

Trump has said that current established policies could sometimes punish good teachers, while rewarding bad teachers. However, research does not provide any definitive proof that the teacher compensation has any correlation to student achievement. (Martha Woodall, Philly.com)

## TRUMP ON THE DEPARTMENT OF EDUCATION

In general, one can assume President Donald Trump would concentrate on a streamlined Department of Education. By reorganizing the reach of the department and its policy-making, Trump wants to severely reduce the department's authority as he attempts to redirect each state's ability to customize their education offerings.

A lot of people believe the Department of Education should just be eliminated. .... If we don't eliminate it completely, we certainly need to cut its power and reach. Education has to be run locally. Common Core, No Child Left Behind, and Race to the Top are all programs that take decisions away from parents and local school boards. These programs allow the progressives in the Department of Education to indoctrinate, not educate, our kids.... I am totally against these programs and the Department of Education. It's a disaster. (Trump, 2015, p. 50)

His intent is to establish stronger local school boards and PTA oversight committees that enact a series of smaller, localized boards to mitigate policy, finances and curricula. His reasoning is simple: based on the strengthening of local education, a decentralized Department of Education would not need the resources it currently uses to run its operations. The net funding realized from lower overhead would be re-purposed to push down to the state level. In this Robin Hood operational plan, states get better funding—by default. Against traditional institutions, this plan champions parental choice and school competition as the vehicles to achieve reform, but it also overlooks—and fails to address—what oversight exist that will ensure that local standards are equitably implemented to ensure that all children have the appropriate level of instruction to be successful and what measures can guarantee that those who do not want equality in education to use the charters as the new discrimination dissension: Separate But Not Equal.

## Trump on Student Debt

A four-year degree today can be expensive enough to create six-figure debt. We can't forgive these loans, but we should take steps to help students. The big problem is the federal government. There is no reason the federal government should profit from student loans. This only makes an already difficult problem worse. (Trump, 2015, p. 58)

Part of Trump's profile is his ongoing insistence that he is a successful businessman and that to be successful in life, individuals must master understanding and the manipulation of money and debt. Having the specter of debt following young workers was one of the proclaimed reasons for establishing Trump University.

Simply put, Trump University was supposed to provide a first-class education to eager real estate want-to-be moguls by utilizing the knowledge and experience of seasoned business practitioners. The university was to offer a diverse curricula, directed heavily online, that would be a gleaming example of how education could be streamlined into a more accessible and affordable option. To this end, Trump was grossly unsuccessful and at this time there are pending and ongoing litigation accusing him of intentionally participating in a fraudulent scheme. The three class-action lawsuits (two cases in California, one in New York) are clear indicators that follow-through and ensuring that the details in a project are executed are not his strong suit.

As it relates to student debt, a large part of Trump's strategy would involve the elimination of student debt acquired through student loans. His idea is to remove the government from making profit from student loan borrowers. The projected result of this action will be an increase in higher education participation since the cost would be lower. It is expected that an increasing general enrollment will reduce the current unevenness of graduates' earning power.

The reality is if Trump's implementation tendency is executed with student debt as it was with Trump University/Institute, then we can reasonably expect that the details involved with crafting an affordable education strategy, that offers all students the opportunity to attend college/university, may be well beyond his reach. During the campaigning period, Ben Carson, the presumed education adviser, proposed a "simpler, more streamlined and transparent financial aid process" (Bencarson.com, Treatment plan, para. 5). Not then, nor since then, has a member of the new political team delved below the 40,000-foot assessment level to determine how this goal would be achieved. This is especially true when one considers that Trump is against tuition-free community college education.

## Trump on History

I was listening to some Europeans once and they seemed to agree that Americans didn't seem to know their roots. Of course, their roots go back far many more centuries than ours and may be easier to decipher because many of us have ancestors from different countries. But it gave me a reason to think about what they said, and I realized in many cases they were right. (Trump, 2010, p. 37)

Recently, while speaking on the American flag at a major convention, Trump reflected passionately on America's pride and the country's patriotism—particularly as it relates to schools and the U.S. education system. According to his statement, he believes by integration the American Legion as an active part of education, that nationalistic values can be imprinted into general education, establishing common values, and bond the nation from the bottom up.

As a centralized part of public education, Trump feels that the nation's education system should bear the responsibilities to education American history and America's legacy heroes. By definition, that policy would become divisive because some Americans, particularly African-Americans—and even though they have a shared history with America–have a greater part of their legacy perspectives and experiences that are different than other American citizens. For example, by law and common thought, Harriet Tubman was property and therefore could be excluded from historic discussion, and minimized to greater America, simply because it was most unusual for one to note or talk about property.

Law and common thought considered her a rebellious woman, a criminal and runaway slave. Consequently, with a historical perspective negated by race, there is a one-sided story and an incomplete and perhaps untrue history fraught with omission (of African American contribution) in any reflective manner or validity. Since slaves were forbidden to read and Blacks in general were discouraged from becoming literate, American policy on education and history was for a greater part of American history, strictly dependent on the color of skin making America greatness in education conditional, contradictable, and an injustice to a quarter of all its citizens.

Another example, to most Americans, Windrow Wilson was known as a great educational president. However, to Blacks he was harsh—setting John Crow laws that skirted support in the flavor of pre-Civil war days. In minority America, Wilson was a racist and constantly denied access to the African American community that helped elect him in a close presidential campaign. Nonetheless, greater America applauded his dedication to the national K-12 infrastructure and his contribution towards making public education a quantitative experience and alternative gateway to the American dream. In regards to America, its return to greatness, and education, the question is: which version of history would be taught in publicly supported schools?

## Trump on Comprehensive education, limited majors and funding

The ode to flaws, in charter-based education, is obvious. At the onset, schools in the inner city would have restricted choices based on residency, location, and transportation. Smaller programs that are more specialized would have trouble competing against larger programs for enrollment. This would intensify the challenges that historically Black colleges and university (HBCUs) and minority-serving institutions (MSIs) have attracting and retaining the best and the brightest students before they are hand-picked and mesmerized by full-scholarships and other inducements that majority institutions can afford as a result of their larger endowed funds and generous alumni giving. If Trump's insinuations that students should choose majors that result in direct employment, then what becomes of history, classics, and much of the liberal arts courses of study. Further, what becomes of the variety of university and college size, type, and offerings that is the foundation and jewel of the U.S. higher education system. There is a real chance that policies like this could increase classism amongst educational levels starting from kindergarten through college, where a student's intellect is completely determined by the institution(s) they can afford to attend.

In conclusion, as stated by author, John Wasik, "Trump's proposals will economically harm students. His approach is poorly conceived and comes up short in addressing the core problems of higher education" (Wasik, 2016).

### REFERENCES

Baker, B. D. (2016, November 30). Exploring the consequences of charter school expansion in U.S. cities. *Economic Policy Institute*. Retrieved from: http://www.epi.org/publication/exploring-the-consequences-of-charter-school-expansion-in-u-s-cities/

Ball, S. L. (1998). Big policies/small world: An introduction to international perspectives in education policy. *Comparative Education, (34)*2, 119-130.

Ball, S. L. (1993). Education markets: Choice and social class: The market as a class strategy in the UK and the USA. *British Journal of Sociology of Education, (14)*1, 3-19.

Ball, S. L., Bowe, R. & Gewirtz, S. (1996). School choice, social class and distinction: The realization of social advantage in education. *Journal of Education Policy, (11)*1, 89-112.

Ganim, S. & Tran, L. (2016, December). Trump's choice for education secretary raises questions. *CNN politics*. Retrieved from: http://www.cnn.com/2016/12/02/politics/betsy-devos-michigan-education-legacy/

Strauss, V. (2016, September 10). If this guy is elected, you can kiss public schools goodbye. *The Washington Post*. Retrieved from https://www.washingtonpost.com/news/answer-sheet/wp/2016/09/10/critics-of-trumps-education-policy-kiss-public-schools-goodbye-if-he-wins/

Strauss, V. (2016, August 19). Trump's perplexing comments about education. *The Washington Post*. Retrieved from https://www.washingtonpost.com/news/answer-sheet/wp/2016/08/19/trumps-perplexing-comments-about-education/

Strauss, V. (2016, March 11). Donald Trump thinks Ben Carson is an education expert. Oy vey. *The Washington Post*. Retrieved from https://www.washingtonpost.com/news/answer-sheet/wp/2016/03/11/donald-trump-thinks-ben-carson-is-an-education-expert-oy-vey/?tid=a_inl

Trump, D. J. (2016, September 8). Trump outlines bold new plan for school choice. Donald Trump website. Retrieved from https://www.donaldjtrump.com/press-releases/donald-j.-trump-remarks-on-school-choice

Trump, D. J. (2015). *Crippled America: How to make America great again*. New York, NY: Threshold Editions.

Trump, D. J. (2009). *Think like a champion: An informal education in business and life*. Philadelphia, PA: Running Press Book Publishers.

Trump, D. J. (2000). *The America we deserve*. Los Angeles, CA: Renaissance Books.

Wasik, J. (2016, July). Donald Trump's college plan needs to go back to school. *Money Watch*. Retrieved from http://www.cbsnews.com/news/donald-trumps-college-plan-needs-to-go-back-to-school/

Whitty, G. (2010). Education, social class and social exclusion. *Journal of Education Policy, (16)*4, 287-295.

Zernike, K. (2016, November 24). For education, an advocate who backs shifting money from public schools. *The New York Times*. Retrieved from: http://www.nytimes.com/2016/11/23/us/politics/betsy-devos-trumps-education-pick-has-steered-money-from-public-schools.html

# CHAPTER TWELVE

## *White Nationalism*

### When America was Black and Red: Latino Muslims and the Reimagining of American Greatness

### Sara Swetzoff

The world is changing and the United States is under new pressures; the status quo is more unsustainable than ever before. Many have sought refuge in white nativism or militant isolationism, seizing onto Donald Trump's promise to "make America great again." Others have stood by in passive uncertainty, while others – still in denial about the historical depth and geographical breadth of American violence – have doubled down in their support for the Democratic Party. Each of these reactions is a type of escapism. Trump's rise indicates the urgent need for an existential national reckoning. What is America? Was it ever great? Is it great now?

Answering these questions is imperative to resisting the Trump agenda. Opposing Trump must reach beyond short-term campaigns to protect preexisting policies and liberal values. We have to dig deeper into the genealogy of American violence and ask how national mythologies and economic structures endemic to the United States brought us to this point. Nothing short of a profound, anti-colonial reimagination of life on this continent will prepare us for a just future. I chose the word "prepare" because injustice is unsustainable and therefore change is inevitable: the question is how gracefully it will happen.

This chapter attempts to reimagine American greatness from the vantage point of the Latino Muslim experience, and particularly the writings of Shaykh Yahya Figueroa Abdul-Latif of the Alianza Islamica in New York City. Throughout his campaign, Trump became known for dehumanizing both Muslims and Latinos. He threatened to expel the former. He called the latter rapists and murderers. He set up these two presumably mutually exclusive groups as the twin anti-Americas: the visible, petty criminal right at our border and the terrorist looming everywhere at once.

Thus the Latino Muslim fundamentally challenges the logic of Trump's rhetoric. The twin anti-Americas in fact constitute one hybrid identity that might be considered the very essence of America: Tejano, Chicano, Taino, Afro-Latino, Afro-Brazilian, Aztec, Maya, Navajo. Both indigenous to the New World and spiritually at home across large swathes of the Old World, the Latino Muslim undermines every assumption of white nativism. The complexity of the Latino Muslim story is not the exception, but rather the forgotten rule of these American continents where Black and Red outnumbered White for many long centuries, and Islam figured prominently in numerous insurrections against enslavement and oppression.

The foreigner is in fact the native, whiteness an imposter. America has always been its greatest at any time and place where Black and Red survived and resisted.

It is essential that this decolonial reimagining of America be differentiated from the tired rhetoric of diversity that we have been so well-trained to evoke in our formulations of American possibility. Such rhetoric, like that deployed during the Democratic National Convention, can only take us so far. It is diversity in the service of nationalism and it fails to address the violence embedded deeply in the nation itself. It leaves us all vulnerable to the inevitable collapse of an unsustainable system.

In his book entitled *White Nation: Fantasies of White supremacy in a multicultural society*, Ghassan Hage compels the reader to confront enduring logics of white supremacy that often underpin multicultural advocacy. Although the book's scope focuses on the rise of the Australian right wing during Australia's involvement in the Gulf War, Hage's detailed analyses of liberal expressions of white supremacy hold many lessons for every Western nation born of Eurocentrism and/or white settler movements. In other words, white supremacy does not just look like the overt xenophobia and racism we identify with Trump. It also looks like progressive appeals for inclusion that actually aim to protect the existing system of privileged whiteness. As Hage explains, "Multiculturalism is not central because the subject itself *is* multicultural. Is it central because it figures as a solution to a White problem."[1]

An example of this phenomenon in American politics is the Democratic Party's recent approach to Muslims. Like many across the political spectrum, the Party has condemned Trump's hateful stereotyping and proposal to ban all Muslims. Yet, by repeatedly referencing Muslim Americans' potential role in combatting terrorism, and by showcasing the family of a Muslim veteran during the convention, the Democratic Party's implicit message is that the American Muslim's belonging hinges upon their willingness to inform on their neighbor or unquestioningly sacrifice their children to never-ending war. What is multiculturalism wielded in the service of a police state and military-industrial empire?

Similar rhetoric is deployed in debates regarding Latino Americans. Trump's threats to build a wall are countered by talking points on immigration reform and the importance of Latinos to the American economy. However, this framing of diversity does not challenge the fundamental

---

1  Hage, p.148

assumption that the American public has a right to decide who is legal and illegal on land stolen from Indigenous Peoples.

It is in the context described above that the story of Latino Muslims is so compelling.

Latinos are the fastest growing demographic in the United States, and Latino Muslims are the fastest growing demographic within the greater American Muslim community. This phenomenon has not gone unnoticed by the mainstream media. In an August article published by Horizons, the magazine of the Islamic Society of North America, Wendy Diaz writes that numerous networks including NBC, BBC, PBS, Al-Jazeera, and Telemundo have all featured stories on Latino Muslims in recent years. Diaz also highlights a surge in interest coinciding with Trump's candidacy.

However, many Latino Muslims do not think of themselves as a new group. On Alianza Islamica's blog, Nuyorican elder Yahya Figueroa Abdul-Latif describes Latino Muslim identity as the reclaiming of a much older Islamic heritage that traces back to Andalucia, the region of southern Spain that was once a thriving model of coexistence ("convivencia") in the Middle Ages. Latino Muslims thus root themselves in the memory of a world that profoundly differs from the Eurocentric capitalist-colonialist world system that supplanted it. In 1492 Ferdinand and Isabella completed the violent Christian Reconquista of Andalucia, the same year Columbus set sail from their shores. As Jews and Muslims were expelled from Spain for being the wrong religion, Africans and Indigenous Peoples of the American continents were cast as subhuman and soulless by a system that accumulated land and wealth through genocide and slavery.

Andalucia as an idea thus encompasses far more than a heritage or cultural lineage: it has become synonymous with an ethic of solidarity against supremacy. It evokes a world of coexistence that was not completely vanquished but rather endured in every instance where those disenfranchised by a Eurocentric world order engaged in co-resistance. Just as Nuyorican Muslims got support and guidance from African American imams back when they first started Alianza Islamica in the 1970s, Gullah-Geechee descendants of enslaved West African Muslims allied with the

Seminole Indians to create autonomous, fortified free towns in the Florida south from the early 1700s. In his 2006 book *The Invisible War*, Y. N. Kly recounts how this powerful alliance later staved off the American military for close to fifty years, during the three Seminole Wars which constituted the longest and most expensive of all the Indian wars waged by the U.S.

It is these examples and others, such the successive Islamic insurrections of enslaved Africans that took place in Brazil during the early 1800s,[2] that illustrate the epistemological unity shared by Afrocentricity, Islamic liberation theology, the Andalucian ethic, and Indigenous resistance against colonialism. Writes Dr. Vesta Daniel, "Unlike the pervasive Eurocentrism, which is monocular and teaches that all contributions of value to the history of the world are European based, Afrocentrism encourages the side by side placement and interweaving of all cultural and/or ethnic groups in the construction of world history and culture."[3] The mention of "interweaving" is particularly salient in the American context, where rich hybridized identities abound. This is the story of Latino Muslims and the reason why their thriving community challenges every way in which white supremacy – of both the nativist and multicultural brands – attempts to divide people and define them by their contribution to the state.

Yet these are not just lessons in interpreting the past. They are also tools for the imagining of our futures. Some call this process decolonization. Some call it economic justice. Others speak of truth, reconciliation, and reparations, both material and spiritual. In recent years, Afro-Futurism and Indigenous Futurism have blossomed as literary genres that radically reimagine existence on these lands we call America.

There are also lessons for those of us who have been raised and raced as White. Ana Olian Amets of the blog *Awakening the Horse People* calls upon North Americans of European heritage to confront our complicity in settler-colonialism and answer the calls of Indigenous organizers. Yet, we cannot heal just by disowning colonial pasts: we must reach back

---

2   K. Kazi-Ferrouillet cites Dennis Walker.
3   Cited by K. Kazi-Ferrouillet.

further to retrieve our own indigeneities and thus find the tools to know who we are, not just who we do not want to be.

Rabbi Rosen of Tzedek Chicago clarifies that the re-indigenizing of religious and cultural identity requires its decoupling from statist nationalisms. His congregation is one of the few Jewish communities to brazenly define itself as non-Zionist, explaining, "While we appreciate the important role of the land of Israel in Jewish tradition, liturgy and identity, we do not celebrate the fusing of Judaism with political nationalism. We are non-Zionist, openly acknowledging that the creation of an ethnic Jewish nation state in historic Palestine resulted in an injustice against its indigenous people – an injustice that continues to this day." In a recent sermon delivered in celebration of Rosh Hashanah, Rabbi Rosen articulates the positivist concept of "Diasporism," in which he celebrates the birth and development of Judaism in the Diaspora. For Rosen, Diaspora is the natural condition of a community that views the whole world as a homeland. He quotes Melanie Kaye Kantrowitz, "Diasporists recognize our identity as simultaneously rock, forged under centuries of pressure, and water, infinitely flexible. Diasporism requires those who know and value past and existing tradition and those who create new ones."

If we will transform the larger game of this political system, then we must imagine beyond the boundaries of its logic, and indeed beyond the physical boundaries of the state itself. The recent and ongoing protests against the Dakota Access Pipeline remind us that we are first and foremost accountable to the land and the water that recognize no state, government or border. Let us envision a collective future that centers Indigenous knowledge of this land while harnessing Diasporism in the service of decolonization.

If you have not already read it, the platform recently published by the Movement for Black Lives is one beautiful place to start.

## Reference

Abdul-Latif, Yahya Figueroa. "Alianza Islamica and Andalucia, Part 3." *The Alianza Islamic Blog: Reviving the Lost History of Latino Muslims in the United States*, September 6, 2016. Retrieved September 15, 2016: http://latinomuslim.com/

Amets, Ana Oian and Christine Blanchly. "Renewal, Remembrance, and Resistance for Decolonizing People of European Heritage." PDF downloaded September 2015, awakeningthehorse.wordpress.com

Diaz, Wendy and Juan Galvan. "The Growing Visibility of the Latino/Hispanic Community." *Islamic Horizons*, Volume 45 No. 4, July/August 2016.

Grosfoguel, Ramon and Eric Mielants. "The Long-Duree Entanglement Between Islamophobia and racism in the Modern/Colonial/Capitalist/Patriarchal World-System." *Human Architecture: Journal of the Sociology of Self-Knowledge*, V.1 Fall 2006, 1-12.

Hage, Ghassan. *White Nation: Fantasies of White supremacy in a multicultural society*. Routledge, 2000.

Rosen, Brant. "Celebrating a New Jewish Diasporism: A Sermon for Rosh Hashanah 5777." *Shalom Rav: A Blog by Rabbi Brant Rosen*. Posted and accessed October 4, 2016: https://rabbibrant.com

Kazi-Ferrouillet, K. "Afrocentricity, Islam, and El Hajji Malik Shabazz (Malcolm X). Originally published by *The Black Collegian* and reposted to *Mr. Vance's World History Blog* on February 10, 2009. Retrieved August 25, 2016: http://mrvanceworld.blogspot.com/2009/02/afrocentricity-islam-and-el-hajji-malik.html

Kly, Y.N., ed. *The Invisible War: The African American Anti-Slavery Resistance from the Stono Rebellion through the Seminole Wars*. Clarity Press, 2006.

# Chapter Thirteen

## *Racism and Discrimination*

### Black Activism as the Face of Terrorism? Donald Trump Pins Black Lives Matter a "Terrorist Organization"

#### Ashley L. Lewis, M.A.

Throughout his campaign for presidency, Republican President Donald J. Trump was most vociferous about his contempt for the Black Lives Matter (BLM) organization and its affiliates. Trump passionately insisted that members of the organization caused disorder and chaos at many of his political rallies. He also accused BLM members and supporters of plotting to avenge Black deaths by targeting innocent police officers. Rather than addressing the distressing circumstances that have led to the deaths of more than 175 African Americans by police since January 2015 (Lowery, 2016), Trump waged an all-out rhetorical war against

BLM and others who openly confront societal injustice. Many were surprised by the vulgar rhetoric that Trump's platform as a presidential candidate allowed him to voice to a much larger audience. Still, others could recall past instances where he clearly communicated disdain for African Americans, only these incidents were less publicized. What should be noted, altogether, is that Trump's rhetoric comes from an age-old discourse designed to neutralize resistance by criminalizing Black activism.

The Black Lives Matter organization officially convened in 2014 after starting off as a twitter hashtag following the acquittal of George Zimmerman for murdering African American teenager Trayvon Martin (McLaughlin, 2016). Members of the organization have since devoted their efforts to addressing the unjust targeting and murders of Black civilians. Trump personally charged these activists with inciting violence against police officers. In a conversation with right-wing political commentator Bill O'Reilly, Trump purported to had "seen them [Black Lives Matter activists] marching down the street essentially calling death to the police" (Flores, 2016). Widespread concerns about BLM even sparked the development of an online petition which urged the Obama administration to designate BLM a terrorist organization. The petition garnered more than 141,000 signatures, but was ultimately unsuccessful as the White House is not responsible for designating domestic terror groups (Flores, 2016).

What's more is that Trump's vile treatment of the BLM protestors who attended his political rallies encouraged his supporters to treat them with the same disdain. During a rally held in New Orleans on March 5th, 2016 where Trump was speaking, a group of BLM protestors were "forcibly ejected" from the rally. One Black male protestor was shoved, kicked, and punched by a Trump supporter prior to being ejected (Galperina, 2016; LoBianco & Killough, 2016). In response to the violence that his supporters inflicted on this protester and others, Trump commented that "maybe he [the assaulted protestor] should have been roughed up because it was absolutely disgusting what he was doing" (LoBianco & Killough, 2016). According to thegrio.com, media initially reported that the protestors who were assaulted were not thrown to the ground, but fell to the ground purposely (TheGrio, 2016). This account was later refuted by a woman who attended the rally and witnessed the entire event.

Not only were Donald Trump's rallies a breeding ground for violence and disrespect, but they served as celebrations of hate toward Black activists. In February 2016, Trump encouraged violence against Black dissenters by expressing his desire to punch a BLM protestor in the face (Chiacu, 2016). During another rally, where one African American woman was taunted by a group of White trump supporters, Trump could be heard lamenting "You know, in the old days — which isn't so long ago — when we were less politically correct, that kind of stuff wouldn't have happened. Today we have to be so nice, so nice, we always have to be so nice." (King, 2016). In Cleveland, Ohio, Trump declared that Black Lives Matter activists should "Go Back to Africa" (thegrio, n.d.). At a later rally in Madison, Alabama, Donald Trump exclaimed that all lives mattered while he requested that six Black activists from his rally be removed for protesting. Hypocritically, Trump, during the removal of the activists, advised his protestors to "love everybody" (Martoskso, 2016). Martosko (2016) offers that people, like Donald Trump, who contend that all lives matter, are often perceived to be choosing to align with police and White supremacists while disregarding Black liberal activists. This completely dismisses their very real experiences with racism.

Inciting malice and hatred for Black Americans is only the tip of the iceberg where Trump is concerned. Among one of Trump's most telling pieces of rhetoric during his campaign was a phrase that may have revealed his true feelings toward African Americans as well his intentions for America's future. This phrase, which became a staple of Trumps verbal campaign, promised to "Make America Great Again". Interestingly enough, this same phrase was featured on red baseball caps worn by White supremacists at Kentucky rally in March 2016. Considering America's turbulent, grossly racist history since its official founding in 1776 (and even before this time), it is a wonder what time in American History Trump considered to be "great", and which time in American History Trump hoped to re-create.

Was he referring to a time where Blacks were abused and extorted for free labor? Or the time in history where Blacks were lynched, beaten, terrorized and targeted without warning? Is Trump hoping to re-establish the "law and order" of the Reagan Era (1981- 1989) which initiated the mass incarceration of African American men and women at disproportionately higher rates than Whites? The same era that noted linguist and author Noam Chomsky believes made it impossible for Black men and women to become a part of American society by waging a racist "war on drugs" (Chumley, 2014)? A careful examination of Trump's statements and actions toward Black Lives Matter activists as well as the greater African American community suggests that any one of these periods in America's dark history would suffice for him, as long as African Americans maintain their roles as subjugated people with efforts to resist injustice being met as they always have; with violence and hate.

Unfortunately, Trumps sentiments regarding Black Americans are familiar to most and have only evolved from earlier epochs of hate in his life. Who can forget the five Black and Latino teenagers that Trump referred to as muggers and murderers when they were falsely accused of sexually assaulting and murdering a White female jogger in Central Park in 1989? The New York Times reported that Donald Trump spent about 85,000 dollars on full-page ads in four New York city newspapers, calling for the young men to receive the death penalty (Burns, 2016). Even after they were proven to be innocent 14 years later, Trump refused to retract his earlier statements, maintaining that they were at fault because they admitted guilt (Burns, 2016). The same racism and bias that was characteristic of Donald Trump during this time prevailed in his recent campaign rhetoric and now sadly will have the opportunity to be fully realized once he is inaugurated.

On November 8th, 2016, Donald Trump was elected to succeed President Barack Obama as President of the United States. Since then, quite a few theories have emerged to explain what many believe to be unexplainable. What would move American citizens to elect an under-qualified, inexperienced, ill-tempered suspected White supremacist as the next leader of the free world? Some believe to know the answer to this very difficult question; There are Whites who allege that Donald Trump's victory can be attributed to Black activism (that which has been directly linked to the Black Lives Matter Movement as well as other Black activist groups with no affiliation to BLM). While insulting, it is not all surprising that conservatives would feel this way.

Leon Wolf is a writer for *The Blaze*, a conservative internet newspaper founded by staunch Republican Glenn Beck. In Wolf's opinion piece entitled, "How the Black Lives Matter Movement Helped to Elect Donald Trump", Wolf contends that BLM activists indirectly supported Donald Trump's election by failing to publicly denounce the ambushes and killings of police officers, and by failing to denounce violence as a means of political persuasion (Wolf, 2016). While it is true that some internet users (of all races) have endorsed violence toward law enforcement (just as some internet users have supported and attempted to rationalize police killings of unarmed Black citizens), many of these users are not affiliated with BLM and they should not be grouped with the whole of concerned Black citizens who are calling for reform in all American institutions.

Further, Wolfe's opinions do not negate very real instances where unarmed Black citizens have been slain or accosted by police. In sum, Wolfe's editorial piece reiterates the criminalization of Black activism and how fear of it is so prevalent that it would drive a nation to elect an individual with ties to people who are unabashed White Supremacists. Trump is alleged to be appointing political figures who are indifferent to Black issues, to his presidential cabinet. Of these are Steve Brannon, former Breitbart executive who holds White nationalist views and is associated with the Alt-right (a white nationalist movement). Brannon will serve as Trump's chief strategist, an appointment that Ku Klux Klan leader David Duke personally co-signed (Kaczynski & M2assie, 2016).

Donald Trump's rhetoric is already having a significant influence on our nation. Hours after the election results were revealed, students at a suburban Detroit middle school taunted Mexican students by chanting "Build a Wall" during a lunch period in the school cafeteria (Jacobo, 2016).

This chant comes directly from a statement that Trump made frequently during his campaign regarding his plans to build a wall at the Mexican border to curtail illegal immigration to the United States. Trump's ethnically insensitive phrases and statements have been regurgitated repeatedly in media outlets since his election. Further, Trump's rhetoric will have very tangible consequences for African Americans. For example, Trump has discussed repealing facets of the Affordable Care Act during his stint as President. The Affordable Care Act (2010) made health insurance accessible to over 2 million adult African Americans (Madhani, 2016). Also discussed during his campaign, Trump would like to reinstate the use of Stop and Frisk on national police forces. Previously used in New York, Stop and Frisk was found to be unconstitutional because it unfairly targeted Black and Latino civilians (Lee, 2016).

Rampant protests ignited across the nation after Trump's election. During one protest, students burned American flags on a college campus. However, Black Lives Matter activists specifically, were singled out for these actions. One White student voiced her concern about these actions to the Washington Post, stating "students from the Black Lives Matter group pulled out American flags and started lighting them on fire". She further contended that this action was "disrespectful to her father who serves in the military." (Ernst, 2016). Again, what can clearly be seen is the scapegoating that has become characteristic of discussions regarding Black activists and BLM, who should be free to petition for acknowledgment of their rights and interests as Whites are free to do without fear of reproach.

Frustrated by the outcry from concerned citizens post-election, Bill O'Reilly commented that the "left" feels that white privilege is oppressive and subsequently wants to marginalize White working class voters. He also suggested Blacks want to take power away from the White establishment in order to change the way that America is currently run" (Shapiro, 2016). This did not sit well with African Americans and other non-White groups. Some believe that O'Reilly's true feelings were revealed in this moment and reflected a much larger sentiment about activist groups who fervently demand equal treatment for people of African descent on a global scale.

In sum, Trump's campaign, his prejudiced rhetoric, and the opinions of those who have loyally supported him all contribute to the prevailing discourse where Black activism is concerned. The discourse says that Back activism is dangerous and should be thwarted the very moment any evidence of it emergences. This way of thinking is reminiscent of former FBI director J. Edgar Hoover and COINTELPRO'S (1956-1971) efforts to dismantle the Black Panther Party in the 1960s. Uncovered documents support that this government-created organization's mission was to "expose, disrupt, misdirect, discredit, and otherwise neutralize African American organizations and leaders" (Taylor, 2014). Among these targeted leaders were Malcom X, Martin Luther King Jr., and the Nation of Islam, all known for their efforts to challenge American racism while seeking to improve life for oppressed Black Americans. It is with this awareness that BLM activist and Co-founder Alicia Garza likens Donald Trump's anti-BLM rhetoric to that of a fascist. While BLM activists work to forge new paths for the safety of Black communities in the United States, she asserts that Trump is looking to usher the nation into a repressive state that gives police the authority to "terrorize Black communities".

Richard Cohen, president of the Southern Poverty Law Center (SPLC), writes that the center has received a flood of requests to have BLM labeled a hate group due to the murders of Police officers in cities around the country (Cohen, 2016). The organization does not meet the SPLC's criteria for hate groups which are defined as groups that "vilify entire groups of people based on immutable characteristics such as race or ethnicity" (Cohen, 2016). Contrary to what Donald Trump alleges, it is actually White Supremacist organizations, like those who ascribe to Alt-right ideology, who mobilize with the intention of harming African Americans and other non-White groups, as is reported by the Southern Poverty Law Center. Unfortunately, however, history has shown that assertiveness among Blacks is likely to be interpreted as violent or threatening in the minds of disagreeing Whites. Cohen (2016) also notes that hate for BLM represents a sense of unease among Whites about how our country is changing culturally, with some Whites believing that gains for

African Americans will come at their expense. It is not up to Whites to supervise the anger, frustration, and discomfort that African Americans feel as victims of injustice, nor the ways that African Americans react to incidents of injustice. In fact, what elevates these feelings is when groups of historically disenfranchised people continue to have their concerns and issues policed by Whites who refuse to address the root of the anger.

Donald Trump's rhetoric and his election as President of the United States illuminates the bigger issue with our society; a society that continues to ignore that racial injustice is alive, well, and warrants the activism of groups like BLM. As people of African descent continue to be dedicated to correcting the injustices committed against them, while others like Donald Trump persist to resist change, could Black activism in America become the face of terrorism?

## References:

Aren't more white people than black people killed by police? Yes, but no. *Post Nation*. Retrieved from https://www.washingtonpost.com/news/post-nation/wp/2016/07/11/arent-more-whitepeoplethan-black-people-killed-by-police-yes-but-no/?utm_term=.00c52eeba46c

Burns, S. (2016). Why Trump Doubled Down on the Central Park Five. Retrieved October 18, 2016, from http://www.nytimes.com/2016/10/18/opinion/why-trump-doubled-down-on-the-centralpark-five.html?_r=0

Chiacu, D. (2016). Hecklers disrupt Trump rally, photographer shoved to the ground. Retrieved October 18, 2016, from http://www.reuters.com/article/us-usa-election-idUSMTZSAPEC2TBIQTGK

Chumley, C. K. (2014, December 11). Noam Chomsky: 'Ronald Reagan was an extreme racist–though he denied it'. Retrieved October 19, 2016, from http://www.washingtontimes.com/news/2014/dec/11/noam-chomsky-ronald-reagan-was-anextreme-racist/

Cohen, R. (2016). *Black Lives Matter is not A Hate Group*. Retrieved from Southern Poverty Law Center: https://www.splcenter.org/news/2016/07/19/black-lives-matter-not-hate-group

Ernst, D. (2016, November 10). Donald Trump protesters with black lives matter burn flag at American university, rile veterans. Retrieved December 31, 2016, from http://www.washingtontimes.com/news/2016/nov/10/donald-trump-protesters-with-black-livesmatter-bu/

Flores, R. (2016). Donald Trump: Black Lives Matter Calls for the Killing of Police. Retrieved from http://www.cbsnews.com/news/donald-trump-black-lives-matter-calls-for-killing-police/

Galperina, M. (2016). Black Lives Matter Protesters Violently Thrown Out of Trump Rally in New Orleans. Retrieved from http://gawker.com/black-lives-matter-protesters-violently-thrown-outof-t-1763066858

BKing, S. (2016). Single most racist word Trump has used this campaign. Retrieved October 16, 2016, from http://www.

nydailynews.com/news/politics/king-single-racist-word-trump-campaignarticle-1.2555694

Lee, M. Y. H. (2016, September 28). Trump's false claim that stop and frisk in NYC wasn't ruled unconstitutional. *Washington Post*. Retrieved from https://www.washingtonpost.com/news/factchecker/wp/2016/09/28/trumps-false-claim-that-stop-and-frisk-was-not-ruledunconstitutional/?utm_term=.a2cb7d01dc54

LoBianco, T., & Killough, A. (2016). Trump pitches black voters: 'What the hell do you have to lose?'. Retrieved from http://www.cnn.com/2016/08/19/politics/donald-trump-african-american-voters/

Lowery, W. (2016). Post NationAnalysis. *The Washington Post*.

Madhani, A. (2016, November 10). Trump's victory leaves black community reeling. . Retrieved from http://www.usatoday.com/story/news/politics/elections/2016/2016/11/10/trumps-victory-leavesblack-community-reeling/93562246/

Martosko, D. (2016). 'All lives matter!' Trump takes on Black Lives Matter protesters at rally as controversy mounts over his REFUSAL to disavow ex-KKK leader's endorsement. Retrieved October 18, 2016, from http://www.dailymail.co.uk/news/article-3468603/Trump-goes-toe-toeBlack-Lives-Matter-protesters-rally-saying-lives-matter-controversy-mounts-REFUSALdisavow-former-KKK-leader-David-Duke-s-endorsement.html

McLaughlin, M. (2016). The Dynamic History of #Black Lives Matter. *Black Voices*. Retrieved from http://www.huffingtonpost.com/entry/history-black-livesmatter_us_56d0a3b0e4b0871f60eb4af5

Shapiro, R. (2016, December 21). Bill O'Reilly: "The left wants power taken away from the white establishment." *Huffington Post*. Retrieved from http://www.huffingtonpost.com/entry/billoreilly-the-left-wants-power-taken-away-from-the-whiteestablishment_us_585a1d05e4b0d9a594567f9d

Taylor, G. F. (2013, December 03). The FBI COINTELPRO Program and the Fred Hampton. Retrieved October 19, 2016, from https://warriorpublications.wordpress.com/2014/12/04/the-fbicointelpro-program-and-the-fred-hampton-assassination/

TheGrio. (2016). BLM protesters violently thrown out of Trump rally in New Orleans. Retrieved from http://thegrio.com/2016/03/07/blm-protesters-violently-thrown-out-of-trump-rally-innew-orleans/

Trump supporter yells 'Go back to Africa' to protesters, black woman replies 'Ya'll brought us here'. (n.d.). Retrieved October 18, 2016, from http://thegrio.com/2016/03/14/trump-supporter-yellsgo-back-to-africa-to-protesters-black-woman-replies-yall-brought-us-here/

Wolf, L. (2016, November 15). Commentary: How the black lives matter movement helped elect Donald Trump. Retrieved December 26, 2016, from http://www.theblaze.com/news/2016/11/15/commentary-how-the-black-lives-mattermovement-helped-elect-donald-trump

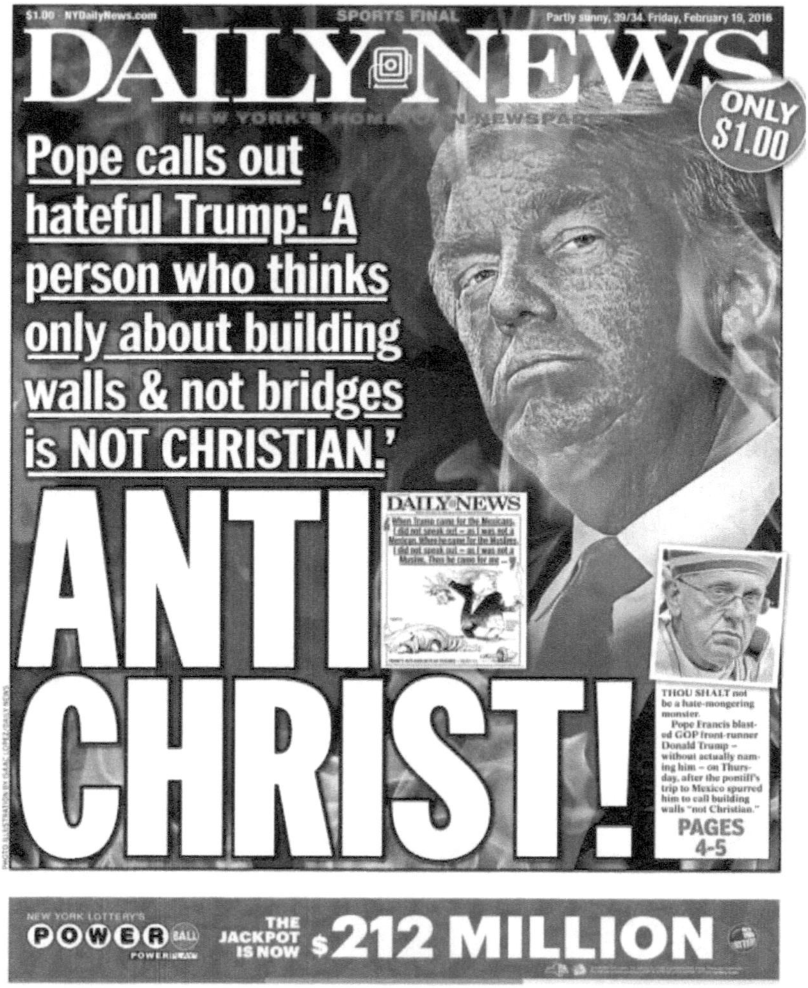

$1.00 · NYDailyNews.com SPORTS FINAL Partly sunny, 39/34. Friday, February 19, 2016

DAILY NEWS

NEW YORK'S HOMETOWN NEWSPAPER

ONLY $1.00

Pope calls out hateful Trump: 'A person who thinks only about building walls & not bridges is NOT CHRISTIAN.'

DAILY NEWS

"When Trump came for the Mexicans, I did not speak out – as I was not a Mexican. When he came for the Muslims, I did not speak out – as I was not a Muslim. Then he came for me ..."

ANTI CHRIST!

THOU SHALT not be a hate-mongering monster.

Pope Francis blasted GOP front-runner Donald Trump – without actually naming him – on Thursday, after the pontiff's trip to Mexico spurred him to call building walls "not Christian."

PAGES 4-5

NEW YORK LOTTERY'S POWERBALL THE JACKPOT IS NOW $212 MILLION

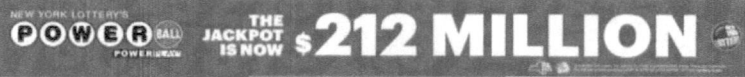

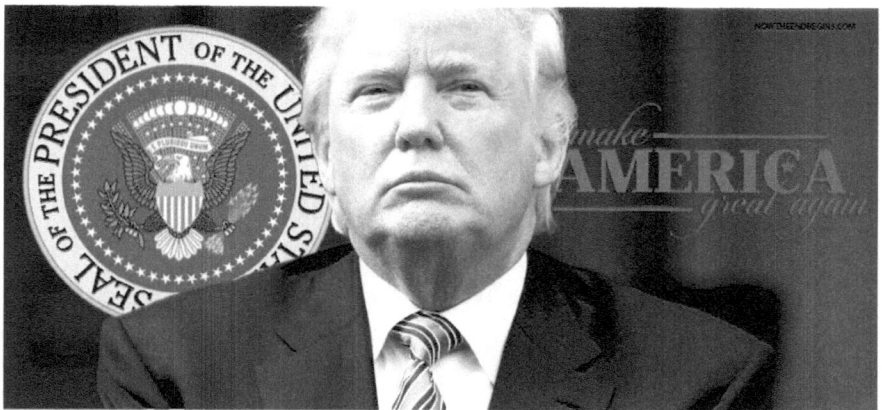

# Chapter Fourteen

## *Politics and Race*

### Linguistic Imperialism: Trump and Making America Great Again

Denise Rosier

**Abstract**

*Make America Great Again!* This was the mantra of the 2016 Republican Party, a kind of rebirth of the Nixonian approach to political campaigning, and a loud echo of those darker periods of racial oppression and strife in American history. Enter Donald J. Trump, trumpeting just how ominously he should be viewed and understood as an activist ready to bring America to some mythical past glory. As the Republican Party nominee, and now as President of the United States, Donald Trump cleverly uses language and words to mesmerize and flatter, to ridicule and scorn, but always to push his agenda, economic, political, and social. Many read the Republican "Make America Great" mantra as part of a white nationalist call to undermine civil rights and voting rights for all Americans, irrespective of race, color, nationality, religion, and national origin (Walters, 2008).

The aim of this research is to categorize and explain Trump's rhetoric and communication style as a nationalist discourse, with imperialist undertones. More significantly, the paper seeks to answer how this fundamental, symbolic and coded language translates into educational policies and regulations that impact marginalized children and youths. Language is pervasive through culture; therefore, it is imperative that we see it not just as words, or accents, or rhetoric, but also as power. This power can be used to implement fear, strip away identity and mask reality by imposing imperialistic ideology using Eurocentric frameworks. What the essay demonstrates is that it is this power that is being translated into the proposed privatization of education coded as charter schools, and the dismantling of government coded as economic savings and the disenfranchisement of HBCUs coded as "Pioneers of School Choice" (Zoppo, 2017)

Using extensive research on Linguistic Imperialism the paper explains that the English language itself is inherently structured to perpetuate "sexism and racism" (Phillipson, Realities and Myths of Linguistic Imperialism, 2010). Linguicism, defined as an ideology structured to promote extreme bias in the division of power (Canagarajah, 1995), is clearly applied in abridging fear of differences as normal dogmatic strategy (Talbott, 2008). In light of the changes in our socio-political climate, the rhetoric manifested in social media, education, and regulatory policies has been drastically reimagined. This paper uses elements of cultural analysis and critical theory, arguing that while Trump certainly is distinguished among American contemporary American politicians for being brazen, intemperate, and imperious, he also personifies white nationalist discourse and ideology. Hence, this research seeks to gauge the extent to which Trump's rhetorical style contributes to white nationalist discourse and ideology. Or, as Bourdieu (2003) asked, how does language perpetuate imperialist ideology?

Trump rose to presidential power on the votes of dispirited whites, whose vanished economic prospects made them susceptible to his cleverly placed ethnic and racial caricatures. His communication style comprised mainly of self-aggrandizing images and symbols present him as a great conciliator and healer, the hero who would swoop in at the last moment to spark a white American renaissance. Of course, not all uses of language aim for imperial ends. Hence our conclusion that language (when rightly used for good ends) can be a fundamental ingredient in halting imperialism, and in preventing it from doing harm.

*Keywords:*

Linguicism, Racial Symbolism, Afrocentricity, Linguistic Imperialism, Racism, White Nationalism, Eurocentric, Diaspora, Identity Construction, Trumpism, White Supremacy

## An Approach

From an Afrocentric framework, Linguistic Imperialism and Linguicism are crucial aspects of critical analysis and cultural theory, to show that there is a weapon of rhetoric being strategically implemented as a means of controlling and perpetuating fear among and within the diaspora. The narrative of animosity within political policies, legislative measures, and the 2016 presidential election, has caused a global imbalance by pitching groups against each other in what resembles a modern day Civil Rights revolution.

## Rationale

Language is the blueprint of our realities. It is not *just words* that are emitted from our lips through a variety of sound vibrations. It is not characters etched on paper to infer or transpose knowledge or ideas. Language is the very fabric of everything that we think, live, feel, breathe, and do everyday of our lives. No socially constructed, race, color, creed, religion, or ideology is immune from language. Like DNA it is the microcosm of everything that makes us tic. For this reason, this topic is not only relevant but also significant to the survival and understanding of why coded language, and symbolic racism play such a large role in political behaviors, and the vigilance that must be manifested to halt the radical play on words, negative symbolism emerged in pictures, caricatures, and policy implementation such as education, which is so critical for marginalized communities.

## Objectives

This paper utilizes a mixed methods approach and two theoretical lenses that consist of Linguistic Imperialism, Linguicism and Afrocentricity as the counter narrative to Trump's rhetoric. I start with definitions of *Linguistic Imperialism as Political Rhetoric and Symbolic Racism*. In fact, this construction is defined as the use of language to extend control over and to perpetuate the subjugation of African and other people. According to Phillipson, "Linguistic imperialism has been traditionally concerned with economic and political aspects of dominance...Later theorists have been concerned with analyzing military, social, communication and culture activities, and the underlying structures and ideologies that link powerful countries" (Phillipson, Linguistic Imperialism Continued, 2009, p. 2). Phillipson explains that, "Linguistic Imperialism presupposes an overarching structure of asymmetrical, unequal exchange, where language dominance dovetails with economic political and other types of dominance" (Phillipson, Linguistic Imperialism Continued, 2009, p. 2). This dominance is prevalent and pervasive, and "can be regarded as a subcategory of cultural imperialism, along with media imperialism (e.g., news agencies, the world information order), educational imperialism (the export of Western Institutional norms, teacher training, textbooks, etc., and World Bank policies privileging Center languages in Education systems" (Phillipson, Linguistic Imperialism Continued, 2009, p. 2).

Linguicism is a term "used to legitimate, effectuate and reproduce unequal division of power and resources (both material and non-material) between groups defined on the basis of ethnicity/cultural/language" (Skutnabb-Kangas, Legitimizing and Delegitimizing New Forms of Racism: The Role of Researchers, l990, p. 77). Unquestionably when used together Linguicism and Linguistic Imperialism generate a tool for critiquing political rhetoric in the media and other systemized communication mechanisms.

Afrocentricity is a powerful contrast to the narrative expressed by many contemporary political pundits. The essence of this concept is agency, location, and respect for the person to assert herself in any situation. Thus, Afrocentricity speaks to growth, self-determination and agency assertion by putting African realities in the center of any situation that involves African people (Asante, The Afrocentric Idea, 1998). Molefi Kete Asante argues that the way of teaching history and culture is often distorted by using a Eurocentric framework that marginalizes African people and handles situations in ways that impact how policy is implemented for continuation of the subjugation of African people (Asante, Afrocentricity: The Theory of Social Change, 2005). Therefore, this current political system must not only be amended, but it must be transformed so that we are able to advance understanding based upon our own sense of agency. In the *Global Intercultural Communication Reader*, Asante and his colleagues say "Afrocentricity constitutes a new way of examining data, a novel orientation to data, it carries with it assumptions about the current state of the African world" (Molefi Kete Asante, 2014). Even more poignant, the education system must be reconstructed in a mass overall to counter the linguistic imperialism agenda that has been implemented in policies thought throughout the country in the education system, capturing young minds and distorting their own self image. Asante writes "On the basis of the Afrocentric paradigm introduced into the philosophical discourse on culture and identity nearly forty years ago I proposed Afrocentric education as a principal road to revolutionary pedagogy and ultimately the total transformation of American education" (Asante, Revolutionary Pedagogy: Primer for Teachers of Black Children, 2017, p. 20). Further more, Harris argues that "recounting our war stories is especially urgent in the arena of politics, mainly because it is the space wherein authoritative decisions (rules, laws, politics, and regulations) and non-decisions emanate, affecting Black and human life in innumerable ways" (Harris, 2016, p. 382).

## Making America Great Again

The rehashing of Reagan's 1980 promise to "Make America Great" (Williamson, 1981, p. 148) slogan appears to be a new tag line for the Trumpism effect. However, for those of us who were not around or too young to remember the Reagan, Nixon and Hoover eras, we have often reacted with shock, trepidation, fear, and uncertainty, simply because of the outcome of the 2016 presidential election. Depression, sadness and protests have marked the win of Trump, who for all intents and purposes, and according to media and political pundits, have taken the United States hostage and no one seem to know how it happened. Many scholars noted, that this should not be a surprise.

This type of upset has happened before, where Trump simply applied the concept of Dog Whistle Politics (Lopez, Dog Whistle Politics: How Coded Racial Appeals Have Reinvented Racism & Wrecked the Middle Class, 2014) to the narrative and rhetoric of his campaign and bogarded his way into the White House. West explains, "public opinion in the United States often is thought to be relatively stable. According to political scientists Benjamin Page and Robert Shapiro in their book, *The Rational Public*, overall citizen views don't change radically over short periods of time. People's opinions about public affairs are deeply rooted in party identifications and ideology, along with personal perceptions related to fundamental issues such as the economy, war, and peace. For those reasons, their perspectives evolve slowly based on social, economic, and political developments" (West, 2016, p. 45).

It appears from the constant chatter on the airwaves and in the newspapers that most of the American public is disgruntled with the state of the union so to speak. Many people tend to think immigrants are taking their jobs (Sanchez), Muslims are terrorists (Terrorism, 2004), women shouldn't be presidents (Faludi, 1991), freedom of choice is murder (Baron, 1989), and freedom of lovers are satanic (Meyer, 2015) and only a bigot billionaire who believe that men have the right to conquer all (Casteneda, 2016), including any woman he so chooses (Sherry, 1992); should be president. The win for Trump despite his hate rhetoric, speaks volume regarding the fear and arrogance of the American populace. So the question remains, who will Trump make America great again for? It appears to be obvious, that it is not for Muslims, Blacks, LBGTQ, Mexicans or Poor Whites. Many scholars are asking this question and the answer is a resounding slap in the face to marginalized communities and across the diaspora. Looking back at history, it is evident that America was great when it was being built on the backs, intellect and charisma of Black people (Tise, 1987); land stolen from indigenous Indians (Deloria, 2013) and Africa was being plundered (Matura, 2011).

Surely Donald Trump knew what he was doing, and he if didn't, he had some very well prepared political strategists and historians guiding him to the most powerful post in the world, the American Presidency. He had the media at a complete loss, by implementing and applying tactics that are beyond the realm of the typical journey of competition for the White House, such as social media. He took a page from the Obama administration book, and lit a fire to it under the proverbial posterior of social media (Harfoush, 2009), that the world was afraid to blink else they miss something. He was prepared by registering the phrase of "Making America Great Again" (Huber, 2016), which was a tag line that the far right who voted Reagan into office loved; and political pundits for this reason, believe that he had his eyes on the white house for decades. As West stated, public opinion don't change much, but they are influenced and reinforced by fear, war, economic and distress (West, 2016).

Reagan, Hoover and Nixon ran the country also at a time when America was in great distress. They used Dog Whistle Politics to speak to the "silent" Majority and Forgotten Americans, which means, White People who yearn for a White America. Dog Whistle politics is a behavior attributed to intentionally using veiled terms to stimulate racial animosity, whipping up popular fears and stroking dangerously and misdirected sentiments. Lopez tells us, that "Dog whistling is widely-and correctly-understood as expressing racially loaded ideas in coded terms. For instance, it uses "inner city" or illegal alien" to stand in for communities of color, and "silent majority" to invoke white people" (Lopez, Dog Whistle Politics: How Coded Racial Appeals Have Reinvented Racism & Wrecked the Middle Class, 2014). It was also noted, that "under the concept of "Dog Whistle", terms like "welfare queen" and "thug" offer prejudiced individuals more acceptable ways for them to say the "N" word without actually saying it" (Lopez, Dog Whistle Politics: How Coded Racial Appeals Have Reinvented Racism & Wrecked the Middle Class, 2014).

Trumpism is a direct spin off from his predecessors' actions, and he used the fears of the "silent" majority to boost him to power. "But there was a darker edge to this connection between politician and people- it was clouded by a "condescending and contemptuous attitude toward the commonality of the American people" (Mason, 2004). Nixon's controversy earned him the name of "Tricky Dick", which is exactly what Trump did to the media. He played a dirty trick on the entire country and won.

## Conclusion

Based on written, spoken, and visual communication, I intend to analyze books, social and online media as well as political campaign messages both current and archived, to show that there was not just racial symbolism being applied to the political campaign of 2015-16. Ultimately, my observations show that the practice of racism in this county is very pervasive and still very alive. From the Hoover era of lynching's, Nixon's rhetoric of getting "niggered", and Reagan "Anti- Civil Rights" policies, Donald Trump is just another president in a long line of hate narrative that is now the modern day lynch DO YOU MEAN "LAUNCH" pad for marginalized communities.

## REFERENCE

Achebe, C. (1976). The African Writer and the English Language. In C. Achebe, *Morning Yet On Creation Day* (pp. 74-84). Anchor Books.

Alexander, N. (2007). Linguistic Diversity in South Africa and the Challenges of the African Renaissance. *South African Embassy*, (pp. 1-35). Berlin.

Asante, M. K. (2005). *Afrocentricity: The Theory of Social Change*. Chicago, IL: African American Images.

Asante, M. K. (2017). *Revolutionary Pedagogy: Primer for Teachers of Black Children*. Brooklyn, NY: Universal Write Publications, LLC.

Asante, M. K. (1998). *The Afrocentric Idea*. Philadelphia, PA: Temple University Press.

Baron, J. (1989). Myside bias in Thinking about Abortion. *UPenn Press*, 17.

Blay, Z. (2016, August 26). *12 Reasons Donald Trump Would Not Be Great For 'The Blacks'*. Retrieved from The Huffington Post: http://www.huffingtonpost.com/entry/8-reasons-donald-trump-would-not-be-great-for-the-blacks_us_56e0729fe4b065e2e3d47e82

Bourdieu, P. (2003). *Language & Symbolic Power*. Cambridge, Massachusetts: Harvard University Press.

Canagarajah, A. S. (1995). Reviewed Work(s): Linguistic Imperialism by Robert Phillipson. *Campbridge University Press*, 590-594.

Casteneda, A. J. (2016, 9 13). Aristotle's Rhetoric in Trump's Hate Speech. *Universidad Panamericana, Guadalajara, Mexico*, 9.

Darwin, C. (2005). *On The Origins of Species by Means of Natural Selection. Adamant Media Corporation*. Adamant Media Corporation.

Deloria, V. (2013). Custer Died for Your Sins: An Indian Manifesto. *SAGE Publications*, 2.

Devenish, H. (1986). *Language and Liberation: Creole Language Politics in the Caribbean*. Londan: Karia Press.

Edlman, M. (1967). *The Symbolic Uses of Politics*. Chicago, Illnois: University of Illinois Press.

Faludi, S. (1991). *Backlash: The Undeclared War Against American Women*. New York, New York: Three Rivers Press.

Fang, M., & Rieger, J. (2016 , September 28). *This May Be The Most Horrible Thing That Donald Trump Believes.* Retrieved from The Huffington Post : http://www.huffingtonpost.com/entry/donald-trump-eugenics_us_57ec4cc2e4b024a52d2cc7f9

Finnegan, T. (2013). No Rights for the Negro which a White Man is Bound to Respect: Lynching and Plitical Power in Mississippi and South Carolina. In T. Finnegan, *A Deed So Accursed* (pp. 55-101). VA: University of Virginia Press.

Galton, F. (1904). Eugenics: It's Definition, Scope, and Aims. *The American Journal of Sociology*, *X* (1).

Harfoush, R. (2009). *Yes We Did: An Inside look at How Social Media Built the Obama Brand.* Berkley , California: New Riders.

Harris, D. T. (2016). Reflections on Political Science. In A. C. Akomolafe, M. K. Asante, & A. Nwoye (Eds.), *We Will Tell Our Own Story!* (p. 402). Brooklyn, NY: Universal Write Publications, LLC.

Huber, L. P. (2016). Make America Great Again: Donald Trump, Racist Nativism and the Virulent Adherance to White Supremacy Amid U.S. Demographic Change. *Charleston Law Review* .

Kamwangamalu, D. N. (2013). Effects of Policy on English-Medium Instruction in Africa. *World Englishes*, *32* (3), 325-337.

Kamwangamalu, N. M. (2004). The Language Policy/Langauge economics interface and mother-tonge education in post-apartheid South Africa. *Langauge Problems and Langauge Planning*, *28* (2), 131-146.

Kendals, F. E. (2006). *Understanding White Priviledge: Creating Pathways to Authentic Relationships Across Race.* New York, New York: Routledge.

LoBianco, T., & Killough, A. (2016, August 19 ). *Trump pitches black voters: 'What the hell do you have to lose?'.* Retrieved from CNN.com: http://www.cnn.com/2016/08/19/politics/donald-trump-african-american-voters/

Lopez, I. H. (2014). *Dog Whistle Politics: How Coded Racial Appeals Have Reinvented Racism & Wrecked the Middle Class.* New York , New York: Oxford University Press.

Lopez, I. H. (2014). *Dog Whistle Politics: How Coded Racial Appeals Have Reinvented Racism and Wrecked the Middle Class.* New York, New York: Oxford University Press.

Mason, R. (2004). *Richard Nixon and the Qeust for a New Majority.* NC: The University of North Carolina Press.

Matura, P. M. (2011). The 'voracious dragon', the 'scramble' and the 'honey pot': Conceptions of Conflict over Africa's Natural Resources. *Journal of Contempoary African Studies, 29* (2).

Mazrui, A. (2016). the Linguistic Balance Sheet: Post-Cold War, Post-Apartheid & Beyond Structural Adjustment. *Course Reader,* 195-211.

Meyer, D. (2015). *Violence against Queer People: Race, Class, Gender, and the Persistence of Anti-LBBT Discrimination.* Rutgers University Press.

Molefi Kete Asante, Y. M. (Ed.). (2014). *The Global Intercultural Communication Reader.* New York, NY: Routledge.

Phillipson, R. (2009). *Linguistic Imperialism Continued.* New York, New York: Routledge.

Phillipson, R. (2010, March 29). Realities and Myths of Linguistic Imperialism. *Journal of Multilingual and Multicultural Development*, 238-248.

Roberts, D. (2011). *Fatal Invention: How Science, Politics, and Big Businesses Re-Create Race in the Twenty-First Century.* New York: New Press.

Roberts, D. (1997 ). *Killing the Black Body: Race, Reproduction, and the Meaning of Liberty.* New York : Random House .

Sanchez, G. J. (n.d.). Face the Nation: Race, Immigration and the Rise of Nativism in Late Twentieth Century America. *University of Southern California ,* 22.

Sherry, S. (1992). The Forgotten Victims. *Vanderbilt University's Institutional Repositiory* .

Skutnabb-Kangas, T. (2010, September 14). Legitimating or delegitimating new forms of racism-the role of researchers. *Journal of Multilingual and Multicultural Development* , 77-100.

Skutnabb-Kangas, T. (1990). Legitimizing or deliegitimating new forms of racism-the role of researchers. *Journal of Multilingual and Multicultural Developement, 11* (1-2), 77-100.

Talbott, J. R. (2008). *Obama Nomics: How Bottom-Up Economic Prosperity Will Replace Trickle-Down Economics.* New York, NY: Seven Stories Press.

Terrorism, a. S. (2004). Combating Al . *The Washington Quarterly Center for Strategic and Int'l Studies, 27* (3), 67-90 .

Thiong'O, N. w. (2003). Consciousness and African Renaissance: South Africa in the black Imagination. *The Fourth Annual Steve Biko Memorial Lecture, University of Cape Town, South Africa*, (pp. 1-11). Cape Town.

Tise, L. E. (1987). *Proslavery: A History of the Defense of Slavery in America, 1701-1840.* Athens: University of Georgia Press.

Walters, R. W. (2008). *The Price of Racial Reconciliation.* Michigan, Michigan: University of Michigan Press.

West, D. M. (2016). Economic Disruption, Political Upheaval, and Social Strife in the 21st Century. In D. M. West, *Megachange* (p. 45). Bookings Institution Press.

Williamson, R. S. (1981). The Reagan Campaign: Harbinger of a Revitalized Federalism. *Oxford Journals, 11* (3/4), 147-153.

Woodruff, B. (2016, July 22). *Meet the Shady Network of Immigration Opponents Donald Trump Loves to Cite.* Retrieved from The Daily Beast : http://www.thedailybeast.com/articles/2016/07/22/meet-the-shady-network-of-immigration-opponents-donald-trump-loves-to-cite.html

Zoppo, A. (2017, February 28). *DeVos Slammed as "Totally Nuts" for Calling HBCUs "Pioneers of School Choice".* Retrieved March 14, 2017, from NBC NEWS: www.nbcnews.com/news/nbcblk/devos-slammed-totally-nuts-calling-hbcus-pioneers-school-choice-n726856

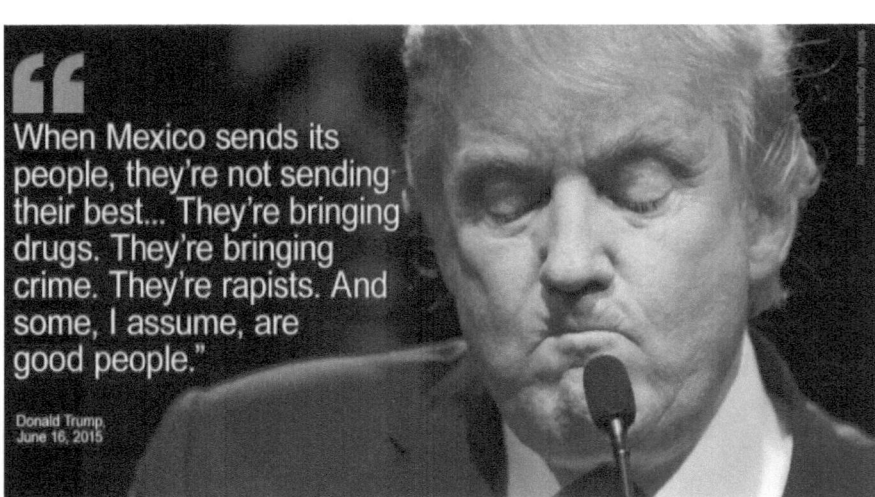

# CHAPTER FIFTEEN

## *Racism and Rhetoric*

### Trump, Eugenics, and the Black Inferiority Complex

### Jaimee A. Swift, Doctoral Student, Howard University, Department of Political Science

*"I have a certain gene, I'm — I'm a gene believer."* [1]

These words are spoken by none other than President Donald J. Trump. Known for his abrasive and abusive rhetoric, which spans the racist, homophobic, sexist and misogynistic gamut, Trump's hate speech was a customary fixture in his campaign. However, his *"I have a certain gene,"* comment — and the countless references Trump has made in regards to his

---

1   (Fang and Rieger 2016)

"intellectual" prowess — it is critical to look at the deeper paradigm of not only what Trump says, but the hegemonic context and construct in which he operates his political machine. Here, Trump's pomposity not only derives from a socio-economic and political, white supremacist framework, but an innate, biological one as well; in which, he believes that his genes and the nature of his bloodline have distinguished him, his family and other 'privileged' members of society from being conflated with that of the lowly masses.

With Trump claiming the "right genes" gave him the "right brain", Here, Trump's pomposity simply community, but their intellectual capacity as well. mmunity is not smart enough to him for what1 111[2] his ideology stems from eugenics, which historically advocated for sexual reproduction with only groups of "superior" genetic breed and therefore, castigates those with "inferior" bio-genetics as menial. The eugenics framework is therefore a scientific, racial theory which adheres to the notions of an inherent, genetic hierarchy, which Trump subscribes to. In spite of his constant pandering to the Black community in efforts to galvanize the Black vote, Trump's ideological and political frame and eugenics is inextricably intertwined, and therefore, not only renders Black people as subsidiary in the social realm, but also biologically deficient and intellectually inferior. Here, Trump cannot separate his eugenic idealism from that of his politics, and his lack of political correctness is telling of his true colors in how he feels about the intellectual capacity of certain communities — especially the Black and the brown ones.

Here, I provide a brief overview of the foundational framework of eugenics theory, and how Trump's political and philosophical discourse to and about the Black community emphasizes his eugenics ideology, ultimately governing his mindset of Black people as intellectually inferior and therefore, genetically subordinate.

---

2   (Fang and Rieger 2016)

## Race, Eugenics, and the 'Intelligentsia'

In 1859, Charles Darwin published his book "On The Origins of Species by Means of Natural Selection"[3], a scientific literature purporting that humanity, just as in animal and plant kingdoms, has a natural selection process; a "survival of the fittest" where "the strong" surpass "the weak" in society. Later known as Social Darwinism, the theory would be the formidable framework for several socio-political movements and actors throughout history, who would brandish Darwin's dogma as a weapon to justify racial and genetic superiority and intellectual segregation. One of the most notorious institutions to use biological determinism to promote racial stratification would be The American Eugenics Society.

Coined by Sir Francis Galton in 1883, "eugenics" (also called the "study of Race Improvement") "is the science which deals with all influences that improve the inborn qualities of a race; also with those that develop them to the utmost advantage."[4] In the book "Killing the Black Body: Race, Reproduction, and the Meaning of Liberty", author Dorothy Roberts expounds on the work of Galton, who believed that since intelligence and character were intertwined, it was imperative "society should take steps to encourage the procreation of superior stock."[5] In order to keep one's genetic pool biologically and intellectually superior, one must distinguish each race's characteristics, as not to breed with subordinates. In Galton's purview, to mate with the Black race, especially, would be a seditious act against genetic purity. Galton writes this passage about the traits of the Black race:

> "The Negro has strong impulsive passions, and neither patience, reticence, nor dignity. He is warm-hearted, loving towards his master's children, and idolized by the children in return. He is eminently gregarious, for he is always jabbering, quarrelling, tom-tom-ing, or dancing. He is remarkably domestic, and is endowed with such constitutional vigour, and is so prolific, that his race is irrepressible." [6]

---

3   (Darwin 2005)
4   (Galton, 1904)
5   (Roberts, 1997)
6   (Roberts, 1997 )

Roberts also asserts in her 2011 book, "Fatal Invention: How Science, Politics, and Big Businesses Re-Create Race in the Twenty-First Century", that humanity is void of biological races and it is proven, scientifically, there are more genetic variations within racial groups than in-between.[7] However, eugenicists used the social construction of race to implement their racism into science; thus, validating their beliefs of genetic and intellectual degeneracy amongst certain racial groups in the United States, most notably Blacks.[8] Operating from a classical liberalist stance and in objection to social programs to "improve the living conditions of the poor" and also in connection with the Ku Klux Klan, The American Eugenics Society (which was formally established in 1925) was notably known for their application of what Roberts' calls negative eugenics, inflicting compulsory sterilization "to prevent socially undesirable populations from procreating." [9] Using IQ tests and cranial capacity analyses to assess intellectual inferiority, whites' racial indifference to Blacks served as the catalyst for eugenicists to implement sterilization and also, castration:

The idea of imposing sterilization as a solution for antisocial behavior originated in the castration of Black men as a punishment for crime. In the eighteenth-century Virginia, castration was imposed on slaves "convicted of an attempt to ravish a white woman." In 1855, the territorial legislature of Kansas enacted a law making castration the penalty for any Negro or mulatto who was convicted of rape, attempted rape, or kidnapping of any white woman. Other state legislatures considered, but failed to pass, similar legislation. Around that time, a Texas physician, Dr. Gideon Linecum, disseminated to lawmakers and the press an essay advocating castration as a deterrent to crime. He supported his proposition with an anecdote about a "vicious, disobedient, drunken Negro" who was suspected of raping women of his own race: "After discovering that he had impregnated an idiot white girl, three men went into the field where he worked and castrated him. Less than two years later I heard his mistress say that he had become a model servant." [10]

---

7 (Roberts, 2011)
8 (Roberts, 2011)
9 (Roberts, 1997)
10 (Roberts, 1997 )

Negative eugenicists' use of compulsory sterilization would also play a critical role in the reproductive freedom in the Black community, especially among Black women. Roberts argues that while castration and other violent, involuntary mechanisms were enforced on the Black community under eugenics laws, the compulsory sterilization of Black women, however, was not always initiated under such regulations. [11]Much of the forced sterilization that was imposed on Black women was enacted by medical doctors, who were given funds from the state to "provide healthcare for these women." [12] These sterilizations were often given without consent nor were they initiated for specific medical needs or concerns; thus, fueling a pervasive, generational mistrust between the Black community and the medical industry. Civil Rights' activist, Fannie Lou Hamer, was a victim of forced sterilization, having a "complete hysterectomy without her knowledge or consent." [13]

While this brief summary of eugenics does not fully capture the pervasive violence and vile actions enacted by many proponents of eugenics theory on the Black community, it serves as a synopsis to showcase the political dogma of Trump and its relativity to the eugenics framework; which governs his bigoted and pernicious responses to the Black people.

## TRUMP, EUGENICS THEORY, AND THE IDEALISM OF BLACK INFERIORITY

> *"All men are created equal. Well it's not true.*
> *Cause some are smart, some aren't."*
> *"When you connect two racehorses, you usually end up with a fast racehorse."*
> *"Do we believe in the gene thing? I mean, I do."*
> *"Some people cannot genetically handle pressure."*

---

11  (Roberts, 1997 )
12  (Roberts, 1997 )
13  (Roberts, 1997)

Trump's statements above — and the countless others that were reflected in a video produced by *The Huffington Post* [14]— are some remarks which the news organization compiled from Trump's speeches and social commentary that uncover and expound upon his eugenicist belief system. A Frontline documentary titled "The Choice" which aired on PBS in September, probes into the backgrounds of both presidential candidates, Trump and Democratic contender, Hillary Clinton, and subsequently, what has cultivated their socio-political aspirations and their leadership systems. In the documentary, Trump's biographer, Michael D'Antonio, noted that his ties to eugenics were initiated at birth; citing that his ideology is that of a "racehorse theory", which Trump believes is a genetic factor, contributing to his and his family's success:

> "The family subscribes to a racehorse theory of development. They believe that there are superior people and that if you put together the genes of a superior woman and a superior man, you get a superior offspring." [15]

Trump's "racehorse" framework is also reflected in his political advertisements. In one of his commercials, The Center for Immigration Studies is noted at the bottom. The founder of the Center for Immigration Studies is John Tanton, a known eugenicist and anti-immigrant extremist, with white nationalist roots. In his many speeches, Trump has also cited data from Tanton's other anti-immigrant group, the Federation for Immigration Reform (FAIR). [16]

In regards to the Black community, Trump's eugenics ideology is rampant and can be found in how he addresses and mocks their concerns, needs, and even socio-economical and political status in the United States. Here, Trump's Black inferiority complex is evident in his extensive and offensive timeline about the Black community throughout his campaign

---

14 (Fang and Rieger 2016 )
15 (Fang and Rieger 2016)
16 (Woodruff 2016)

trail, and even prior to it. In August, during one of his speeches addressing a predominantly white community in Dimondale, Michigan, he elicited a quipping question to the Black community, which reinforced not only stereotypical notions, but is telling of his skewed perception of all "the Blacks" and their "lesser" place in society:

*"You're living in poverty, your schools are no good, you have no jobs, 58 percent of your youth is unemployed — what the hell do you have to lose?"* [17]

Here, Trump's statistics on Blacks in America living in poverty are askew, as according to the Henry J. Kaiser Foundation's survey on poverty rate by race and ethnicity, shows that the majority of African-Americans do not live in poverty. Also, his metrics on Black employment rate was too, wrong: the unemployment rate for Black youth is 18.7 percent and not 58 percent.[18]

Endorsed and supported by members of the Ku Klux Klan, most notably by David Duke, a white nationalist and former Imperial Wizard, his stance towards "black-on-black" crime and the Black Lives Matter movement is too, revealing of Trump's outlook on the notions of Black intellectual subservience. Instead of addressing institutional and structural forces that have culminated the pervasive disenfranchisement of disadvantaged groups, Trump overlooks such hegemonic order and instead views it from a classical liberalist function of one's individual work ethic and also their genetics, as a reason for their lack of success in American society:

*"Look, it is a disaster the way African-Americans are living... We'll get rid of the crime. You'll be able to walk down the street without getting shot. Right now, you walk down the street, you get shot."* [19]

While these statements are fairly recent, Trump's supremacist comments about the Black community and their intellectual capacity are not

---

17  (LoBianco and Killough 2016)
18  (Blay 2016)
19  (Blay 2016)

some new phenomena. In 1991, Trump allegedly said that "Laziness is a trait in blacks, according to the former Trump Plaza Hotel & Casino president John R. O'Donnell." [20]

"According to a book written by former Trump Plaza Hotel & Casino president John R. O'Donnell, the real estate mogul once said in 1991 that "Laziness is a trait in blacks." He was allegedly referring to a black accountant working for Trump Plaza, and added, ""Black guys counting my money! I hate it. The only kind of people I want counting my money are short guys that wear yarmulkes every day." The kicker is that Trump, in a 1999 Playboy magazine interview, did not even *deny* saying those things. He admitted O'Donnell's allegations were "probably true," but insisted it didn't matter because he was obviously a disgruntled employee."[21]

In efforts to revitalize his "relationship" with the Black community and to distance himself from his father's ties in Klan riots, although Trump has recalibrated his campaign to appeal to Black voters by visiting Black churches in Cleveland and Detroit and hiring Omarosa Manigault as his campaign's African-American outreach director, Trump's pandering too, also reflects a political tactic that views Black people as intellectually inferior for this reason: he acts as if the Black community does not see, understand, or comprehend that his newly found interest is only to garner votes for his political prowess.

While Blackness and political partisanship are not monoliths nor do they do not exist in vacuums, Trump's belief in Black intellectual inferiority is so acute, that he presumes the Black community is not smart enough to see him for *who* and *what* he really is — a white supremacist, a racist, and eugenicist, who has no regard for the not only the physical or political status of the Black community, but their intellectual capacity as well.

---

20  (Blay 2016)
21  (Blay 2016)

## Reference

Blay, Z. (2016, August 26). *12 Reasons Donald Trump Would Not Be Great For 'The Blacks'*. Retrieved from The Huffington Post: http://www.huffingtonpost.com/entry/8-reasons-donald-trump-would-not-be-great-for-the-blacks_us_56e0729fe4b065e2e3d47e82

Darwin, C. (2005). *On The Origins of Species by Means of Natural Selection*. Adamant Media Corporation. Adamant Media Corporation.

Fang, M., & Rieger, J. (2016, September 28). *This May Be The Most Horrible Thing That Donald Trump Believes*. Retrieved from The Huffington Post: http://www.huffingtonpost.com/entry/donald-trump-eugenics_us_57ec4cc2e4b024a52d2cc7f9

Galton, F. (1904). Eugenics: It's Definition, Scope, and Aims. *The American Journal of Sociology*, X (1).

LoBianco, T., & Killough, A. (2016, August 19). *Trump pitches black voters: 'What the hell do you have to lose?'*. Retrieved from CNN.com: http://www.cnn.com/2016/08/19/politics/donald-trump-african-american-voters/

Roberts, D. (2011). *Fatal Invention: How Science, Politics, and Big Businesses Re-Create Race in the Twenty-First Century*. New York: New Press.

Roberts, D. (1997). *Killing the Black Body: Race, Reproduction, and the Meaning of Liberty*. New York: Random House.

Woodruff, B. (2016, July 22). *Meet the Shady Network of Immigration Opponents Donald Trump Loves to Cite*. Retrieved from The Daily Beast: http://www.thedailybeast.com/articles/2016/07/22/meet-the-shady-network-of-immigration-opponents-donald-trump-loves-to-cite.html

# Chapter Sixteen

## *Islamophobia*

### Trump's Anti-Muslim Rhetoric and the Implications for Clinical Social Work Practice

#### Stephenie Howard

Anti-Muslim and Islamophobic discourse in the United States predates the attacks of 9/11; however, since that time, American media outlets have broadcasted and propagated news of terrorist attacks committed nationally and abroad, inciting fears of a homeland under attack by adherents of Islam (Ogan, Willnat, Pennington, & Bashir, 2014). This narrative of terrorism has been exploited by Donald Trump in his presidential campaign. Indeed, a few months after he announced his run for office, Trump (2015) released a press statement calling for the "total and complete shutdown of Muslims entering the United States" (n.p.). He supported his proposal with vague and less than credible research

(Gunter, 2015) suggesting that large segments of the Muslim population harbor "great hatred for Americans" (Trump, 2015, n.p.).

In several iterations of his immigration policy, Trump relaxed his ban on Muslims and introduced a policy of "extreme vetting" (White, 2016, n.p.). As reflected in the transcript provided by White (2016) of Trump's town hall speech, Trump framed the policy as a strategy for thwarting the spread of "Radical Islamic" ideologies and practices to America (n.p.). While upholding a temporary suspension of immigrants from Muslim countries, he advanced an ideological screening test to exclude individuals with values that he suggested run counter to gay rights, women's liberation, and religious freedom. Additionally, for Muslims who gain admittance into the US, Trump implored them to assimilate into mainstream American culture as an indication of their allegiance to the country. Finally, in this speech, Trump put upon "moderate" Muslims the onus of preventing terrorism and profiling individuals in their communities (n.p.).

Trump's hate rhetoric falls into the 24 hours a day, 7 days a week news cycle, influencing the sentiments of Americans towards Muslims. In fact, a recent study found media exposure of Muslim-related issues to be positively associated with anti-Muslim and Islamophobic attitudes among American respondents (Ogan, et al., 2014). Thus, considering the widespread coverage of Trump and his hate rhetoric, it should be no surprise that Muslims residing in the US are experiencing increased anti-Muslim and Islamophobic hostility and scrutiny (Shammas, 2015). As evidence of such, a brief case study is presented below. The client's name has been changed to protect her identity.

## Case Study

Tahera is a 12-year-old Muslim girl from Saudi Arabia. After moving to the United States, Tahera began demonstrating changes in her religious practices. In particular, Tahera wore a headscarf every day in Saudi Arabia as a reflection of her understanding and observance of the commandments of God; however, she discontinued the practice of veiling shortly after transferring to an American public school. Tahera expressed concerns that her headscarf functioned as a symbol of Islam and her peers appeared to conflate terrorism and extremists with Islam and Muslims. As such, she felt it necessary to be submissive and accommodating in order to distance herself from the terrorist stereotype. However, she found these acts of submission to be inauthentic and demeaning. In order to minimize their identification of her as a terrorist without compromising her integrity, she decided to abandon wearing the headscarf. Without her headscarf, she reported feeling a better sense of belonging and acceptance by her peers. However, she also reported significant feelings of guilt and shame for not veiling herself in public and new somatic pain and anxiety symptoms to include panic attacks. She attributed these feelings of distress as well as any negative events and personal adversities to God's displeasure in her decision not to veil herself. It was apparent that her abandonment of the practice of veiling caused her clinically significant distress.

## IMPLICATIONS

### *Assessment*

Because it is clear that social workers will come into contact with Muslims who are negatively impacted by this culture of Islamophobia, it is imperative that an assessment of exposure to differential treatment and discrimination be integrated into clinical services with Muslim clients (Hodge, Zidan, & Husain, 2015). This assessment should be sensitive to both overt and subtle forms of discrimination as well as the intersectionality of race, gender, and class (see Nadal et al., 2012). Social workers should be cognizant that Muslim women may be more vulnerable targets for Islamophobic victimization by virtue of their veil as a symbol of Islam (Zempi, 2014). Additionally, it should be noted that Black Muslims may have difficulties identifying which of their identities is targeted and may spend inordinate time and energy ruminating over the incident and how to respond (Sue, 2010). As such, clinicians should be sensitive to any disclosures of discrimination and respond with validation, competence, and compassion, being careful not to participate in victim-blaming or the minimization or rationalization of the client's experience (Bryant-Davis, 2007).

If it is determined that a Muslim client has experienced Islamophobia or religious discrimination, then it is critical that social workers identify the long and short term impacts. Towards this goal, social workers should process the incident with the client from a cognitive, emotional, and behavior standpoint (see Sue, 2010). This discussion should help the client to organize and understand how he or she perceived the incident, his or her immediate reaction, the meaning that he or she attached to the incident, and the cumulative impact overtime to include changes in mood (Sue, 2010). Social workers should also be attentive to any changes in behavior, as, as evident in the case study, it may be experienced as a loss of religious integrity that manifests in clinically significant distress.

*Treatment*

Social workers are called by an ethical and professional mandate to intervene in the lives of Muslim clients adversely affected by the climate of Islamophobia (NASW, 2008). Such interventions should be driven by the values, traditions, and belief system of Islam (Husain & Hodge, 2016). Indeed, scholarship has demonstrated the importance of integrating religion into clinical practice for Muslim clients who place Islam as a central force in their lives (Abu Raiya & Pargament, 2010). Even more, scholars have found advantage in helping Muslim clients to draw on Islamic religious coping methods to deal with stressors (Abu Raiya & Pargament, 2010). Towards this goal, Muslim clients may be served by Islamically modified cognitive behavioral therapy (Husain & Hodge, 2016). This clinical intervention adapts traditional cognitive-behavioral statements to reflect Islamic values. This modality of treatment is useful in helping Muslim clients to identify and reframe harmful schemas into more adaptive patterns of thinking as consistent with their value set (Husain & Hodge, 2016). In doing so, therapists may be able to help Muslim clients to understand the impact that exposure to Islamophobia has had in their lives and to ameliorate its harmful effects.

In addition to therapeutic interventions, support groups for Muslims may also be instrumental in redressing the harmful impact of exposure to Islamophobia. These groups may afford Muslims a safe space to discuss their concerns regarding religious matters and to conceive of solutions collaboratively (Ali & Bagheri, 2009). Muslims may also come together in these groups to negotiate their religious identity and its expression within the context of exposure to discriminatory treatment and bigotry (Ali & Bagheri, 2009; Mubarak, 2007). These group experiences may build upon their individual and collective power to respond to instances of Islamophobia.

Special clinical attention should be given to Muslim children exposed to religious discrimination. From an Eriksonian perspective, healthy development is dependent on feeling secure, competent, and accepted by others (Erikson, 1980). Exposure to Islamophobia conveys messages that are directly antagonistic to these ego-gains. However, early intervention may aid in preventing detrimental outcomes among this population. In the clinical setting, social workers can assist Muslim children in understanding the relationship between religious discrimination and internal conflicts and to reframe negative self-talk with positive affirmations (Garber, Frankel, & Herrington, 2016). While there remains a need for more developmentally-sensitive cognitive-behavioral interventions for children, clinicians should aim to tailor treatments to match children's social-emotional skill-level (Garber, Frankel, & Herrington, 2016; Lickel, MacLean, Blakeley-Smith, & Hepburn, 2012). Muslim children may also benefit from being connecting with other Muslim children to help normalize her experiences and to aid in problem solving around exposure to Islamophobia.

## Conclusion

With Trump securing nearly half of the country's vote for president, it is difficult to deny a culture of Islamophobia and bias in America (McCormick & Niquette, 2016). The Trump victory speaks to a prevailing indifference for the marginalization and oppression of the Muslim population at best and a widespread bias for Muslim persons at worst. The widespread acceptance of Trump's hate rhetoric also conveys to Muslims that they do not belong in America and are not welcome. As evident in the case study presented in this paper, these messages of Islamophobia may manifest in clinically significant distress among Muslims. As such, social workers should be prepared to assess for exposure to differential treatment and religious discrimination among Muslim clients and to identify and address its impact. Such services should be informed by extant scholarship, which have provided models for culturally sensitive interventions for Muslim populations. With informed and culturally sensitive attention to the needs of Muslim clients, social workers can help to mitigate the deleterious impact of Trump's hate rhetoric on Muslim clients.

**REFERENCES**

Abu Raiya, H., & Pargament, K. I. (2010). Religiously integrated psychotherapy with Muslim clients: From research to practice. *Professional Psychology: Research and Practice, 41*(2), 181-188.

Ali, S. R., & Bagheri, E. (2009). Practical suggestions to accommodate the needs of Muslim students on campus. *New Directions for Student Services, 125*, 47-54.

Bryant-Davis, T. (2007). Healing Requires Recognition: The Case for Race-Based Traumatic Stress. *The Counseling Psychologist, 35*(1), 135-143.

Erikson, E. (1980). Identity and the life cycle. New York, NY: Norton.

Garber, J., Frankel, S. A., & Herrington, C. G. (2016). Developmental Demands of Cognitive Behavioral Therapy for Depression in Children and Adolescents: Cognitive, Social, and Emotional Processes. *Annual review of clinical psychology, 12*, 181-216.

Gunter, J. (2015, December 8). *Trump's 'Muslim lockdown': What is the Center for Security Policy?* Retrieved from http://www.bbc.com/news/world-us-canada-35037943

Hodge, D. R., Zidan, T., & Husain, A. (2015). Depression among Muslims in the United States: Examining the Role of Discrimination and Spirituality as Risk and Protective Factors. *Social Work, 61*(1), 45-52.

Husain, A., & Hodge, D. R. (2016). Islamically modified cognitive behavioral therapy: Enhancing outcomes by increasing the cultural congruence of cognitive behavioral therapy self-statements. *International Social Work, 59*(3), 393-405.

Husain, A., & Ross-Sheriff, F. (2011). Cultural competence with Muslim Americans. In D. Lum (Ed.), *Culturally competent practice: A framework for understanding diverse groups and justice issues* (4th ed., pp. 358-389). Belmont, CA: Brooks/Cole.

Lickel, A., MacLean, W. E., Blakeley-Smith, A., & Hepburn, S. (2012). Assessment of the Prerequisite Skills for Cognitive Behavioral Therapy in Children with and Without Autism Spectrum

Disorders. *Journal of Autism and Developmental Disorders, 42*(6), 992–1000. http://doi.org/10.1007/s10803-011-1330-x

McCormick, J. & Niquette, M. (2016, Nov 9). Trump wins presidency in divided nation, may lose popular vote. *Bloomberg.* Retrieved from https://www.bloomberg.com/politics/articles/2016-11-09/trump-defeats-clinton-in-stunning-upset-that-rocks-markets

Mubarak, H. (2007). How Muslim students negotiate their religious identity and practices in an undergraduate setting. *Social Science Research Council.* Retrieved from http: www.ssrc.org/publications/search/

Nadal, K. L., Griffin, K. E., Hamit, S., Leon, J., Tobio, M., & Rivera, D. P. (2012). Subtle and overt forms of islamophobia: Microaggressions toward Muslim Americans. *Journal of Muslim Mental Health, 6*(2), 15-37.

National Association of Social Workers (NASW). (2008). *Code of Ethics* (rev. ed.). Washington, DC: National Association of Social Workers.

Ogan, C., Willnat, L., Pennington, R., & Bashir, M. (2014). The rise of anti-Muslim prejudice: Media and Islamophobia in Europe and the United States. *International Communication Gazette, 76*(1), 27-46.

Shammas, D. (2015). We are not all the same: Arab and Muslim students forging their own campus communities in a post-9/11 America. *Journal of Muslim Minority Affairs, 35*(1), 65-88.

Sue, D. W. (Ed.). (2010). *Microaggressions and marginality: Manifestation, dynamics, and impact.* Hoboken, NJ: John Wiley & Sons.

Trump, J. D. (2015). *Donald J. Trump statement on preventing Muslim immigration* [Press release]. Retrieved from https://www.donaldjtrump.com/press-releases/donald-j.-trump-statement-on-preventing-muslim-immigration

White, D. (2016, Aug 15). Read Donald Trump's Ohio Speech on Immigration and Terrorism. *Time.* Retrieved from http://time.

com/4453110/donald-trump-national-security-immigration-terrorism-speech/

Zempi, E. (2014). *Unveiling Islamophobia: The victimization of veiled Muslim women* (Doctoral dissertation). Retrieved from ProQuest.

# Chapter Seventeen

## *Racism and Rhetoric*

### An Unfair Burden: Donald Trump's Rhetoric and Latino Families

Paula Lezama
University of South Florida
Latino/Minority Kids

My eight-year-old daughter expressed great concern during the recent Republican primaries about Donald Trump's candidacy. I tried to ease her fears (and mine) by telling her that someone like him will never win. Yet, months later, my daughter's distress skyrocketed when she heard that indeed he had won the Republican Party nomination. Not only was her mom wrong, but the person who so openly loathed us Latinos (and other non-white Americans for that matter) had won!

Her concern was justified, and in fact, I was concerned as well. His hateful speech is well documented by different news outlets,[1] e.g. "When Mexico sends its people, they are not sending the best...They are bringing drugs. They are bringing crime. They are rapist..." He also argued that if president he will build a "great, great wall" in the US-Mexico border. Trump even sent a detailed letter to the Washington Post explaining how he will forced the Mexican government to pay for the wall, among others, by confiscating remittances from Mexicans in the US.[2] In regards to the legal battle over Trump's University cases, he argued that the Judge has inherent conflict of interest as if Mexican heritage. Also, during a rally in New Mexico he tweeted: "The protesters in New Mexico were thugs who were flying the Mexican flag. The rally inside was big and beautiful, but outside, criminals!"[3]

However, immigration in the US is a very complex issue with migrants coming from all over the world, legally and undocumented as well. Even more Latinos in the US come from different national origins, not only Mexican. Finally, crime and migrants are not always correlated, and such a comments only reinforce negative stereotypes and misinformed people.

In this scenario, no wonder my daughter worries about her parents and relatives being sent back to our home country, Colombia, and that she would be kept in the US, as she was an American-born citizen. I explained to her that we are still waiting for the final vote on the presidency, and that he had just won the Republican Party nomination and not the U.S. presidency. I really had concluded that my daughter was just overly-sensitive. But later, I was sadly surprised to read the Southern Poverty Law Center report entitled, "The Trump Effect: The impact of the Presidential Campaign on our Nation's Schools." She was not alone in her anxiety.

---

1  http://www.forbes.com/sites/doliaestevez/2015/11/04/prominent-hispanic-intellectuals-call-donald-trumps-hate-speech-dangerous/#67cfc7fe42a1
2  https://www.washingtonpost.com/apps/g/page/politics/memo-explains-how-donald-trump-plans-to-pay-for-border-wall/2007/?tid=a_inl
3  https://twitter.com/realDonaldTrump/status/735465352436408320?ref_src=twsrc%5Etfw

As it turned out, her fears were widely shared by other kids, teachers and families alike.

The report (Costello, 2016) argues that:

*"Fears are pervasive. Students tell teachers they are worried about deportation, having their families split, being put in jail or attacked by police, losing their homes, seeing their places of worship closed, going into hiding and being sent to detention camps. Some Muslim students think that, if Trump becomes president, they will have microchips implanted under their skin."* (p. 7)

Since children cannot vote, they are rarely consulted about elections; however, the fact that they too are expressing such apprehension and fear is a telling indication of how far the negative impact of Mr. Trump's incendiary language has gone. The amount of media coverage he has received has only exacerbated this negative impact.

Contrary to popular belief, almost two-thirds of the U.S. Hispanic population is U.S.-born. There are approximately 36,938 million US-born citizens of Hispanic origin, approximately 61% of the US Hispanic Population (FFF: Hispanic Heritage Month, 2016). Thus a great proportion of US citizens are bearing an unfair burden caused by an ill-intentioned and discriminatory discourse. They are reporting social distress and social identity threats related to the perception of their group affiliation[4].

If kids are experiencing an "alarming level of fear and anxiety" in schools as documented in the report, no wonder similar fears can be felt at home. Parents now have to juggle an uncertain and hostile social environment while reassuring their kids at home that their country accepts them and that they are an important part of the nation, as they have been taught from grade one with the Pledge of Allegiance.

---

4   According to Ellemers et al. the social context offers social resources as well as threats to individual's sense of self. Basically, social identity threat relates to the sense of danger individuals report when the groups to which they belong are called into questions (2002).

## Kids as "Trump's Supporters"

It is precisely in the contrast between the symbolic significance of the Pledge of Allegiance and Trump's hate rhetoric that we can take a glimpse at the far reaching impacts this election will have on the social fabric of this nation. In a scenario in which a steady theme behind Trump's 2016 political campaign has been his shameless race-baiting on Latinos, Muslims, African-Americans (and of course women); the idea of "...One nation... indivisible...with liberty and justice for all," is under attack and our kids are bearing an unjust burden on all sides of the political spectrum.

Let us note that the negative effects are not only borne by kids belonging to minority groups, but also by kids whose families are Trump supporters, as they are being encouraged to reproduce hostile language and behavior in their social interactions. According to the report, "The gains made by years of anti-bullying work in schools have been rolled back in a few short months. Teachers report that students have been "emboldened" to use slurs, engage in name-calling and make inflammatory statements toward each other" (p 10). Students taunting fellow classmates with phrases such as: "When Trump wins, you and your family will get sent back," and "I am supporting Donald Trump because he was going to kill all of the Muslims if he became president!" are becoming more and more frequent.

Research on the impacts of bullying on the bully argue that bullies themselves suffer some various additional risks. For instance, Copeland et al. (2013), reported that after controlling for childhood psychiatric problems or family hardships, bullies have a four to five times increased risk for anti-social personality disorder (described as a lack of empathy, lying, and criminal behavior.) In addition, bullies are more likely to abuse alcohol, tobacco and marijuana. They are more likely to face criminal convictions for antisocial behavior, including unusual amounts of traffic violations. Finally, they are also more prone to have long-term relation issues, including abusive behaviors towards their spouses and children (Smokowski et al., 2005).

Kids learn to distinguish what constitutes appropriate social interaction behavior mainly from what they see in adults. Thus, allowing children to see adults and especially presidential candidates berating and spewing insults like water drops on a rainy day, and at the same time gaining considerable popularity, is little short of giving them an approved school course on how to desecrate the ethical values of this nation.

As Dr. Briscoe-Smith (2016) argues:

*"The way our most influential grown-ups behave and speak about women, immigrants, and each other matters. When a presidential frontrunner claims that all Mexicans are rapists or that Muslims should carry a special ID, those are not innocuous sound bites. They can become part of the foundation of how children understand our government, civic life, and relationships. And they can seep into the smog that affects children, influencing how they get along with others and how they view themselves."*

Thus, when thinking of the deep negative impact that such a hostile and bitter rhetoric can have on our society, it is important to note that we are all victims. We are all being victimized by a political environment that preys on our most fundamental human values, making our schools and our communities the battlegrounds of the unreasonable.

Even people within Trump's own Republican Party understand the dangers of a Trump presidency as well as the damage that is already being inflicted upon the character of the nation. Case in point, 2012 Republican presidential nominee former Gov. Mitt Romney (R-MA) interview for CNN's *Situation Room*. Mr. Romney's exact words were: "Presidents have an impact on the nature of our nation, and trickle down racism and trickle down bigotry and trickle down misogyny — all of these things are extraordinarily dangerous to the heart and character of America" (Breland, 2016).

## Hope as the Antidote to Fear Mongering

Touching on another discussions with my eight-year-old daughter, I would like to mention an anecdote related to the ill-disposed imaginary that Trump's rhetoric creates inside and outside the US national borders in our families.

While visiting our home country, Colombia, this past summer, my daughter was curious about our reasons for migrating to the U.S. In honesty but also out of respect for her youth, I have told her (superficially) of the profound impacts that conflict and violence have had on the people of my country, and that her own mother has not been immune to those losses. A very superficial discussion of guerrillas, paramilitaries and corrupt government officials, including the armed forces and police, immediately lead her to conclude that indeed her own country, America, was a far better option. On second thought, she was not as sure of that last statement if Trump did win the presidency and the police indiscriminate killing of young African-Americans, Latinos, Native Americans and other vulnerable citizens continues. How will be fare in America if these circumstances continue to occur? Then, with a somber reflection she remained silent.

Indeed, coming from a country that has been ravaged by violence, narcotraffic and conflict for over a half century, a country where polarization and everyday violence have taken a huge toll on our communities and on our capacity to come together in our shared humanity, I cannot help but feel outraged and deeply saddened by this U.S. election and its surrounding context of acrimonious racism and discrimination.

On the other hand, I accept as true that as humans we are very resilient beings. Latinos in this case have come from difficult lives abroad, many of them having risked their lives in the pursuit of a better life, hoping those efforts and risks will pay off in the long run. It is as if being hopeful is part of our cultural make-up, thus, despite the circumstances, we cannot help but also feel hopeful that, in the end, our shared humanity will allow us to see that those imaginary separations of race, ethnicity, religion, national borders, etc. are only that, imaginary etiquettes used by those in power to instill fear, divide and gain support for their selfish agendas.

Truly, it is impossible not to be hopeful and inspired by the courageous actions of those who stand up against bigotry, discrimination and the corruption of the public sphere. I personally feel hopeful seeing groups like the Occupy movement; Black Lives Matter; protesters against the North Dakota oil pipeline; the protests around the world pressuring developed nations to accept refugees fleeing the extreme poverty and wars in their countries; people everywhere advocating for sustainable production and consumption patterns so global warming is halted and the worst case scenarios of climate change are avoided. And of course, the people in my country, Colombia, resisting polarization and advocating for the end of the more than a half century of conflict that has devastated our communities. These social movements give us back hope in the midst of crisis. [5]

These contrasting realities and our inner need to keep hoping inspire us to not only hope but also to pray that just as we have been able to materially advance our living conditions, we are going to be able to share that progress with all our fellow humans, coming together in respect and solidarity.

## Fueling Compassion as the First Step

As Amartya Sen stated, "We live in a world of unprecedented opulence... And yet we also live in a world with remarkable deprivation, destitution and oppression" (2000; p. xi). The first is driven by the noteworthy human capacity to innovate and create new possibilities, while the second is fueled by our greed and selfishness. At any rate, human emotions and abilities are in constant interaction, creating step by step the societies that we live in.

Hence, it is in this moment of crisis and of deep fear that we need to ask ourselves, what is the type of society we want our kids to grow up in? Is it a society where the value of a person is determined by his or her skin color, religious affiliation or national origin? Or do we want them to grow up in a community where their character is the marker by which they are going to be measured? Do we want a society that preys on the vulnerable, and strips away not only the possibility of material comfort, but also their lives, dreams and hopes? Or do we want a society that is able to come together in its shared humanity and accept that dignity and respect for all is a fundamental pillar of a peaceful and prosperous nation?

---

5   https://www.theguardian.com/world/protest

Once a resolution has been made on the ethical ends that we as society want to pursue, it is important to question also what is it that we are willing to commit in the fight for such a noble aim? As my grandmother used to say, "The longest trip always starts with the first step," meaning that our first step in this ominous social situation is to go out, look and talk to our neighbors and rediscover that as "us," they are human beings trying to forge a good life for themselves and their families, and start building from there, if not friendship, at least mutual respect as fellow citizens within a democratic nation.

Although humans have shown through history a deep capacity for wrong-doing, there have also been telling examples of our capacity for empathy, altruism and self-sacrifice in the wake of tragedy. The latter have sparked in us not only the need to move beyond the fallacy of the evolutionary imposition of the survival of fittest; but also to discover new understandings of emotions, among them, compassion.

Compassion, defined by Adam Smith (2011) as, "...the emotion which we feel for the misery of others, when we either see it, or are made to conceive it in a very lively manner" (p.3). According to Dr. Keltner (2004), recent research on the subject has concluded that there is not only a biological component as the basis of compassion, but also a social evolutionary one. In a way, humans are wired to feel empathy towards the suffering of others, thus cultivating compassion is the starting point of a healthy community. In Dr. Keltner's words, "What's more, a sense of compassion fosters compassionate behavior and helps shape the lessons we teach our children."

As a consequence, developing and nurturing compassion and tolerance towards others while hoping and working towards the cultivation of healthy societal interactions is our shared responsibility. Still, I do believe that everyone is entitled to their own madness, but as a society we have not only the need to protect ourselves from propagating fear mongering, but also the obligation to our little ones to shield them as much as possible from the negative effects such behavior can have on their wellbeing and future possibilities. The latter being a concern that I experience on an everyday basis just by virtue of being the mother of a little Latina girl.

## Final Thoughts

In sum, no matter what the outcome of this present election year is, collateral damage to the social fabric has already being inflicted for generations to come. It will take not only courageous and honest leaders, but also an active civil society that understands the deepest meaning of American values, to mend the damage and rebuild trust where it has been desecrated.

Still, as our Hispanic heritage has taught us and our dear singer and poet Facundo Cabral so righteously expressed: "Goodness is more abundant, but not noticeable because it is quiet: a bomb makes more noise than a caress, but for every bomb that destroyed millions, there are millions of caresses that nurture life." Hence, those of us who see beyond appearances are called to nurture not only our own lives, but the lives of those disenfranchised from our political system. In the meantime, we are also called to keep hope.

Thus, in hope, we can only keep working on giving society the best version of ourselves while hoping that common sense, solidarity and empathy will help restore faith in the social contract that binds us together in our commitment to this country and the global village. In the meantime, it is good to remember that reciprocity is a good starting point for any type of social interaction, meaning, treating others as you want to be treated never fails!

**REFERENCES**

Breland, A. (2016, June 10). Romney: Trump will cause "trickle-down racism." Retrieved September 30, 2016, from http://www.politico.com/story/2016/06/mitt-romney-donald-trump-trickle-down-racism-224209

Briscoe-Smith, A. (2016, April 13). How to Talk with Your Kids about Donald Trump. Retrieved September 30, 2016 from http://greatergood.berkeley.edu/article/item/how_to_talk_with_your_kids_about_donald_trump#

Copeland, W. E., Wolke, D., Angold, A., & Costello, E. J. (2013). Adult Psychiatric Outcomes of Bullying and Being Bullied by Peers in Childhood and Adolescence. JAMA Psychiatry, 70(4), 419. doi:10.1001/jamapsychiatry.2013.504

Costello, M. B. (2016, April 13). TEACHING THE 2016 ELECTION The Trump Effect. Retrieved September 30, 2016, from https://www.splcenter.org/sites/default/files/splc_the_trump_effect.pdf

FFF: Hispanic Heritage Month 2016. (2016, July 28). Retrieved September 30, 2016, from http://www.census.gov/newsroom/facts-for-features/2016/cb16-ff16.html

Keltner, D. (2004, March 1). The Compassionate Instinct. Retrieved September 30, 2016, from http://greatergood.berkeley.edu/article/item/the_compassionate_instinct

Smith, A. (2011). The Theory of Moral Sentiments. Kapaau (T.H.): Gutenberg.

Smokowski, P. R., & Kopasz, K. H. (2005). Bullying in School: An Overview of Types, Effects, Family Characteristics, and Intervention Strategies. Children & Schools, 27(2), 101-110. doi:10.1093/cs/27.2.101

Ellemers, Naomi, Spears, Russell and Doosje, Bertjan (2002) Self and Social Identity. *Annual Review of Psychology*, Vol. 53: 161-186 (Volume publication date February 2002)

# Chapter Eighteen

## *Racism and Rhetoric*

### 2 Faces of Evil, Donald J. Trump as the Poster-Child for Political Eurobliviousness!

### Aaron Smith, PhD: Temple University

He has been described as a political Savior by some, and an unfit Anti-Christ by others. He is a polarizing public figure who often appears to be equally revered and reviled. His political leadership continues to raise even more questions than his signature hairstyle. He is Donald J. Trump. In addition to being an unlikely candidate for the President of The United States of America, I view Donald Trump as one of the most politically, racially, and intellectually emblematic figures found within contemporary society. Most telling perhaps is Trump's ability to engage, embody and advocate for a political base that represents a destructive historical phenomena that I describe as Eurobliviousness. In this discussion, I will point out the many ways Donald J. Trump's effective rhetoric, political maneuverings, and popular appeal are rooted in Eurobliviousness and the crippling contradictions of the White identity.

Eurobliviousness is a cancerous cultural cocktail of delusion, division, distortion and death. Eurobliviousness is when willful ignorance and cognitive dissonance are multiplied exponentially by the cultural, historical weight of racial oppression, and this plays a critical role in the formation and maintenance of White identity within the global system of racism/White supremacy. This phenomenon has propelled Donald Trump and his campaign to the heights of Republican politics and non-partisan ignorance.

A recent Pew Research Center poll found that roughly four in ten African Americans are doubtful that the U.S. will ever achieve racial equality. This pessimism is due, in large measure, to White America's history of displaying cross cultural cognitive dissonance according to experts like Dr. Joy Degruy (author of Post Traumatic Slave Syndrome). In an article about Degruy's work in the *Huffington Post*, titled "Whites and the Fear Caused by White Supremacy," Rev Dr. Susan Smith reports, "DeGruy says that when Americans exist with the contradictions presented by the Constitution they suffer internal psychological conflict, 'cognitive dissonance.' They have to convince themselves that the treatment of black people by whites was not bad, but that black people were bad and therefore deserved what they were getting."

This reluctance of many Whites (like Donald Trump) to alter their existing internal narratives, even when faced with contradicting factual information is increased exponentially when dealing with polarized analyses concerning racial inequality. These disparities are particularly exacerbated when assessing inequities directly impacting African Americans. This sociologically toxic perceptual distortion is so deeply rooted in what actor/activist Jesse Williams recently referred to as "the idea of Whiteness" that I found terms like willful ignorance and cognitive dissonance only scratched the surface of what I describe as Eurobliviousness.

## Trump-the face of racist/anti-historical ideologies, when rhetoric can't Trump reality: Saying it doesn't make it so.

This so-called deserved destiny is manifested in Trump's rhetoric on immigration (who belongs and who doesn't). One of the greatest examples of the contradictions between racism and reality can be found in Trump's celebrated yet non-existent relationship with the African American community. Despite numerous disparaging remarks that Trump has made about people he has referred to as "The Blacks," a disconnect persists that leads him to believe that he has a positive, productive, and potentially politically reciprocal relationship with African American voters. For instance, while campaigning in Diaomondale, Michigan he asked Black and Brown voters, "What have you got to lose"? Such contradictions were highlighted in the online source Gawker.com in a piece titled, "The Collected Quotes of Donald Trump on "The Blacks." Here Donald Trump is quoted as saying, "Black guys counting my money! I hate it. The only kind of people I want counting my money are short guys that wear yarmulkes every day." He also expressed his view that, "Laziness is a trait in Blacks" (Gawker 2016). Trump's inflammatory quotes are then juxtaposed with his Eurobliviousness regarding his own place or role in racial harmony and reconciliation, as he states, "I have a great relationship with the blacks. I've always had a great relationship with the blacks." This degree of dissonance is reminiscent of the Pew poll that I referenced earlier, and dominant culture's consistently profound inability to accurately assess its relationship with those whom it dominates.

In the case of Trump, this distortion has been magnified to the point where he views African Americans as having more advantages in American society than their White counterparts (yes, more advantages). Trump states, "A well-educated black has a tremendous advantage over a well-educated white in terms of the job market. I think sometimes a black may think they don't have an advantage or this and that... I've said on one occasion, even about myself, if I were starting off today, I would love to be a well-educated black, because I believe they do have an actual advantage." Gawker.com 2016. This ignorance of true history is critical to the maintenance of the current American social order and the White identity. In this regard, Donald J. Trump is ignorance incarnate.

## TRUMP AS THE EMPEROR WITH OLD IDEOLOGICAL CLOTHES. THOSE WHO THINK LIFE IS A GAME MAY BE PRONE TO PLAYING TOO MUCH.

When Parker Brothers shapes your political policy, the game of life can quickly descend into a game of lies. Donald J. Trump has lived in a virtual monopoly game for most of his adult life. In this metaphoric contest of windfalls, wealth, and worth, Donald Trump has played many roles, including the role of trust fund baby. In his book, "The Art of the Deal," Trump explains that he started out with around $200,000 after graduating from college. This figure includes real estate his father helped him obtain. Trump reportedly inherited $40-$200 million when his father died in 1999. He was worth $1.6 billion at this time, estimated by Forbes magazine. Trump has been quoted as telling an interviewer, "It has not been easy for me, my father gave me a small loan of a million dollars." This economic component is foundational to Eurobliviousness and the myth of meritocracy. People who identify as White often lend more credence to hard-work and self-determination, lofty tales of picking themselves up by their boot straps and being desirous of freedom and liberty as factors that attribute to current wealth inequalities, stratified mainly by race. A more accurate, empirical historical analysis would include discriminatory laws, acts and customs including (but not limited to) chattel enslavement, Indian removal, The Head-Right system, The Homestead Act, and housing discrimination as contributing factors influencing economic racial disparities.

When Donald Trump rails against hand-outs, welfare, and undocumented workers taking jobs from decent Americans, he is feeding a bigoted non-historically contextualized beast. This ideological beast of

White men's burdens has been baptized in the colonial rhetoric of Manifest Destiny, domesticated by the signers of the Constitution and multiplied considerably by neo-conservatives, Tea Party loyalists, and reprobate Republicans of all types. Seemingly unbeknownst to Trump supporters suffering from acute Eurobliviousness, this beast has been dying a slow painful death since it was born and suffered a potentially fatal blow in 2008 with the election of Barack Obama. Long before millions of people rejected the idea of a Black man in the White House, Donald Trump and his father Fred were being accused of keeping Black men and women out of housing owned by White men.

Donald J. Trump also played the role of slum lord. A *New York Times* article titled, "No Vacancies for Blacks, How Donald Trump Got His Start and Was First Accused of Bias," points out that as Trump assumed a leading role in the business, the company's practice of turning away potential black tenants was painstakingly documented by activists and organizations that viewed equal housing as the next frontier in the civil rights struggle.

The Justice Department undertook its own investigation and, in 1973, sued Trump Management for discriminating against blacks, naming both Fred Trump, the company's chairman, and Donald Trump, its president, as defendants (Mahler, Elder 2016). The lawsuit resulted in what Trump described as "a minor settlement" (according to a *Washington Post* article about the case, Kranish and O'Harrow 2016). Part of this settlement prohibited Trump from being made to admit guilt, which appears to be a staple of his personal and political character. Currently we are watching Donald Trump performing an amalgamation of *two truths and a lie, truth or dare,* with a seemingly war mongering desire to engage in an international game of *Battleship* that can yield cataclysmic nuclear results. If the inner and outer child of Donald J. Trump is ever empowered to turn his tantrums into our tyranny, his Eurobliviousness could result in our obliteration.

Thankfully, despite the fact that we use such terms, the political arena, complete with scores, turns on competitive races. The informed among us readily realize that Presidential politics is not a game; however, when ignorance is exacerbated by material abundance, Trump can represent how a person can simultaneously become the owner of everything and knower of nothing.

Some of the other faces of Donald include: Trump as the habitual liar, and (allegedly) Trump as the misogynistic sexual predator. These attributes create a most unfortunate blend of ambition, ambivalence, and arrogance. This mix of dissonance and disrespect is Donald J. Trump, father of false confidence, Mr. Fragility, bka **Trumpty Dumpty**...

When Trumpty-Dumpty dreamt of a wall/

Trumpty Dumpty set up his fall.../

All of the Pundits/

His family and friends/

Couldn't do enough to make Donald win!

If it is true that pride comes before the fall, then the countdown for Donald Trump's next disastrous, self-destructive demonstration is due any day now.

**REFERENCES:**

http://www.huffingtonpost.com/rev-dr-susan-k-smith/the-fear-caused-by-white-supremacy_b_8958652.html

http://gawker.com/the-collected-quotes-of-donald-trump-on-the-blacks-1719961925

http://www.nytimes.com/2016/08/28/us/politics/donald-trump-housing-race.html?_r=0

https://www.washingtonpost.com/politics/inside-the-governments-racial-bias-case-against-donald-trumps-company-and-how-he-fought-it/2016/01/23/fb90163e-bfbe-11e5-bcda-62a36b394160_story.html

# Chapter Nineteen

## *Misogyny*

### Donald Trump: Racism, Rhetoric, and Women

### Anjerrika Bean

*"Laziness is a trait of blacks." "I have a great relationship with THE blacks. I've always had a great relationship with THE blacks." (Parham, The Huffington Post, 2015) "You know, it doesn't really matter what [the media] write as long as you've got a young and beautiful piece of ass." Like you wouldn't have your job if you weren't beautiful." "If Hillary Clinton can't satisfy her husband what makes you think she can satisfy America?" "I've said if Ivanka weren't my daughter, perhaps I'd be dating her." (Bahadur, The Huffington Post, 2015)*

~Donald Trump~

I was born in beautiful, brown skin, and that is all I know. Despite the criticisms of some, I have learned that my Black is beautiful, and nothing will take that away from me. It has been motivating to watch President Barack Obama, someone who looks like me, run the White House for eight years; and, even more inspiring to witness First Lady Michelle Obama tackle serious social and political issues with grace, poise, dignity, and intellectual respect. Michelle Obama embodies everything Black women, like myself, aspire to be: Black, empowered, and free. Through eloquent speech, such as her statement "'I wake up each day in 'a house that was built by slaves. And I watch my daughters two beautiful intelligent, young black women, playing with their dog on the White House Lawn'" (Huffington Post, 2016), she faces issues head on while simultaneously motivating people to strive for their full potential.

However, the dream of succeeding in previously unimaginable and unattainable spaces as a Black woman is now on the cusp of either thriving under Hillary Clinton, potentially the first female President, or suffocating under Donald Trump. Throughout his presidential campaign, Donald Trump has used his platform to promote bigotry, demagoguery, and chauvinism, as evidenced, in part, by his constant suggestions of blindly deporting multiple ethnic groups (e.g., illegal Hispanics and refugees) upon being elected. All women and minorities are suffering from his hateful words, but this paper will focus specifically on the role of his harmful rhetoric and ideology on the degradation of Black women.

In 2008, the election of the first Black President forced race into public discourse. When people who spew hateful messages through propaganda and mass media outlets are forced to take responsibility for these actions, victims of these prejudiced messages will feel less ostracized from society and live more freely. This is noteworthy, because Donald Trump's hateful rhetoric against female minorities will further marginalize an already oppressed group of people.

Primary findings in *The African American Women's Voices Project* showed 90% of the women surveyed reported experiencing discrimination, and 10% remember being called a "nigger" at one point in their lives.

Additionally, 69% of respondents reported experiencing discrimination in the workplace relating to hiring practices, salary equality, and promotions (Shorter and Gooden, 2003). A presidential nominee who uses his/her platform to degrade non-white males is intentionally dismantling American culture by subconsciously pushing a white supremacy agenda. As seen throughout history, American culture has been irrevocably damaged through the teachings of slavery, Jim Crow, and the rise of capitalism that led to commodifying Black women's bodies and children. Electing a president with a similar harmful platform is likely to have similar irrevocably damaging results: stunted economic growth and a divided American population.

Ronald Ackers' social learning theory, which I will refer to in this paper as SLT (Ackers, 2013) is heavily grounded in symbolic interactionism. The primary assumption of his SLT is that the learning process that occurs within interpersonal interactions and different situations produces both conforming and deviant behavior (Cullen, Agnew, & Cox, 2014). According to SLT, social learning begins in childhood, continues through adolescence, and shapes behaviors exhibited during adulthood. Sutherland also viewed criminal behavior as a process in which a person engages. There are practical examples of how we learn behavior from our leaders. Parents dress their children up for holidays like political figures, and encourage them to be embrace and adopt their political ideologies.

Therefore, one must consider what the next generation of children will learn from Donald Trump if he is elected president. Do we want them exposed to a mass objectification of women and marginalization of minority groups? Donald Trump's behavior is criminal, and, sadly, American taxpayer dollars are funding his protection as he globally spews hate. Americans are at a crossroads. Tell me, what will be our fate America?

**REFERENCES:**

Akers, R. L., & Sellers, C. S. (2013). *Criminological theories: Introduction, evaluation, and application*. New York: Oxford University Press.

Bahadur, N. (2015, August 19). Donald Trump's Religion and Political Views. Retrieved August 31, 2016, from http://www.huffingtonpost.com/entry/18-real-things-donald-trump-has-said-about-women_us_

Blay, Z. (2016, July/August). Why Michelle Obama's "I live in a White House built by slaves' quote is vital. Retrieved August 31, 2016, from http://www.huffingtonpost.com/

Cullen, F. T., & Agnew, R., Wilcox, P. (2014). *Criminological theory: Past to present: essential readings*. New York: Oxford University Press.

Jones, Charisse, and Kumea Shorter-Gooden. *Shifting: The Double Lives of Black Women in America*. New York: HarperCollins, 2003. Print.

Parham, J. (2015, July 24). The Collected Quotes of Donald Trump on "the Blacks" Retrieved July/August, 2016, from http://gawker.com/the-collected-quotes-of-donald-trump-on-the-blacks-

# Contributors Affiliations and Titles

## EDITOR

*Introduction*

**Daryl Taiwo Harris, Ph.D.**
Associate Professor
Department of Political Science
Howard University
Washington, D.C. 20059
dbharris@howard.edu

## FOREWORD

**Michael D'Antonio**
Author, Screenwriter, Political Pundit
Long Island, New York
www.michaeldantonio.net

## PREFACE

**Ama Mazama Ph.D.,**
Professor
Department of Africology
Temple University
Ama_mazama@hotmail.com

**Molefi Kete Asante Ph.D.**
President, Molefi Kete Asante Institute for Afrocentric Studies
Professor and Chair
Department of Africology
Temple University
masante@temple.edu

**Brian L. Wright, Ph.D.**
Assistant Professor
University of Memphis
blwrght1@memphis.edu

**Jemimah L. Young, Ph.D.**
Assistant Professor
University of North Texas
jemimah.young@unt.edu

**Donna Y. Ford, Ph.D.**
Professor and Endowed Chair
Vanderbilt University
donna.ford@vanderbilt.edu

**Anjerrika Bean**
Doctoral Student
Department of Sociology
Howard University
anjerrikab@yahoo.com

**Aaron Smith, Ph.D.,**
Assistant Professor
Department of Africology
Temple University

**Paula Lezama**
Assistant Director
Institute for the Study of Latin America and the Caribbean (ISLAC)

University of South Florida
plezama@usf.edu

**Clarence Lusane Ph.D.**
Professor and Chair
Department of Political Science
Howard University
clarence.lusane@howard.edu

**Asike Jude Ph.D.**
Department of Philosophy
Faculty of Humanities
University Of Port Harcourt, Nigeria.
A lecturer of Philosophy with vested interest in Public Policy and its Impact on African Culture, Conflicts, Politics and Development.
asikejude@yahoo.com

**Kola Abimbola Ph.D**
Associate Professor
Department of Philosophy
Howard University
kolapo.abimbola@howard.edu

**Ashley L. Lewis, Doctoral Student**
Howard University
Department of Communication
Culture and Media Studies (CCMS)
ashleyleplewis@gmail.com

**Justin Gammage Ph.D**
Assistant Professor
Department of Africana Studies
California State University, Dominquez Hills
Marquita Pellerin-Gammage Ph.D
Associate Professor

Department of Africana Studies
California State University, Northridge

**KenZoe Brian J. Selassie Ph.D.**
Assistant Professor and Chair Department of English
Foreign Language, and Mass Communication
Benedict College
kenzoebrian.selassie@gmail.com

**Denise Rosier, aka Ayo Sekai**
Doctoral Student
Department of Political Science
Howard University
dmarosier@gmail.com

**Luqman Abdullah Ph.D.**
Department of Political Science
Howard University
Luqman2511@yahoo.com

**Stephanie Howard**
Doctoral Student
Department of Sociology
Howard University
stephenie.howard@bison.howard.edu

**Aitza Haddad, Esq., Ph.D.**
Department of Communication
Culture and Media Studies (CCMS)
Howard University
amhaddadlaw@gmail.com

**Ann-Marie Waterman, M.A.**
Assistant Dean, School of Law
Howard University
a_waterman@howard.edu

**Jaimee Swift**
Doctoral Student
Department of Political Science
Howard University
jaimee.swift@bison.howard.edu

**Sara Swetzoff**
Doctoral Student
Department of African Studies
Howard University
sswetzoff@gmail.com

www.ingramcontent.com/pod-product-compliance
Lightning Source LLC
Chambersburg PA
CBHW020643300426
44112CB00007B/220